THE BIG MONEY

*Seven Steps to Picking Great Stocks
and Finding Financial Security*

FREDERICK R. KOBRICK

Simon & Schuster Paperbacks
New York   London   Toronto   Sydney

SIMON & SCHUSTER PAPERBACKS
Rockefeller Center
1230 Avenue of the Americas
New York, NY 10020

First Simon & Schuster paperback edition 2007

SIMON & SCHUSTER PAPERBACKS and colophon are registered trademarks
of Simon & Schuster, Inc.

For information about special discounts for bulk purchases,
please contact Simon & Schuster Special Sales at
1-800-456-6798 or business@simonandschuster.com.

Designed by Elliott Beard

Manufactured in the United States of America

1   3   5   7   9   10   8   6   4   2

The Library of Congress has cataloged the hardcover edition as follows:
Kobrick, Frederick R.
The big money : seven steps to picking great stocks
and finding financial security / Frederick R. Kobrick.
p.   cm.
Includes index.
1. Investments—United States. 2. Stocks—United States.
3. Finance, Personal—United States. I. Title.
HG4910.K62   2006
332.63'22—dc22   2006042236

ISBN-13: 978-0-7432-5870-8
ISBN-10:   0-7432-5870-3
ISBN-13: 978-0-7432-5871-5 (Pbk)
ISBN-10:   0-7432-5871-1 (Pbk)

For Sherrill, Jacob, and Samantha

CONTENTS

THE BIG MONEY

CHAPTER ONE

ANYONE CAN BECOME RICH

One Stock, BASM, and the Seven Steps

America won the Revolutionary War. Although the reasons are complicated and involved strategy, perseverance, supplies, and more, we know from our school days that the British relied on an outmoded way of fighting. They were very well organized, marched in a straight line, and stood tall in their bright red coats when they fired.

In contrast, the Colonials were more free-form, hid behind trees, and fired when ready. Comedian Bill Cosby had a routine in which he played the captains of two teams, the Red Coats and the Settlers. When the captain of the Settlers won the coin toss, Cosby then asked him what he wanted.

The Settlers' captain said that the enemy team had to wear those bright red coats, approach the Settlers in a straight line, and fire only when commanded to, while the Settlers could hide behind rocks and trees and fire at will. We have always laughed at this, and put a lot of faith in that part of what we learned in school. The regimentation of the British undermined their ability to fight this type of war. The Colonials' flexibility and new ways of fighting were instrumental in helping them win a war against a much larger and better-equipped army.

America won its independence.

What if I told you that most investors today are practicing a form of "Red Coat Investing" that undermines their ability to become truly wealthy?

I would add that there is a way to win your own independence from inflexible, counterproductive investing. It is through very easy yet solid techniques that I and many other investors with top records have used for decades to capitalize on great stocks. It is not magic, nor does it work while you sleep. You have to actually learn the key techniques of how to recognize a great company and a future winner and then know how to hold on so you can create wealth.

First you have to free yourself from old ways of thinking. Next, you need a "compass," so that you can direct your attention to some critical but simple things. Haven't you always wanted to recognize, buy, and hold one of the companies that have made stock investors 100X (100 times) their money? (Throughout the book I use X to denote multiples—thus here it means "one hundred times the value of the original investment.")

This book is about the compass, and about Seven Steps that are the simple but highly effective procedure you use, so you can stop beating yourself. It is not a manual with complex instructions, but in contrast, it uses entertaining true stories from my decades as a stock picker, with lessons. This is the way most of us learn most quickly and effectively.

Over time, you'll be able to work with more confidence and less frustration, and have a far better chance of making the big money. While this can be triples and quadruples, I think of the "big money" as more like making 10X, 25X—even 100X or 200X—your investment by owning the greatest companies, and owning them with true insights and patience over the long term. This will reward you with a second form of independence: being independently wealthy.

Since computers arrived on desktops in the early to mid-1980s, investing has not improved, nor has it improved with the arrival of the information age. For most people, information overload has simply made it much tougher to pick stocks in order to become wealthy. People look for almost everything, lacking focus and the secrets of what to look for. Those secrets of how and what to focus on are revealed herein. By simplifying and focusing, your chances of getting rich go up enormously.

My college English-literature teacher taught us that there were only seven great themes in all literature, so every book, movie, or play embodies one of those themes or a derivative of one of them. Well, there are a few more than seven themes (or principles) in all of investing, but not many. Almost all of the best growth-stock investing revolves around certain themes of how a company makes its money, grows, and thereby provides great stock wealth to its shareholders.

When we can recognize things that have occurred before, investing becomes much more simple. Each great company has a business model that it should describe in very straightforward terms: how it will grow, be very profitable, and protect itself from competitors. Learning to recognize the things that really matter gives you that critical focus and helps you avoid drowning in the flood of information available in this information age. Thus you can concentrate on the relevant aspects of that business model, the strategy and key assumptions a company makes, and, of course, how good its management is. I will outline how you go about finding this relevant information and how to focus on four critical factors, or BASM: **B**usiness model, **A**ssumptions, **S**trategy, and **M**anagement. Investors who learn to focus on BASM become the investors who invest for the greatest gains.

The earnings that companies generate do create the stock gains over a relatively long period of time, but there is a lot of confusion and noise in the short term. The reporting and accounting techniques in the "numbers game," and even fraud and lying, can all seem like one of those English garden mazes to most of us at times. Thus I regard earnings as the "golden eggs" that create stock gains, but what I call the "golden goose"—BASM—is actually responsible for generating those golden eggs.

Still, our universal human instincts, foibles, and responses often get in the way of good investing. These foibles include greed, which can be a positive force if controlled, but a negative force when emotions run high. Next come lack of patience and lack of regard for time horizons, or insensitivity to benchmarks. Another critical and very human mistake is trying to predict short-term market moves and basing all good stock investing on high-risk factors, a strategy that almost always torpedoes great investing. Central to all great investing is substituting knowledge for emotions and building the right kind of knowledge to make the big money.

To use BASM and the tools and concepts of successful investing, we need to stop doing the things which, although typical of human behavior, constitute beating ourselves. We need, then, to follow the Seven Steps:

- knowledge
- patience
- disciplines
- emotions
- time horizon
- market timing
- benchmarks

The Seven Steps and BASM combine in a very fluid and natural way to allow you to invest for the big money. Learning to use these things is not very hard. You can see how they work in the examples I offer in this book. You will be using what is, in effect, the case method, which is the core learning tool of Harvard Business School, many of the other top business schools, and most great law schools (although my own experiences, recounted here, and yours will be much more effective than anything you learn in school). It seems to work far better than other methods. It is experiences that make investors great, and these experiences can help to make you great—meaning rich.

Did you make an early prediction that the Asian crisis would hit in 1998, or that the bull market would peak in March 2000? Most of the time, people cannot accurately predict early in a season the two teams that will be in the Super Bowl or World Series; nor can they predict the weather, or even some of the most important things that happen in their personal lives. We all like to feel that we can predict certain things, but we also know that reality says we rarely can do it accurately.

But when I get to know the CEO of a company well, I can start to understand how he or she will react to new situations. Although you may not be able to actually meet with CEOs, you can certainly read up on their track records, public statements about their company, and articles about them—in short, get to know what you truly need to know about them as you learn the techniques in this book.

Today, the Internet and other resources make it possible for you to learn all about who a CEO truly is. You can find out things right at your desk that I and other professionals had to research through travel, meetings, and phone calls.

You can predict the behavior of your closest family members and friends in certain situations, so even if you cannot predict the behavior of CEOs quite as well, you can still separate the great ones from the rest. That's what it's all about.

Identifying great CEOs and understanding the best corporate business models can make you very wealthy. The system of identifying those investing elements that I describe over and over again is what most great investors have found through their experiences—like those in the cases we look at here. It is the best way to make a lot of money, and over the years I refined what many of us used into the key four elements of great companies and great stock picks. Thus BASM—the four elements—is how you can identify and predict the companies whose stocks will generate the big money for investors.

I will never forget a warm spring day in Chicago more than a dozen years ago, when a man came up to me from the crowd after I had made a presentation to a large group of investors in the mutual funds I managed. He was in that portion of mutual-fund investors who also liked to buy some individual stocks to try to get rich. He made it clear to me that, for him, the best part of the presentation was not my fund per se, but my stories about how I picked the best stocks. Years of talking to investors have reinforced the fact that those who want to get rich crave the same kind of stock stories that professional investors tell each other over lunch.

These investors felt that they learned and benefited not so much from rules, books, or articles but from hearing about the experiences of successful investors. I immediately recognized how profoundly important that principle was, for not only had I learned from my own experiences and from great investors I knew, but I had also learned a lot from the very beginning by embracing the experiences of someone who was interviewing me for a job before I graduated from business school. It was one great story, but sometimes that is all it takes.

Over years of talking to individuals and giving presentations, I acquired a lot of insight into their problems and challenges, and always tried to make them feel confident that they could own and concentrate on a few stocks—or even try to become rich from just one stock. Naturally, I also talked a lot about how I invested their money that was in my mutual funds. That is why I was there. They asked questions about how I picked stocks and said they would love to hear story after story. I told them that those of us who did well at stock picking loved the stories too and we told them to each other. The stories are not just interesting and entertaining, but the best way for both money managers and individual investors to learn and then act on what they had learned. This is why I decided to tell some of these stories in this book. As I said, I want to give investors a compass for navigating their way to financial independence while having the simplicity of approach and confidence to act on what they learn and put some real money to work.

Obviously, learning but not acting on what you have learned won't get you there. Sure, we all know that, but emotions and lack of a compass to direct us to what to learn is a pretty common problem for investors and one that often blocks action.

My good friend Ben Bloomstone, a veteran broker, once waited in line at a Starbucks coffee shop in Seattle many years before Starbucks even went public. He saw how terrific the operation was and how much he and the other customers loved it all. Yet Ben had no real way of assessing how the company would differ from countless competitors, and never focused on the key things (what I came to call BASM), so he never bought its stock. Although he wonders today why he did not buy Starbucks on its first offering, I think he would not have hesitated had he known the principles of BASM—he would have owned it, and it could have made him a fortune. Another good friend, Vic Linell, wonders why he sold Microsoft each time the market scared him, or some other factor made it seem as though the stock would plunge, only to see Microsoft shares dip temporarily and then continue to go up and make fortunes for many other people.

These two friends have been two of the top institutional brokers in the country, providing great research from their brokerage firms to leading investment professionals. Yet they got too busy doing a great job in their professions, and they never had a system of stock picking that was different from those used by their research analysts. Research analysts do great research but think differently from money managers, and are generally not very good stock pickers. (Good analysts understand the importance of BASM, but they don't follow the logic of the Seven Steps—and that makes a big difference.)

Why do I make this unequivocal statement? Because I began my career as an analyst and evolved into a stock picker. Instead of imposing the detailed history of my own career on you at this point, I will unfold the parts that will help you, through stock stories, as the book goes on, showing you why BASM and the Seven Steps have made me very successful—and how they showed me the way to help a lot of others make a great deal of money.

My experience is the reason this book is about stock picking, not securities analysis.

In August 2005, as Google celebrated its first anniversary as a public company, its stock was roughly 4X the price at which it had gone public. Many bulls and bears had trouble understanding the price.

Approaching its initial public offering, or IPO, the Internet search-engine developer was the subject of a huge amount of press and fanfare, since its product was so popular. The debates about how expensive the stock was approached the same high levels as debates on national issues or major sports championships. Most of these debates took fundamental approaches using some concepts of securities analysis, but I did not see any of them really get into the key issues that BASM focuses on—that is, would Google be viewed just as a hot product and hot stock, or as a great company to own and follow?

As Google comes into a period when it will contend with the key factor all potentially great companies must face—competition (Google's is from Yahoo and Microsoft), it will be BASM once again that will define how we track Google's progress and judge whether it will belong in the ranks of the great ones.

HOW DID I DO IT?

Like most investors, I learned from experience and used each experience as a stepping-stone to understand how great investors identify business models and pick winners.

The very first stock story I heard, at a lunch down on Wall Street in 1971, made a great impression on me, and I used what I heard over and over again; it set a tone for my entire career. It is something that, I think, will help many other investors:

I was about to graduate from Harvard Business School and had spent the morning interviewing with a great group of security analysts from a large Wall Street firm. Now I was having lunch with their boss, the director of research. The interviews had gone extremely well; I sensed a good rapport between me and the analysts. This lunch seemed to confirm that in the course of nonstop conversation.

I had been impressed with the analysts, and I was even more impressed with Dave. Unlike some research directors I had met, he was not so much an administrator as he was a mentor and teacher. "I want to develop stock pickers," he had said, adding, "I want a bunch of real investors in my department. That is what this business is all about." He and I knew that many analysts do in-depth research and turn out very impressive reports, but they may not know how to pick the right stock at the right time to make their clients a lot of money.

As our long lunch drew to a close, my host took the check and pulled from his pocket a huge roll of bills that looked as if it could choke a water buffalo. My eyes grew wide in wonder. I couldn't help asking Dave if he always carried around so much cash.

"Oh, I guess so," he replied casually. "I have a lot of money in a drawer, and I just pull out a bunch when I think I need some. Frankly, I don't think about money at all. I started with nothing and became very wealthy investing, and I don't need to work. I come to work because it is fun, and I love it, and I love picking great stocks."

THOSE DEFINING MOMENTS IN LIFE

Most of us can remember a few moments in life that were "defining." That is to say, something set us on a new or different course or made a big difference. This was one of those moments for me, and I have never forgotten it. The seemingly simple stock story that he told me established the basis for a large part of how I came to invest. That one story made a big difference for me.

First, I recognized on that day that I should always try to work in organizations with great people who knew a lot about investing, rather than try to get most of my information from technical journals or texts. I had read about "grand masters" in investing and other areas of life, and it seemed as if one should learn the best and the most from a master. But I had always envisioned this type of person as very famous and had not realized that many masters did not have their name in lights.

Dave was the first person I had ever spoken with at length who had become very wealthy from picking his own stocks, so I was eager to hear more.

He told me that he had invested in a bunch of small, fast-growing companies over time, and some worked better than others. He felt that while everyone should have a portfolio, or group of stocks, that had future growth potential, ones that made sense for him or her, he had always believed that it was smart to also have a few stocks that had the possibility of making one rich.

One day he invested in Xerox. The company, formerly known as Haloid, had a technology that it was perfecting and selling in 1959. The stock went public that year and was trading over the counter, so he bought it. Xerox, the first automatic office copying machine to use regular paper, was listed on the New York Stock Exchange in 1961. Because its price had been appreciating strongly, it became much better known, and the gains accelerated. He went on to say that he read all he could about the new technology and the market reception, the lack of real competition, and the potential for the company. Xerox had been relatively unknown before then, as was the new technology that enabled its machines to make paper copies from printed pages. Back then, everyone used low-tech methods—such as carbon paper, slipped in between sheets in a typewriter—to make copies.

After reading and understanding all about how the company operated, Dave still had not been satisfied, since there was no assurance that this new technology would pay for itself and actually flourish. One of the more important things he did was to talk to other companies' purchasing people, who actually bought the machines; he also spoke with many of the users in some nearby Wall Street offices. He chatted with clerks and secretaries. He asked good questions about their usage patterns, what they liked and did not like, and what would make them buy more copiers. That gave him a real feel for the state of the market and gave him enough relevant information to make his own back-of-the-envelope calculations.

Dave used common sense and estimated how many machines could be sold as technology improved; as prices dropped; and as marketing, distribution, and awareness all were projected to show reasonable expansion. He worked out a weak case, a really strong case, and a middle-of-the-road case. Just from these calculations, it was plain that the potential for earnings growth was huge. Dave had what he needed and wanted in common-sense terms, but he also could look at real numbers on one piece of paper. The simplicity and logic of it all were very impressive, and today I still love so-called models of a company's future earnings that can be made simple, straightforward, and logical.

As much as I benefited from training in my early investment days, it was the practical applications of this commonsense approach that started me on a track that became my personal methodology in most things, including talking to airline pilots, truck drivers, and baseball-card dealers, over the years, to name just a few. In this situation, as the Xerox stock had climbed higher, my lunch partner had known more, had greater confidence, and had bought more. The ups and downs of the market would affect the stock price, of course, but he bought on dips because he had great faith that this company would persevere. He told me that the more knowledge he had, the more money he made; and the more money he made, the more he wanted to know.

I could understand why many investors and businessmen were skeptical about the new product, as they wondered whether buyers were just experimenting with this new toy that seemed to make copies that were so much more expensive than those done with, say, carbon paper. Remember that this great boom period for Xerox occurred before personal computers, and even word processors, appeared in offices. It was just as appropriate to be highly suspicious of brand-new, untested products, services, and markets back then as it is today. Skepticism is a reflection of a healthy sensitivity to risk, and it manifests itself either in staying away from what is feared or unknown or in working to gain the knowledge to clear up some of the doubts and uncertainties, one way or another.

The doubters—there are always plenty of bears for every great idea—felt that the cost of the machine would be far too high for a really broad market to develop, and the copier would not pay for itself in a business that cared about costs and expenses, which is virtually every business. Moreover, the copies came out damp with ink, the machine made noise, and the process was slow. In these early days, nothing at all had been solidly proved. But this company had a product in an early stage and was selling into an immature market, and unlike most of the Internet companies of the 1990s, Haloid Xerox did have some earnings, good management, and a solid business model.

Up to now, Dave had made pretty good money on various investments, like many other investors. But, while many investors over the years held, for example, Xerox, Microsoft, Medtronic, Home Depot, Toys "R" Us, and many others at just the right time in their early years, most investors took a profit and got out way too early, missing the chance to build a fortune with a few stocks, or one stock. Countless investors were shaken out of great stocks because something happened that made the overall market go down, and they just plain bolted for the door.

The difference was that they did not build deep knowledge of the company behind the stock—the kind of deep knowledge that keeps you in the stock when the market fluctuates, the kind of deep knowledge that makes you want to buy more stock, and the kind of knowledge that keeps you in the stock for a very long time.

If you look at an old stock chart from that period, you see that after adjusting for splits, Xerox stock would have sold for about $4 around the time Dave first bought it; some dozen years later, it had hit $160 per share. He had made 40X his money, essentially a lifetime's fortune, and that was that.

That period in which my new friend Dave made his fortune was the real golden era for Xerox. Later it would see its fortunes get better or worse. Many of those periods in which the challenges were poorly met had to do with its own management. So Xerox in the following decades presents us with other great lessons to learn, and we will be coming back to this company. Clearly, though, I had learned a great lesson from my friend—a lesson that would launch me on a quest early in my professional years. The quest I speak of is with me even now.

This book is about doing what Dave did.

Using stories that are both educational and entertaining, *The Big Money* reveals the best methods to simplify stock picking and to stop defeating ourselves. You will hear from one of the greatest investors of the 1920s and see how he describes investors beating themselves almost a century ago. This, unfortunately, is still the case with most people today. We are all emotional creatures, and busy and swamped with information and data, but far too many of us have no obvious "navigation chart."

The lessons from each story are universal in the sense that they can be applied to many, many stocks, not just one, and not just in one industry. The theme of simplifying investing is paramount, and this book is not built on numbers or concepts that you need experience to use. This book is for everyone out there willing to spend a few hours a week reading and focusing on a few key factors that can make you the big money from one stock or just a few stocks.

I ask people, "How are you going to recognize the next Microsoft, or the next Home Depot, Dell, Nike, or McDonald's, if you do not really understand how we recognized those companies in the first place?"

McDonald's did not invent either hamburgers or fast food, and Nike did not invent running shoes. Both, however, became the clear leaders of their industries. Microsoft did not invent computer operating systems, word-processing software, or spreadsheet software programs, yet it became the market leader for all of these products.

Home Depot did not invent hardware stores or retailing (though it did pioneer something of its own), and Dell did not invent computers (though it too was a pioneer). Not only that, but in their early years, when these companies were just lifting off, they were not first in their industry. Every one of these companies came from behind. You will be both interested and entertained by these examples, and you will find that the lessons in the following stories can make you rich by helping you to recognize what makes a company and its stock potential sources of great wealth.

All of these companies, and many more that you have heard of—and a long list that you have not heard of—had a few key things in common. These things were ideas that were translated into strategy, business plan, and action.

Over time, companies like Cisco, Dell, Microsoft, Home Depot, Wal-Mart, and others have made investors hundreds of times their money (and in some cases thousands of times, as with Wal-Mart). Yet many more stocks were there for the taking. Some were good gains, some were great gains, and some could make patient investors wealthy for the rest of their lives.

I do feel that most people should have the bulk of their retirement money in mutual funds or with financial advisers or both, so that they are not burdened with managing their retirement account. But I also feel that everyone can use the methods I have developed, own a few stocks, and concentrate all of his or her investment time on the "wealth" stocks, with the objective of becoming truly rich.

It is not just the famous names that can make you rich. You will find a story about a company named Molex in Chapter 2, why I invested in it, and how it did pretty much what Cisco did. You will be witness to the inside battle between Apollo Computer, the leader in work-station computers in the early 1980s; and Sun Microsystems, which replaced Apollo after a tough fight, and went on to make investors over 200X their money.

The battles are endless. Consider what happened when Sears, Roebuck and Co. was king of retail in this country and celebrated its dominance by opening the 110-story Sears Tower in Chicago in 1973. The Sears Tower was the world's tallest building (until 1996), housing the headquarters of America's most successful retail and catalog operation. Analysts back in the seventies projected that Sears would keep its number one spot for a very long time. They were wrong, very wrong. The reasons why Sears fell and Wal-Mart rose are directly related to business model and management, and if one looked hard at the key elements of their stated strategies, what the management was doing, and the main parts of the business model, instead of just extrapolating the momentum of earnings and analysts' estimates, it was all there to see.

Perhaps investors might remember tremendous gains from Zapata Corporation, or Schlumberger, both in the energy business, and perhaps not. Maybe some will know that Quaker Oats and Ralston Purina each had their periods of 700 percent and 800 percent gains in only a few years, or that Rite Aid, the drugstore chain, once went from $4.75 per share to $55 in about twenty-four months. It is easier to remember that Disney went from $4.50 to $120 in one six-year period (1966 to 1972), while McDonald's multiplied investors' money by 50X during that same time. But many will not be aware that MGIC, a good financial company that professionals as well as individuals owned, rose from $1.70 to $96.

The point is that you cannot always predict which business sectors will produce great gains in a given period. Sometimes the gains will come from the technology sector, sometimes from retail or media companies, and at other times from interesting companies that are just doing a great job while other companies in their industry sector are stagnating. Most of the time, it does not matter whether a company is a drugstore or a software company. What does matter is whether it has an open-ended market opportunity and a great BASM to take advantage of that opportunity.

This is not a history book; it is a book of great lessons to teach you to recognize what will make you rich. Nevertheless, history shows us which companies have generated the huge gains for stockholders and why. We all need this perspective in order to recognize great investments in the years ahead. Investors who wonder how Google will fare are far better off if they understand what happened to all the great search-engine companies that came earlier, from Alta Vista and WebCrawler to Lycos and others, concentrating on companies' descriptions of how they would grow and be profitable—the business models.

Besides, just as in military battles, chess, and elsewhere, all the great moves repeat again and again. Business models can be virtually the same, even if the products or services sold are different. That's why Molex taught me things that helped me to recognize and make huge money from Cisco. The key parts of BASM were the same for these two companies.

I listen carefully as debates rage today about Google—the "poster child" for what people hope is the big opportunity stock—and others such as Apple and its iPod, Netflix, TiVo, nanotechnology companies, and more. Debates over Google are most often about its valuation based on price-to-earnings ratio. But for every time investors wish they had sold a "seemingly" expensive stock, there are many instances when they sold stocks that could have made them rich, because they had no guide other than "conventional valuation arithmetic"—they didn't know what to look for.

It is disappointing how many students and investors I talk to do not really understand how Microsoft or Dell or others came from behind to win. They need to know how these things happened if they are to recognize which companies are to be the biggest successes of tomorrow. So picking a winning stock cannot be like a second-rate general trying to fight the last war; it is all about understanding themes that will occur over and over again, in order to recognize how to win the next war. You can be sure that the management of the great companies understands the history of the winners' business models. So do the best investors.

Thus, to spot Google and nanotechnology and stocks of the future, we move away from the conventional—"Red Coat investing"—and use BASM and the Seven Steps.

The most successful managers and strategists are true visionaries who have learned the right lessons from the past and stand by their commitments even when things are tough. Nike's Phil Knight battled against Reebok, and he led Nike to victory in the contest to be number one. The same goes for Microsoft's Bill Gates, who battled Lotus (which had the early spreadsheet lead of 70 percent market share); and Dell, which came along five years after Compaq, when Compaq seemed invincible.

To me, these same stories are going to repeat again and again, with only the names changing. The Internet battles already fought and won were very much decided by the factors of BASM. The Internet is just beginning to transform our lives and how we do business, and successful investing will mean understanding why eBay and Amazon and Yahoo have done what others could not do. New Internet companies will not end with the arrival of Google. There will be many more. The Internet age has only just begun. More new technologies will continue to arrive in this age of science and discovery. Nanotechnology, or the science of the very small, which focuses on things that are the width of a human hair or less, is already finding new ways of doing things. As in any new, exciting area, there will be mania stocks and there will be great investments, and one needs to know how to recognize each.

Some investors ask me how you tell the difference between a stock like Krispy Kreme Doughnuts, which became a mania stock (irrationality prevailing), and Google, which seems to be a solid company so far. There are some good lessons in this book that will answer those questions and many more that are front and center in today's markets and in the markets of every era. These lessons will help you with many stocks in the future.

I enjoy comparing Apple Computer in its early years with TiVo in its early years, since the lesson is a good one. Investors who have no idea of what happened to former great technology companies that "owned" their industries' number one position, including Wang Laboratories, Digital Equipment Corporation, Lotus Development, and Compaq Computer, will find that they will become much stronger tech investors if they know the outcomes of these great battles, and the reasons for victory and defeat.

Finally, there are even simple ways of dealing with potential fraud or financial reporting problems, and using BASM and the Seven Steps in this regard as well.

Have you heard of Sambo's restaurants? Well, just as Molex taught me things that led me to recognize what Cisco really was when Cisco made its public debut, in the 1970s Sambo's taught me to recognize what Enron really was in the 1990s.

Everything repeats. This is a huge plus, and a huge secret to making money with stocks. Learn to recognize things that you will see again and again, and you will be way ahead of many other investors. This is true equally for winners and losers. In this book you will learn how to recognize the themes and the stocks. All of these themes involve BASM and the Seven Steps.

Nonprofessional investors have big advantages over professionals. Among other things, they do not have to provide elaborate reports to committees in order to justify buying or selling and get the votes required to support such decisions. Professionals do have some advantages, but individuals have many more. There is a world of great opportunity if you simplify and focus only on the specific knowledge that you need. This knowledge leads to confidence, and that, with some disciplines, leads to big money.

This book is for people who want a clear, simple way to add to their mutual funds and investments with some stocks that can make them truly wealthy. It is for all of the countless millions more who want to know the stories, the concepts, and the lessons that will guide them to win their own freedom from inertia and from the old ways of investing.

Looking at earnings is important, of course, and I will discuss how one does this, but it is the golden goose that creates those earnings on which we must focus in order to simplify and to understand the great stocks. BASM, or some version of it, worked very well for me in my stock selection and in building a record that was one of the five best in the country for fifteen years. It has also worked for many more of the best stock pickers in the country.

I hope you enjoy the stories, gain from the lessons—and then go out there and, as Phil Knight would say, "Just do it."

CHAPTER TWO

KNOW WHAT YOU OWN

Knowledge

To succeed in business, to reach the top, an individual must
know all it is possible to know about that business.
—J. PAUL GETTY

HOW IT WORKS

Some people today have heard of Molex, and many have not. Almost
nobody had heard of it many years ago when I first invested in it. I became
familiar with it and bought it on the company's initial public offering in
1972. I made a lot of money and owned it more than once.

Over time the stock gained almost 20,000 percent or 200X its initial
price, so the stock performance made it a "Cisco" long before Cisco appeared. Some specific things about the Molex management and business
model made it similar to Cisco. That helped me to recognize what Cisco
could become when I was studying Cisco as it went public almost two decades later. This is one of those great examples of why certain things in history create the basis for recognizing tomorrow's big-money winners.

Molex, located amid cornfields in Lisle, Illinois, was a tiny electrical
connector company that went public in 1972. I was then working at
Wellington Management Company and was assigned to be the analyst on

this company. Although I knew little about technology companies, what I had read about tech companies and stocks interested me. I was a bit nervous, of course, because I did not fully understand the factors that made technology companies and products good, or what made them successful.

What I quickly found out is what most individual investors need to know: if you look at BASM and the factors that make any company good or great, you will be able to invest in technology with greater ease and better results. You do not need to be an engineer, and you should not go down the "let's play engineer" route and thus get confused by so-called techie language.

I did not stay nervous all that long. I read some more and found that the specific technology products a company sells can be less important than how the company manages the development and evolution of that technology, how it works with its customers, how it markets its products and services, and finally, how it manages itself. There were, and there are, a lot of good technologies, but very few good, let alone great, technology companies.

I do not want to minimize the importance of great technologies, new or old. But think of the technology as the "ante" to get into the "game"— the competitive battle for customers and market share. Think of BASM as the way those companies that win are able to do so. Good technology companies, like all other types of businesses, rank very highly on the four factors of BASM. That leads to the most important aspect of high stock valuations: repeatability. Many, if not most, tech investors are attracted to companies with "hot" products. They become trapped in the stocks as companies fail to carry the great product successes forward and achieve repeatability. Then investors end up with disappointing profits or even lose money.

When I first went to see the management of Molex, I will never forget how convincing the top people were. They didn't try to sell me on their company, but they did convince me that they really knew their mission and how to achieve its objectives. They had great credibility with me, and over the years that turned out to be warranted. They were not promising the moon, and they were not announcing technologies that would conquer the world. The Krehbiels, the family who ran Molex, were a solid midwestern family management team who had worked together for years to grow the company, which had been founded in 1938 to manufacture inexpensive molding materials for toys and flowerpots.

Now they wanted to use their great storehouse of manufacturing knowledge and years of experience to enter a more dynamic market. They had chosen electrical connectors, because they looked a few years ahead and believed that electrical connectors would have a great future.

This is a great example of the assumptions component of BASM. Molex made assumptions about why electrical connectors would be a great business to be in, and those assumptions were critical to its success. (Years later, Microsoft made assumptions that the marketplace would want standard software and would not hop around from one hot product to another. These assumptions made the company willing to make no profit at all on some early offerings just to "lock up" customers.)

The proliferation of electronics that use connectors, from autos and VCRs to Pepsi vending machines, meant a huge moment of opportunity.

You have probably seen connectors—components made of plastic with wires coming out of them. You will find them in just about every electrical product you can think of. Using sophisticated connection devices instead of, say, soldering parts together makes manufacturing cheaper and more competitive, allows for upgrades, and improves product performance.

Connectors are used to connect a personal computer's hard drive (major memory storage, or disk drive) to the rest of the PC, including the "brains," or central processing unit. They do much the same with a long list of things in your car, including the engine, dashboard, and headlights. From televisions to vending machines, the machines that use connectors represent a huge market.

Most of the time, great companies are not limited to serving little niche markets, but correctly pick product or service areas that will have enormous if not unlimited markets to sell into.

This end market is made up of companies that manufacture all sorts of things. Ever since connectors replaced old-fashioned soldering, the pressure has been on the connector companies to make devices that are progressively lower in cost yet significantly improve product performance. Companies that do this win the juicy contracts.

I held these connectors in my hand and could see that manufacturing had to be expert and keep to fine tolerances. It was easy to see that you had to have a low failure rate and had to be very competitive on the cost. (If a connector was defective, you couldn't put it in the "refurbish" bin—you trashed it.) I looked at some of the customer order ledgers management showed me and could see that the customer had started with small orders, showing that they were "trying out" Molex in the days when AMP, the biggest and most prominent manufacturer around, was the leader in this industry. (AMP is still the biggest, but is now part of the Tyco conglomerate.) I see Molex, which is growing faster than AMP, as the innovation leader.

The company's statements and reports seemed consistent with what was going on in the world. The folks at Molex wanted everyone to know them, to read about them, and to understand their business models, assumptions, strategy, and management strengths. They knew that doing this would show us that they wanted to be the best—and that they really could be.

Acquiring in-depth knowledge leads to genuine confidence. Both are essential to make the big money. Knowledge was an early key to investment success for me. It became the first of what I eventually thought of as the Seven Steps to successful investing.

I learned in high school physics the old story about the bird flying past the window. An unsophisticated observer might assume that the bird would just fly on and on in the same direction indefinitely, but a thoughtful person would not extrapolate that way. So I did not assume that what I observed would just continue on indefinitely. Analysts extrapolate as much as they analyze in some cases, using earnings as well as corporate product cycles. This is one of the all-time greatest pitfalls that prevent people from making big money: assuming too much.

What my research was aimed at, then, was what could change as well as what could repeat. What did Molex have to do to repeat product cycles, continue innovation, and get contracts? I did not know this on day one, but I learned that Molex had three of the most important things a company could have if it is going to be a huge winner:

1. taking market share from other worthy competitors
2. having a huge or open-ended market opportunity
3. knowing exactly how to lock in customers and work closely with them

Keep in mind that I did not know BASM then. In my early days as an investor, I learned BASM from companies like Molex. You can learn the same things from the cases in this book and then invest with this knowledge in mind.

I believed what Molex's management said about its product development efforts, and thought it was right about the huge potential market it envisioned. I knew from my own reading and research that there were many things going on in the world that would create this huge market and drive very high growth.

In fact, it all really did happen. Today Molex supplies five connectors to a Pepsi vending machine, nine connectors to a typical scanner, four connectors to a washer or similar appliance, and seven connectors to a cable-television box, just to name a tiny fraction of the products that make up its end market.

What I liked the best is what I could see *on the surface.* I could use rough numbers and see great market dynamics. What the management said to me was also stated in company releases and annual and quarterly reports. It all lined up and was very straightforward.

What I most wanted to know was whether I would be foolish if I extrapolated the great near-term growth and market-share gains over a considerable period. Many small companies can achieve initial success but cannot repeat that success year after year, particularly as they grow larger.

As I said earlier, Molex had been a family-managed firm since its inception. I read recently about how unusual it is for family managements to make it to a second, let alone a third, generation. According to some experts, only 4 percent of companies are still family-dominated in the third generation. Molex is still family-dominated today, and very successful.

I liked management a lot, and that was step one in becoming a believer.

· · ·

Next came a closer look at Molex's business model, which centered on being as profitable as possible while avoiding debt, and, very important, working closely with customers in order to anticipate and meet or exceed their needs. This enabled Molex to be exceptionally good at designing what customers would want most, and having products that performed at the top. Molex wanted a very broad product line so that it could fill *all* needs, and avoid being stuck in a niche.

The key to me was how working with customers and spending a lot of energy, time, and money on this major activity made up the heart of a winning business model in this industry. All the Krehbiels and the other management people I talked to at Molex obviously had dedication and credibility—what they said and what they did hung together. You will see that this is not always so easy to do. Many, many companies say that they work with their customers, but as you read their annual reports and examine the annual reports of competitors or customers, you will see the difference between those who really do what they say and say what they do, and those that do not. "Staying close to the customer" is hard, and expensive, but it pays off. Companies such as Molex, Cisco, Home Depot, and Wal-Mart have a business model that is heavily weighted toward understanding the most important needs of customers and then creating a way of meeting those needs, present and future.

An average company does not develop a deep enough understanding of customers' present and future needs. Most companies have a "financial fear factor" that keeps them from doing what it takes, since they often make short-term decisions to maximize profits. Spending money on customers' needs, though, maximizes future profits and growth and helps to lock in customers—a critical element in repeatability.

So lots of companies give lip service to working closely with customers, but it is quite difficult to do while also maintaining expense control and profit margins at winning levels. Many managers talk this game, but few can actually deliver. This is why identifying "management that can execute" is one of my three buy disciplines, discussed in chapter 4, "Buy and Sell Disciplines."

What I learned from Molex was a key factor that helped me to make the huge money we later made in Cisco, differentiating it from the many other companies that all wanted to do the same thing in those early days of computer networking and switching. I recognized the greatness of the business model and the execution abilities. Both stocks made the big money for investors and are examples of the fact that everything really does repeat. Learning to recognize these key elements of success early will give you the knowledge and confidence to buy tomorrow's big winners.

Making a lot of money with Molex was a classic case of how knowledge goes hand in hand with wealth. Successful investors start with knowledge. The more knowledge you have, the more money you will make.

Naturally, because markets and stocks have volatility, knowledge is a great asset to have. Knowledge brings confidence, and confidence is what keeps people in stocks that are undergoing price pressures yet continue to have great growth in earnings. Confidence is what helps successful investors to buy more shares when prices dip, while investors who do not know what they own become emotional and sell out of fear and lack of knowledge.

Knowledge reduces risk. As Ralph Waldo Emerson wrote, "Knowledge is the antidote to fear." When you have knowledge, you can invest a lot more money to make far bigger gains. Thus, *know what you own*, and why you own it.

KNOWLEDGE IS POWER

In investing, as in many other areas of life, success often depends on knowledge. In the case of Molex, some simple analysis and common sense provided me with the knowledge I needed to make a lot of money.

Plenty of other investment companies bought Molex's public offering. We got a little stock and made some money, but not a lot. Not long after that, the market started to react to a bad economy and took Molex down quite a bit. Because of our deep knowledge, we went against the market drop, taking advantage of the short time horizon and sellers' emotions. So we bought the bigger position we had originally wanted but couldn't get

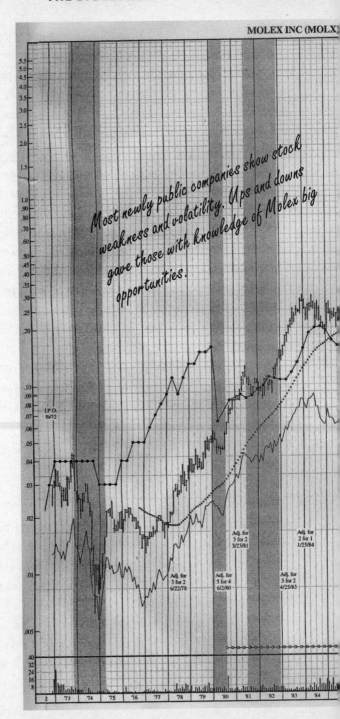

MOLEX INC (MOLX)

Most newly public companies show stock weakness and volatility. Ups and downs gave those with knowledge of Molex big opportunities.

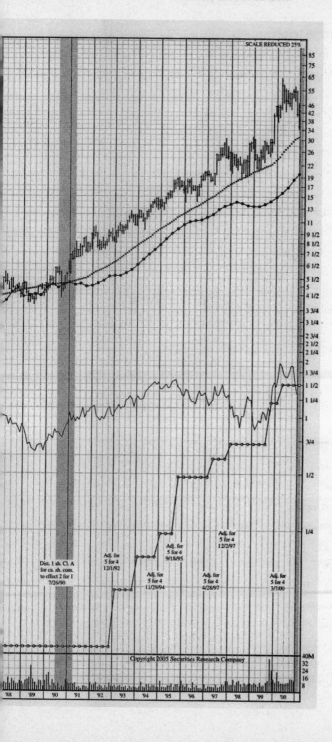

SCALE REDUCED 25%

Dist. 1 sh. Cl. A
for ea. sh. com.
to effect 2 for 1
7/26/90

Adj. for
5 for 4
12/1/92

Adj. for
5 for 4
11/29/94

Adj. for
5 for 4
9/18/95

Adj. for
5 for 4
4/28/97

Adj. for
5 for 4
12/2/97

Adj. for
5 for 4
3/7/00

because of heavy demands for the IPO. The stock quadrupled, then paused and went sideways for a little while, and then tripled after that. Nothing goes straight up, and very often the market action of a stock unduly influences people who lack sufficient knowledge about what they own and, consequently, fail to follow the right buy and sell disciplines. (As you know, I'll discuss buy and sell disciplines in chapter 4.)

Over the long term, Molex sales went from just over $17 million to over $2 billion in a bit more than three decades, an expansion of almost 120X. Profits multiplied even more as margins improved, going from $1.78 million to $858 million at the peak, or 482X. The stock, adjusted for splits, went from 33¢ to $61 at the peak, or 185X.

Most tech companies do well for only a few years. They rise quickly but soon begin to fall behind their competitors. Continued long-term success makes the great companies special. Repeatability of results flows from a great business model and leads to longevity.

> **You can observe a lot by watching.**
> —Yogi Berra

It did not occur to me in my early days that a parking lot could be a great source of information for investors, but ever since I heard from a colleague about a McDonald's parking lot, I do not count out anything.

When I began to cover McDonald's for our company, I visited with management, talked to good Wall Street analysts, and read everything I could. I expanded my knowledge. I also made it a point to talk to franchise operators. I even walked into restaurants to see if there were patterns or trends or other bits of information that I could pick up. I liked to talk to people who used the products. I wanted to know what it was that made people go to McDonald's in droves, particularly more so than to other hamburger restaurants.

I remembered what Dave had done to acquire so much knowledge about Xerox at the very beginning.

I saw with my own eyes and heard from customers that consistency, quality, and cleanliness were there, and were very important factors. Those factors were built into the core of the McDonald's business model, so it became evident that a hamburger restaurant does not succeed just on tasty food. It must be differentiated; the restaurant needs a real business model that can stand the heat of the competitive kitchen, so to speak.

I had tried very hard to get all the portfolio managers at Wellington Management Company to buy the stock, but the group in Philadelphia (I was in Boston), led by legendary "value stock" buyer John Neff, had always felt the stock was a bit expensive. They were unsure whether the company could stay differentiated long enough to justify the higher price. But one day I heard in the morning investment meeting over the speakers that connected our offices that John Nyheim, a senior associate of Neff's, had bought the stock into their portfolios.

I asked Nyheim about it. I was pleased that the group had done so, but I noted that they had resisted buying earlier for the reasons I mentioned (and because John had stated that he personally did not like the burgers).

John said, "Yes, Fred, that is correct. But first of all, I now go there because my kids love it, and they make me go. Second," he added, "when I go there, it is always full and hard to park at. And third, it is the only place I go where there is a full array of every car, from the Volkswagen Beetle to the best Mercedes. This company serves a very broad market with mass appeal—*that* is a great market!"

These things had changed his mind. I could see that John Nyheim, a great investor, had an open mind, which is one of the best weapons of a great investor. Great investors do change their opinions. They are not trying to declare the truth; they are trying to find it.

Moreover, John was doing what I liked to do—he was looking at the users of the product and studying the marketplace. One does not need to learn great lessons every day—there are only so many—but one has to remember them and *use* them. That is how great investors become great, and that is how to make money in stocks.

As I studied McDonald's more and more over time, I realized that what looked simple was not. Management had designed brilliant, complex systems to achieve uniformity, quality, and cost controls, all of which supported great prices. *Sustainability* and *repeatability* are two things always to look for. They do not come out of thin air, they do not come easily, and they never result from luck. They come from the M in BASM. *Management* is what makes the difference.

COMMONSENSE INVESTING

Chiefly the mold of a man's fortune is in his own hands.
—SIR FRANCIS BACON

Whether it was Molex or McDonald's or others, common sense showed me how to evaluate the markets they served. Working up some very basic numbers led me, as it would lead any investor, to the same conclusions I would reach by studying BASM. In other words, BASM is the golden goose, and the earnings are the golden eggs. Over time this earnings growth will translate into great stocks.

Even though one could work up very complex earnings models for McDonald's and all other companies, all you need to know is whether you think the company will meet or beat Wall Street estimates. You are not trying to persuade somebody else to buy, nor are you writing a report. What you want to know is whether or not the company is going to grow strongly, and make or exceed the earnings estimates that are already out there. Common sense and a pencil are all you need.

I looked at how tiny a share of the restaurant market McDonald's (MCD) had, and knew that if it executed well, it could grow strongly for many years before it had much of a share. Then, I looked at the company's projections for opening new restaurants, and the revenues of the whole company, divided by the number of stores out there, to get the average amount of revenue and profits per store (annual report), for starters. Even though new restaurants take a little time to get to good profitability, it was easy to see from these numbers that MCD would grow very strongly, and I felt that the P/E of the stock did not reflect that outlook (see chapter 4 on how to measure stock price to earnings and to growth rates in a simple way). My own arithmetic on this, which is easy even if you do not like math, said to me that estimates could easily be low. Reading about the brilliance of the company's systems gave me knowledge and confidence that execution would be great. Execution from BASM and the number of new restaurants that were opening told me to buy.

Keep in mind that with all quality stocks, the professionals do not have any advantage over anyone reading this book. What Dave did with Xerox or John with McDonald's demonstrates that. If you want to get rich from stocks, and understand BASM, and if you have common sense and a desire to do a little work, and thus seek knowledge, then all it takes is finding one truly great stock—just one.

RECONNAISSANCE AND THE "AMBER ROOM"

During my first visit to McDonald's, when I was a young securities analyst researching and following this company, I spent an entire day at the company's headquarters in Oakbrook, Illinois. That was the moment I got to look into the very core, as it were, of the company. One of management's senior executives took me to a special area.

"This is what we call our Amber Room," my host proudly asserted, as he showed me a modest room dimly lit by amber light. Stepping through what was much like the hatch of a ship's compartment, I found myself standing in a room with a circular floor, most of which was taken up by a circular water bed. The walls formed a conical shape, sweeping upward to a point. "Scientists have found that amber light, coupled with a relaxing atmosphere, stimulates those brain waves most responsible for creativity. Creativity and innovation are central to our future and to maintaining our leadership position in our industry," the executive concluded as he observed my reaction to this fascinating environment.

That visit to McDonald's certainly showed me that this one could indeed be the big one. Those on the management team were driven to be the best, they were highly creative, and they were thinking a lot about how to be successful for a long time to come. All of that is good, but those things alone did not make McDonald's great. As I describe later, I visited with the managements of the major airlines, and they were all driven to compete, but that did not make them great. I had visited with a bunch of restaurant managements and had not yet seen a company that could be called a great company. So what was it about McDonald's that made it a great company? You may seldom (if ever) be able to travel to far-flung locations and meet with managers of companies that interest you, but today, unlike my early days, we have the Internet with huge amounts of information on company Web sites, and we have Regulation FD (Fair Disclosure) from the U.S. Securities and Exchange Commission (SEC), which states that companies cannot give professional investors (or anyone else) private information that they do not release publicly.

So you *do* have the advantage. You get all the information and do not have to fly back home and write a report or get the approval of a committee. You can look at your research and buy.

Moreover, there are plenty of companies worth getting to know in depth that have operations right in your city or town, particularly national chains and franchises. Go in there and look at the company from a *customer's perspective*. Get a real feeling for the location and the facility, and experience how the company delivers its service or products. This is what the military calls reconnaissance. Before you make your move, find out what the terrain is like—become familiar with a company's reality, not just abstractions about it or what management claims.

Real confidence comes when you have read the annual reports and releases from management, and then looked for yourself. It may sound too simple, but, in fact, ensuring that what they claim about themselves and what their customers think of them are the same will help you identify winners.

The first thing I could see about McDonald's is that it was inherently innovative. The company devised a system to deliver a hamburger that had a distinctive taste (and mass appeal) coupled with a lower price than the burger you got at the diner just down the street.

Low price was important, but quality, service, and cleanliness were crucial parts of the business model that really attracted customers. Through research, McDonald's created and maintained a great set of operational systems. It is far tougher to maintain such systems than it is just to stick with low cost and prices. McDonalds' brilliant, innovative systems enabled it to do what nobody else could do: make all the hamburgers consistently good and make them taste exactly the same, every day, at every store. This was the greatness that had even competitors offering compliments.

Being an innovator is a good thing, but being the first one out with a product is not necessary for success. Sometimes the companies that race to be the fastest with innovations have trouble maintaining growth, particularly if they do not have systems to handle rapid growth. When Ray Kroc bought out the McDonald brothers in 1961, there were a number of fast-food restaurant chains in the United States. None that existed at that time became great long-term investments for outside shareholders. Hamburgers were certainly not new, having originated in their modern form, on a bun, at the 1904 World's Fair. Then, in 1921, White Castle was born in Wichita, Kansas, serving small burgers on buns. It grew to be the first chain restaurant of its type, standardizing what it served.

White Castle did really well, and a bunch of imitators sprung up, none nearly as good. But White Castle never expanded aggressively, never developed a broader menu, and never developed the essential operational systems, real-estate plan, or financing to be a megachain. It stayed in the cities, failing to expand into the lucrative suburban markets. Without the kind of systems that McDonald's developed, a suburban expansion probably would have failed. But the tiny burgers and onions were popular, and in some areas still are. (White Castle also established a market share in supermarkets, where you can buy those good old little burgers in the frozen food section.)

Howard Johnson's, born in the 1920s, did very well for decades, but it became a full restaurant, with locations only on highways and primarily serving travelers who wanted a full meal, so it was neither burgers-only nor fast food. Even after the oil embargo of 1973 almost killed the company, and it closed many units, the founder built it back over time. Not until later, after his son took over, did it became poorly managed; it then went from a great American success story to second-rate—one of the most telling examples of how *management makes the critical difference.*

Burger King was born in 1954. (Wendy's came along right about the time I was deeply involved in my investigation of McDonald's, and went public in 1976.) Burger King was an excellent competitor. But McDonald's

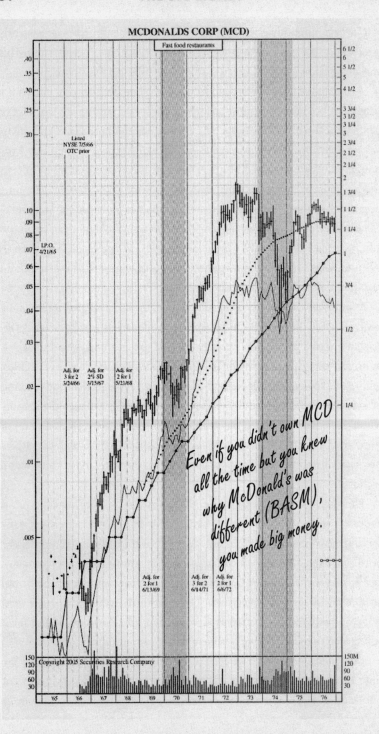

MCDONALDS CORP (MCD)

Fast food restaurants

Listed
NYSE 7/5/66
OTC prior

I.P.O.
4/21/65

Adj. for
3 for 2
5/24/66

Adj. for
2% SD
3/15/67

Adj. for
2 for 1
5/21/68

Adj. for
2 for 1
6/13/69

Adj. for
3 for 2
6/14/71

Adj. for
2 for 1
6/6/72

Even if you didn't own MCD all the time but you knew why McDonald's was different (BASM), you made big money.

Copyright 2005 Securities Research Company

had a culture that impelled it to never rest and to constantly broaden the menu, which, in turn, led it to expand from lunches to breakfasts and dinners. The company relied heavily on the experience and ideas of franchisees, many of whom were bright and aggressive and came up with winning ideas. For instance, the Big Mac was conceived by a franchisee, as was the Egg McMuffin. Culture matters a lot, and McDonald's had a winning culture. If you, as an individual investor, wanted to see the effect that culture had on operations, all you needed to do was eat at the nearest McDonald's and watch how the staff functioned and how they related to customers. Reconnaissance!

All of the things I have mentioned contributed to McDonald's being a truly great company. When one really got to know McDonald's as a company, though, it became clear that the core secret to great management success was operations.

Ray Kroc wanted to buy the couple of restaurants from the McDonald brothers because he felt that with a successful plan the restaurants could be made much better. His plan included dropping barbecued beef (which took too much time to prepare and to eat), and concentrating on hamburgers. Kroc wanted to grow a big chain and developed a strategy to make this possible. More important, he felt that he needed systems that would manage the costs and standardization of menu, service, and profit margins for every unit.

WAVING THE MAGIC WAND

So, while competitors were expanding, including selling lots of franchises, Ray Kroc played the tortoise and expanded slowly for a few years, while implementing his systems. This was like waving a magic wand, because these highly sophisticated systems made the operations very profitable and created a framework for growing the world's largest restaurant chain over time.

McDonald's (MCD) stock rode a number of waves of appreciation, as the company pushed forward to expand rapidly. The stock went public in 1965, and rose by 33 percent the first day—and then did not do anything much for months. Soon, though, it tripled in a year, and then tripled again in the next two and a half years. So its first few years made McDonald's a tremendous investment for many. Around the time I was first visiting and getting to know MCD, it was planning aggressive expansion.

I realized, when I saw the amount of detail and the brilliance of the systems, that what MCD was doing could be repeated over and over again, and therefore I could see no limits to its growth. I came back to Boston from Oak Brook and made my first recommendation of the stock. Some of the portfolio managers bought it. This was not a new public offering, and since the stock had done so well, many who did not look closely at this company would not buy it, fearing that its nice run was over. They did not see that it could grow to be a major gain over time.

We bought the stock at about $15, and within twenty-four months it was $60, and that was just the beginning. McDonald's has made a lot of people rich over time. One did not have to buy it on the first day. We did extremely well even though we bought years after the IPO. (I was still in school at the time of the IPO.) My hat is off to those with knowledge and patience who bought the IPO. Over a thirty-year period, 100 shares bought on the public offering would have cost $2,250 and grown in value to about $1.8 million, so a $10,000 investment would be worth $8 million.

Many people made fortunes along the way. Those who bought at higher prices often had the knowledge, and thus the confidence, to invest much more money. Thus they made more money.

McDonald's was my first great company. I saw that it had taken control of its own destiny. While Wendy's and Kentucky Fried Chicken (KFC) did, well, MCD became the clear leader. Even KFC had to marvel at how McDonald's outdid everybody else in standardizing all of its restaurant units. The systems meant easier, faster, more profitable expansion, and customers were happy at the standardization of the three key things that they could see and that McDonald's emphasized: quality, freshness, and cleanliness.

YOU NEED A SYSTEM

Everybody who plays blackjack and some other casino games hears about people who try to develop a system to beat the house. Well, in many industries and companies, a proprietary system is the company's equivalent of beating the house. It helps the company to beat the competition by doing things better while also achieving higher profits and growth to drive stock prices. Management plans the strategy and implements the business model—the path to profitability—but management has to execute the details of the plan. An investor needs as much relevant knowledge about these factors as he or she can acquire.

Knowledge is such an important element in differentiating companies that slip and slide from those that excel that I want to go into a little detail so you can truly understand what differentiated MCD, and still differentiates it. Operational differentiation and excellence are concepts that will apply to many companies that you will invest in.

For instance, we know that Intel has excelled over the years by continually coming out with the best new microprocessor chips to serve as the brains for personal computers. The Intel systems create repeatability, so for decades big computer manufacturers felt that Intel would always have reliability in its new chips, not just new chips. When Apple recently wanted to switch from IBM chips, for a number of reasons, including lowering the amount of heat radiated by a chip, it could have chosen a cheaper chip from a clone of Intel chips. But Apple chose Intel for reliability and repeatability as well as lower heat radiation and other characteristics.

Many investors do not know that one of the core reasons for Intel's huge success with its customers, aside from great product research and development, is that it spends a fortune on research and development in *production* methods and systems. In other words, after you have a winning semiconductor design, you have to produce it with the lowest number of defects and rejects and potential problems with chips. To produce huge numbers of chips quickly, ship them to customers fast, keep costs in line, and ensure a minimum number of defects, you need awesome production systems. These systems have to be intelligently designed, and they cost lots of money. Intel was smart to do this.

So, what kind of systems do you need for a hamburger chain? Well, your customers are not going to be happy if they have been to one or more restaurants where they wait only 110 seconds for their fast food then go to another one in the same chain and have to wait several times that long, let alone taste any difference in the same food. That is bad business. It costs the restaurants goodwill and money. McDonald's is a company that understands that if the hamburger bun is presliced all the way through, not just partly, it saves time and money and speeds up the process. Originally, the first wave of operational elements that Ray Kroc introduced allowed the company to lower the price of hamburgers from 30¢ to 15¢, maintaining profit margins, but obviously bringing in many more diners at that price, driving up total volume and profits.

Details like how many hamburger patties to a pound, how long to toast a bun (17 seconds), and how much sanitizer to use when cleaning the shake machine (1 packet for 2.5 gallons of water) are crucial. Systems also provide feedback to store managers, so that they can see how they are doing relative to system averages and best and worst stores in many areas of measurement. McDonald's management knew exactly how many rows and columns of burgers would cook on a grill, that a higher temperature grill had to be used for the Quarter Pounder, and that the grill must be scraped clean after each batch, no matter how busy the store was. That was supposed to take 15 minutes. You can read a great deal about these things; it is all there. The important thing to know as an investor is that all of this can be important to making companies like McDonald's, Starbucks, Wal-Mart, Federal Express, and many more great companies. Watch for these things in the future.

Nothing is left to chance in the best-managed operations. Ray Kroc credited the systems with McDonald's early dominance of the industry. By 1979 Wendy's had an 8 percent market share; Burger King, 11 percent; and MCD, an amazing 35 percent.

This is one model of what makes a great company great. Many models are similar, though, which is why I chose this example. Also, many analysts feel that the restaurant business is as management-intensive as any other business, the competitive environment is as tough as that in any industry, and restaurants have as high a casualty (failure) rate as companies in the tech sector. Each company that was really successful in growing profits and stock price had to have management that could demonstrate real execution as well as ideas, innovation, and leadership. For Wendy's, it was Dave Thomas, and for McDonald's it started with Ray Kroc, but he wisely brought in great people.

AN EXISTING MARKET, SERVED BY EXPRESS

McDonald's came into an existing market and just plain did things a lot better. The real great growth stories are those about companies with really big markets or demand and an opportunity to do it better. There is a long list of small companies that became big this way. Companies that fill a niche do not necessarily get really big or become great, but they can. The niche, though, limits them, so bigger companies often acquire them.

One huge market that had no technology attached to it was package delivery. Just as locating restaurants intelligently and lowering prices and raising quality can enlarge a market that has already demonstrated growth, so can technology increase the growth and size of the package-delivery market. That is exactly what happened with Federal Express (FDX), now known as FedEx.

Just as Ray Kroc had the vision to start things off right, maintaining slow growth until the systems and management team were in place, the genius of FDX was Fred Smith, who had a vision of what could be done for express delivery of important packages. In fact, Smith wrote a paper while an undergrad at Yale University about the methods and routes used by airfreight shippers and why they were inadequate. He maintained that a system should be developed for time-sensitive shipments of things such as computer parts, medicines, and electronics. After graduating from college and serving in the military, Smith went into the aviation business and, before long, crystallized his ideas about how to get people their packages in two days or even overnight. This idea revolutionized how an industry did business and became a standard for rapid delivery. But it took great management and a lot of systems and technologies to get there.

FedEx is one of the most ingenious business ideas ever. This business was located in Memphis, a city that had good airport weather almost every day of the year and was centrally located relative to the big markets to and from which shipping was done. Memphis was the ideal choice. From a few Falcon jets, the company has grown into a huge fleet of planes, numbering almost seven hundred. Many people felt that sending everything through Memphis had to be stupid and costly—how could it make sense to route a shipment that was to go from Miami to Atlanta, or even to Jacksonville, Florida, through Memphis? But Fred Smith had a system to track load factors on each plane in each city, and he had most planes at some point with an 80 percent load factor (80 percent of capacity), which is very high and very profitable. Also, it was not just what he was doing, but what he was *not* doing. He was not scheduling flights between hundreds of different cities every night.

The real genius of the FedEx business model is in understanding what is so costly about the delivery business, and also what is the key factor that causes delivery failures. The big cost is in the planes: the capital needed to lease or purchase them, the costs of maintaining them, and paying pilots to fly them. Smith figured out that if you fly everything to one city and then out to the various locations around the country, you can do that with a fraction of the planes and crews that would be needed if you tried to go from every single city served to every other city served, point to point. This efficiency meant lower costs that, in turn, pumped up the company profits, and kept prices charged to customers reasonable relative to alternatives.

Second, the system of having a central point from which to receive and ship turns out, in a complex operational sense, to simplify things so much that failures to deliver on time become very rare. That reliability is critical to becoming number one in the industry.

The core of the business model was the central shipping city, so that costs, prices, and reliability could be maintained at levels nobody else could match. That is what makes a company great, especially since this was a system that was geared for almost unlimited growth and repeatability of results.

Interestingly enough, in the mid-1990s there was an article in a major business magazine about what happened with interoffice mail in the Merrill Lynch New York City headquarters. The system was terribly constructed and broke down under heavy volume. Sending something to another department on another floor should have taken hours, but it was beginning to take days. So professionals at Merrill who had to send reports and documents to another part of the building started to FedEx them for overnight delivery. The packages would be picked up around 5:00 P.M., flown to Memphis, then flown *back* to New York City the same night, and delivered by 10:30 the next morning!

It worked great until the bills started to mount up and a reporter got wind of it. The story was embarrassing for Merrill, to say the least, and very complimentary for Federal Express. Here is the interesting part: If an investor just read that one story, which showed how great FedEx was, and bought the stock on the basis of this information, that individual would have made several times his or her money in a few years. Naturally, I recommend reading and research, and the more knowledge the better. Yet sometimes things are quite straightforward, and your research is geared to looking for what generates repeatability or prevents competitive intrusions. In the cases of McDonald's and FedEx, it was the systems part of the business model more than other things, coupled with imaginative management, which let you know that they intended to win and probably would.

GREAT COMPANIES ENDURE, BUT THEY MUST BE BUILT OVER TIME

Companies are born with the potential to be great. But we cannot know how they will do until they are tested. So we watch, and we study, and we decide whether or not we are going to invest.

Without going into numbing detail, it can be said that FedEx had the same attention to systems and details as did McDonald's from the very beginning, and that is what made it so tough for anybody contemplating coming in as a competitor. Every night, a long stream of planes circles in the Memphis sky, waiting to land, while a large number of highly trained people on the ground unload, scan, and wait for each arrival while simultaneously working on each subsequent departure. It is a system built to manage the details, involving a high degree of technology and human training.

As great as Fred Smith's original vision is, without the systems and culture and a management that can execute, competition would have made FedEx just one of a group of tough competitors. Instead, it is the king, just as are Intel, Microsoft, and McDonald's in their own worlds.

A company shows its greatness by demonstrating how flexible its business model is and how recurring its successful operations are under the stresses of changing conditions and competition. Good investors read and try to know as much as possible about the flexibility built into that business model.

That is how you track Intel, Microsoft, and Home Depot, and it is how you will track Google as competition tries to knock that company off.

Federal Express stock was a great buy in 1978 when the company went public. A number of us bought it and made several times our money in just a couple of years or so, but going forward there were very big gains to be had. Over time, the company's package volume has become more sensitive to the ups and downs of the economy by virtue of the fact that Federal Express has become so large and has become involved in so many economically sensitive customer businesses. It has returned about 75X one's money over time, but the returns have slowed down as the company matures.

Does that mean FedEx is no longer a great company? I think it is still a great company, because it uses technologies and superior management to grow. Great companies can slow or become more mature, but they keep adapting and maximizing opportunities, which is what FedEx does. In contrast, Xerox was more of a great product than a great company, and actually failed to exploit most of the great new technologies developed by its own research people.

The top management people in Xerox were risk-averse and did not have or build a "technology" culture, which would have made a huge difference. Federal Express build a technology culture to support its future from its early years. Eventually, Xerox became complacent. As its patents expired, it should have expected exactly what it got: ferocious competition and inroads from the Japanese and others. So think of early Xerox as you think of any current "hot" technology company, and remember that the business model later failed. There was no *repeatability*.

BASM REMAINS THE KEY

Remember, do not invest in products, invest in the golden goose that creates both the product cycles and the earnings growth. That golden goose is defined by BASM.

Go back to the four defining attributes of great companies: business model, assumptions, strategy, and management. Even more important, look at these examples of companies that can evolve and control much of their destiny. Not many technology companies qualify as great companies. First of all, many are so wrapped up in aggressive product introductions that they fail to pay sufficient attention to developing and changing their business model and management as circumstances dictate. Second, many tech companies have customers that are economically sensitive, and this, in turn, makes them economically sensitive, which means that many do not deliver reliable, steady growth. Repeatable results are essential. The tech companies that do become great are those that "renew" themselves, like Intel, or that have near monopolies but also innovate all the time, like Microsoft, or that have brilliant and resilient business models, like Dell.

Many of the companies we will discuss later fit the definition of great companies that should be held even if they become somewhat overvalued at times. Sell disciplines (described in Chapter 4) are essential, but when you know you have a great company, it pays to make an occasional exception and let the company stay in the portfolio even if the stock is a bit overvalued. That is why "mechanical" methods of investing, which emphasize inflexible rules or principles, so often fail to help investors make the big money.

Cisco was overvalued by conventional standards at times. But I thought it might be on its way to greatness, so I bought some stock in the initial public offering and watched Cisco closely, keeping track of its market share, how happy customers were, and how it executed the basics we have

CISCO

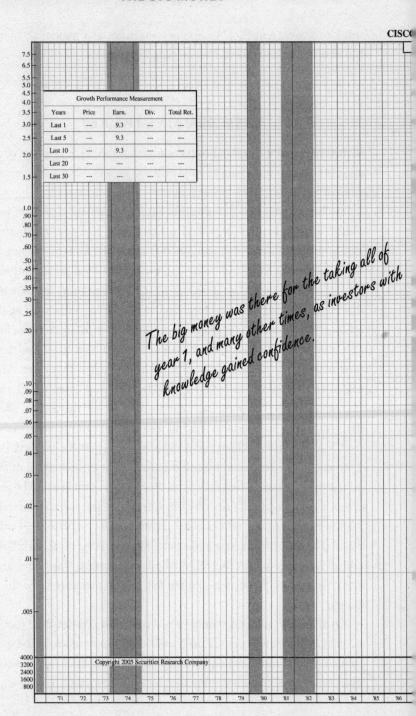

Growth Performance Measurement				
Years	Price	Earn.	Div.	Total Ret.
Last 1	---	9.3	---	---
Last 5	---	9.3	---	---
Last 10	---	9.3	---	---
Last 20	---	---	---	---
Last 30	---	---	---	---

The big money was there for the taking all of year 1, and many other times, as investors with knowledge gained confidence.

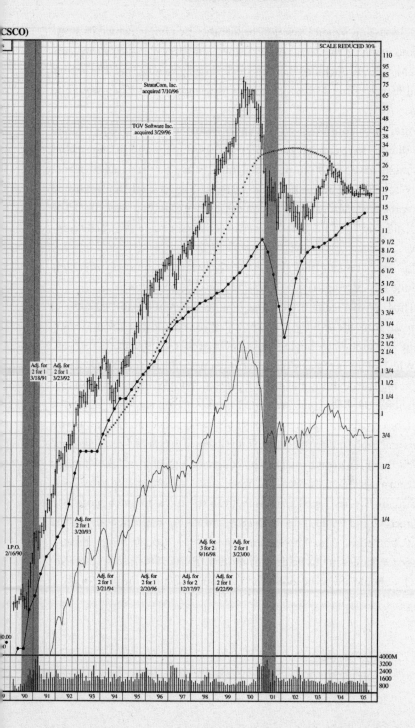

(CSCO)

SCALE REDUCED 30%

StrataCom, Inc.
acquired 7/10/96

TGV Software Inc.
acquired 3/29/96

Adj. for
2 for 1
3/18/91

Adj. for
2 for 1
3/23/92

Adj. for
2 for 1
3/20/93

I.P.O.
2/16/90

Adj. for
2 for 1
3/21/94

Adj. for
2 for 1
2/20/96

Adj. for
3 for 2
12/17/97

Adj. for
2 for 1
6/22/99

Adj. for
3 for 2
9/16/98

Adj. for
2 for 1
3/23/00

110
95
85
75
65
55
48
42
38
34
30
26
22
19
17
15
13
11
9 1/2
8 1/2
7 1/2
6 1/2
5 1/2
5
4 1/2
3 3/4
3 1/4
2 3/4
2 1/2
2 1/4
2
1 3/4
1 1/2
1 1/4
1
3/4
1/2
1/4

4000M
3200
2400
1600
800

'90 '91 '92 '93 '94 '95 '96 '97 '98 '99 '00 '01 '02 '03 '04 '05

been discussing. When I saw how brilliantly Cisco implemented its strategy and managed the details of its business, and how it created strong customer loyalty, I concluded that this stock would go a long way. The lessons I had learned from Molex helped me to recognize that Cisco would be great.

After Cisco doubled in price, many investors took their profits because they did not have enough knowledge of the company and did not realize they might have a great one on their hands. It was after the double that I actually bought a lot more and did an eighteen-bagger. That 18X was over a few years, and then we made lots more money than that over time. The stock did over 200X investors' money over its first decade as a public company.

Just as we bought Intel after the 1987 stock crash, on many occasions we added to Cisco as market corrections took the price down.

Thus, as you really understand how to differentiate the exceptional company from the ordinary, you know that you should give it some leeway on the valuation, since buying those stocks back is so difficult.

Which of the many new Internet companies will succeed? Think of success as high profitability and growth, protection from competition, and repeatability. BASM is what I rely on. I think Amazon could develop to be great, but it needs to further tweak its business model and raise return on assets and profit margins. I do think it is likely to get there. I certainly hope so. Jeff Bezos is a great manager who conceived a great idea. Like Kroc and his team at McDonald's, Bezos has broadened Amazon's menu, so to speak, because he has developed systems that can sell and ship much more than just records and books. I do think eBay and Yahoo! meet the tests and are great companies. Yahoo! is certainly going to give Google some pressure. Other companies in this field have not yet established themselves as great.

One should always be looking to find, buy, and hold "the great one."

CHAPTER THREE

HOLDING ON TO BECOME RICH

Patience and the Other Steps

Patience and perseverance have a magical effect, before which
difficulties disappear, and obstacles vanish.
—JOHN QUINCY ADAMS

. . . And right here let me say one thing: After spending many
years in Wall Street and after making and losing millions of
dollars, I want to tell you this: It never was my thinking that
made the big money for me. It was always my sitting. Got
that? My sitting tight! It is no trick at all to be right on the
market. You always find lots of early bulls in bull markets and
early bears in bear markets. I've known many men who were
right at exactly the right time and began buying or selling
stocks when prices were at the very level that should show the
greatest profits. And their experience invariably matched
mine—that is, they made no real money out of it. Men who
can both be right and sit tight are uncommon. I found it one
of the hardest things to learn. But it is only after a stock
operator has firmly grasped this that he can make big money.
. . . That is why so many men in Wall Street who are not
at all in the "sucker" class, not even in the third grade,

nevertheless lose money. The market does not beat them.
They beat themselves, because though they have brains, they
cannot sit tight.

—JESSE LIVERMORE

This remark is made by Jesse Livermore in Edwin Lefèvre's great book about Wall Street, *Reminiscences of a Stock Operator*, written in 1923. It is a short, classic work. While written as a work of fiction, the story is apparently based on the true experiences of Livermore, the legendary stock investor. All of us have seen how many, many investors have owned stocks that would have made them very rich if they had only had a combination of knowledge and patience, and just held on.

Patience makes people the big money when they know that they own the right stock, because they have real depth of knowledge. They also know that to stick with a great company you have to set some benchmarks, starting with a three- to five-year time horizon. One of the biggest mistakes investors make is owning extraordinary companies but treating them like ordinary companies from which an investor gets ordinary returns. The great ones must be held over an extended period if investors wish to earn the big money. Companies that make you 100X or 200X or far, far more unfold and grow over a period of years, not months. Along the way there are bumps in the road, plenty of bears, and downswings and sellers.

The combination of knowledge and patience will take you from 30 percent gains to triples and quadruples, and on to the big-money stocks that make you truly rich. Even though you can make plenty of money along the way, you need to be patient with your best winners and give them the time they need to grow and prosper if you want to be wealthy.

Even the majority of stocks, though, test human tendencies to be impatient, so two other of the Seven Steps come into play in order to cope with these tendencies: buy/sell disciplines and benchmarks. Thus, for most growth companies, you measure, over a reasonable period of time (three years is good, but five is even better), your investments' performance against those of comparable investments.

For companies that have the potential to be great, you measure their performance (i.e., earnings and market share) against the goals they set for themselves. Reading company reports, you will find that the better the company, the more specific its goals. Great companies issue their own report cards. The lesser ones do not do this very well, and often can only offer excuses because they are losing to the great companies. Market-share gains and losses are core indicators to watch, but they must be watched for a few years to allow strategies to unfold and also to let stocks perform and make you great profits. It is not enough to just say, "Hey, when you own the greatest companies, do not sell them. Hold on to try to make 10X or 100X your money, or more—that is what the best stocks can do."

It is a shame that so often investors treat the stocks of potentially huge winners just the same as those that are ordinary. You may sell a stock after a 30 percent quick gain and feel great—if it is a company that really doesn't show you that it has the elements of great BASM. But if you are thinking more about taking a quick profit than getting really rich, and you sell, you may well find yourself watching the stock go on to double or triple after you sold it. Naturally you are reluctant to buy it back at much higher prices, so typically it is gone. If it is on its way to greatness, it might ultimately multiply investors' money by 200X. All you need is one, so understanding how to combine the elements of BASM with the Seven Steps is the way to go, starting with the patience and benchmarks that can help you to keep and capitalize on that one if you have bought it.

Even 200X your money is far less than what the best stocks have done, by the way. It is peanuts compared with the gains from companies such as Dell and Wal-Mart.

As I mentioned in chapter 2, I learned some important lessons from Molex that I applied to Cisco when that company came along.

Cisco exhibited a "Molex style" in working closely with customers in product development, creating new routers and switches to control, direct, and send Internet traffic to where it should go. Its products were more than just technologically great, though. The company met customers' most important needs and anticipated future needs by spending money, time, and energy to work closely with customers. This required a huge, concentrated effort and investment.

Cisco had made two great assumptions early on. It decided as early as the 1980s, before the public was using the Internet, that the Internet would be huge. The company took an early lead in designing products specifically for switching and routing Internet traffic. Cisco also made a second assumption: that customers would rather have systems from one vendor and not have to continually understand who has the best new products. Company leaders felt that if they had the best products—or even just competitive products—and had the customers locked in with great customer service, they would win. These proved to be the winning strategies and assumptions when executed well.

In 1994 the Federal Reserve Board thought that current economic strength would cause inflation. In response, the board started to tighten credit and raise interest rates. This response was unnecessary, as there was no increase in inflation, but it did cause a bit of a scare for people who key in on short-term market events. NASDAQ suffered a short, sharp drop. Some Cisco (CSCO) holders decided to cash in, after Cisco had already delivered huge gains in just a few years. The stock dropped about 50 percent. As I saw it, many people did not understand the potential of Cisco and never bought it back. There were some investors who were lacking in knowledge, confidence in the future, and thus patience.

Later in this book, we will come back to Cisco, but the point here is that recognizing that a core part of the business model was similar to what I had found in Molex gave me confidence. Once I had an understanding of Cisco, BASM gave me the knowledge, and so I could be patient and hang on to make the big money.

I have read that the average tech stock generally stays really strong for only about three or four years, since tech is so tough. By then most companies are having trouble with innovating, or with customer retention and competition. If you think about it, where have most of each year's great IPOs gone? Acquired, faded away, merged, or down other paths to obscurity. It is very Darwinian: only the fittest survive. Thus, it should have been clear to most observant investors that Cisco would be a winner over a long period, because it was close to the customer, and customers loved it. The company had a strong management and business model and terrific product development, and the industry outlook for networking was fabulous.

Sellers of Cisco lacked knowledge and patience, and walked away from a huge, classic opportunity.

Because investors have so much information, and buy so many interesting initial public offerings, there are many, many investors who own the right companies at one time or another. But most of the time they don't have sufficient knowledge about those companies. Consequently, they get out too soon and stay out for too long. Knowledge acquired from reading is the start. Then the compass of BASM simplifies the task of navigating the overwhelming amount of information out there.

Patience is not only a virtue, it's a necessity. All too often impatience costs investors dearly, because they might have only "intellectual patience"—they know what to do but just can't fight their emotions and the market swings. If investors do not have buy/sell disciplines or benchmarks or a compass, their emotions and intellectual patience will continually be tested by the volatility in the market.

Combating these emotions is why we need the Seven Steps.

SIMPLE RULES OF THE ROAD

You must have a good reason to hang in there with a quality stock. If you have enough knowledge about that company, then you have some idea of its long-term future, and you must have the discipline to stick with your conviction. You will apply discipline based on knowledge. And if what you know about the company is confirmed because management does what it says it will do, then your rational, informed conviction grows stronger. That means you have faith in the company's future, and you decide what you can reasonably expect in terms of performance over a reasonable period of time. What are you looking for when you set benchmarks for performance?

You are looking for metrics, starting with growth. Growth in earnings will grow your investment over time. Metrics show you how the company's BASM is working for investors. All companies must do what they have said they will do. That starts with growth in sales and growth in earnings that are better than those of their competitors, so they take market share and perhaps become number one. Profits divided by assets, or return on capital (ROC, which is the same as return on assets), is a critical metric for all companies and a key predictor of future growth. Some take the equity figure on the balance sheet and divide profits by equity—return on equity (ROE)—which is fine. But that does not take into account debt financing, so ROC plus ROE is the metric I look at. Another metric that tells you how a company is doing relative to others is profit margin—both the gross margin (sales less cost of sales divided by sales) and the net margin (profits before taxes divided by sales). Do not use formulas, but just learn to compare companies against other companies in the same industry, since it is all relative, and you are looking for winners and the best bet, not for absolute numbers.

If you read annual reports, you will also find metrics that managers give for their own industries. For example, same-store sales (announced frequently) for retailers tell you how stores open for equal amounts of time are doing relative to the prior period. Other metrics include loan figures for banks, traffic figures, and load factors (seat miles filled by passengers versus seat miles of capacity flown) for airlines, and so forth. You can find this information and apply it in a commonsense way to determine the health of a company as you acquire deeper knowledge and know what to expect. Operating metrics are like hits and runs in baseball: they show you what is going on. Good companies make it easy for you to learn this.

The point about using metrics is to make an informed judgment about a company's potential to glimpse the future. Projecting what a company can earn, or earnings power, is one key to staying in the stock. This sort of knowledge will give you confidence that you have a great company, or even a very good company with competitive strengths and excellent management. Circuit City (CC) was not yet a great company in 1982. But it was a leader in the new concept of specialized electronics retailing. Electronics retailing was beginning to broaden beyond traditional stereo systems to a much greater array of products. That meant Circuit City was an emerging company in an emerging industry with enormous opportunity.

This is when you want to do some work to gain knowledge, and thus gain confidence, so you can know whether to be patient. Investors feared that the weaker economy of 1982 would cause a period of weakness in Circuit City's sales. Yet this was actually the very moment when the company's strategy was about to yield great results. If you just took some time to stay close to the fundamentals—the ROC and ROE that I just described—you might have predicted a very nice trend of rising earnings going forward.

Circuit City made some very important assumptions, starting with the assumption that people would always want new, exciting electronics products in the marketplace at virtually all times, and that they wanted to shop at a store that had the most product offerings. Circuit City had to convince people that it had more products to choose from, and at lower prices. So it spent on deep and broad inventory and figured that if it could lower prices on some high-visibility, popular items, consumers would make Circuit City their destination for all electronics. In that case consumers might buy far more than what they originally intended—that is, they would be coming in to browse, finding a lot that was exciting, and buying things they had not thought about.

Holding massive amounts of inventory to have that depth and breadth is very expensive, and the small retailers could not come close. Circuit City's gamble paid off. Its assumptions were correct, and it got the huge volumes needed to make it all profitable.

In the recession of 1982, many money managers and I were increasing our positions in stocks that looked cheap, like Circuit City. Too many people sold, forcing the stock price to drop by more than half over a few months. Earnings did not suffer a long decline, and very soon moved sharply higher. That is the beauty of a well-managed emerging company. People still bought at Circuit City. The BASM was sound, and the execution and product selections were brilliant. My studying the company over a reasonable time period gave me confidence, which in turn made me patient.

The stock had actually turned around before the earnings, so there were good reasons to anticipate better performance, as is almost always the case in a company with the right BASM. In less than a year, the stock had tripled; in about twenty-four months, holders saw 5X their money. On and on it went, until after thirteen years the long-term holders would have made 100X their investment. Naturally, there were some more downdrafts along the way, so investors again had the choice of bailing out under fire or buying and making doubles, triples, and quadruples in few years.

Experienced and successful investors know that swings in the market and headlines in the financial press do often collapse investors' patience and cause them to get sucked into the great sin of market timing: trying to judge the near-term direction of the market. I and the great stock pickers strongly believe that there is enough proof for us to conclude that not only is market timing impossible, but it also takes people out of great stocks that could have made them rich.

The market moves in the short term as the result of many economic and financial factors that change rapidly, as well as because of investors' psychology and perceptions. These factors are far too complex to predict. So even though there are always people who claim to have systems, using charts or computers or other methods to predict the market, the greatest stock pickers I know do not allow themselves to get sucked into believing this. We concentrate on stocks, not short-term market gyrations. I will have much more to say about this in a later chapter because attempts to time the market are so common—and so harmful to investors.

The buy and sell disciplines that I discuss in chapter 4, part of the Seven Steps, are another tool to help investors to be patient, avoid market timing, stay with winners, and focus on stocks, not on market volatility and headlines.

Over and over again, investors get into many small companies as they come public in new, very promising industries that offer the highest potential for the future. But a lack of differentiation, a lack of good metrics and yardsticks, or a failure to recognize that the management and business models of those companies are weak means that many investors get fooled by lots of hot stocks with good stories behind them and good price action. If the companies are not able to support high prices by virtue of great operations, the stocks just come back down to earth and cancel the profits that were racked up early.

It is wise to remember that it is not hot products that win in the long term and generate the big money, it is great product cycles that repeat again and again, and give both customers and investors confidence. Most tech companies start with a hot product and get some investors' money, but few can repeat this success with new product development and execution.

The few companies that can repeat great product cycles do so because of great BASM, pure and simple. It's easiest to track metrics for the great companies, since theirs are typically glowing success stories in their financial releases.

Many investors regularly get into a bunch of hot stocks, make quick profits, and then get out. They pat themselves on the back for making 30 percent, 50 percent, or even 100 percent in a very short time. But they are relying on luck and hunches, and lack the knowledge that leads to the kind of rational conviction that enables them to be patient over the long term. They don't understand that hot can get cold overnight for a company with only average management. They may be able to act quickly and take a profit. But building real wealth comes over time.

LEARNING WHICH COMPANIES DESERVE YOUR PATIENCE

During the great Internet boom of the 1990s hundreds of Internet companies arose and excited investors with tales of future glory. iVillage (IVIL) was one of them.

Although iVillage looked great initially, like Martha Stewart Living .com and some other so-called women's sites, it soon became apparent that iVillage was not unique. First, lack of uniqueness meant many other Web companies springing up and offering similar content on their Web sites. Second, the lack of a unique product meant that they could not convert most of their Web site visitors to paying customers.

The company was founded in 1995, and went public in late March 1999. Its IPO was initially priced at between $22 and $24 per share. In the euphoria of the day, however, it was actually brought out somewhat higher and traded as high as $95.38 that same day, closing at $80.13 per share.

The stock soon went on to a high of about $121. But then, not long thereafter, it began a decline all the way down to about $0.67 per share. It has climbed moderately since then. I could see that the lack of a proprietary product and the presence of a growing number of competitors doing something similar meant that iVillage did not have a path to decent profitability.

iVillage continued to lose money until late 2004. It appears that if the company had not raised so much capital from its hot initial stock offering, it might have gone bankrupt. IPO money is why so many Internet companies with highly questionable business models are still around.

A great many people who understood that there were no earnings to use as a metric failed to look for other metrics that would be useful. Most important, they did not study the business model to see if there was a true route to profitability. That is the number one thing to look for in a business model, along with growth and protecting against competition. The business model should explain clearly how the company can achieve profitability.

iVillage is a Web site with some good content. It gets hundreds of millions of hits, or visits, per year, according to the company. That fact attracted investors, but a lack of differentiation and a lack of something valuable enough to consumers that they would pay for it were the problems.

In contrast, Martha Stewart Omnimedia (MSO) went public around the same time. It had great products, branding, image, management, and a solid business model. In other words, it was a real company, and a good one. (Martha's legal saga notwithstanding, the company may just go on to regain its strength.)

Martha Stewart had come to understand her market and customers over many years before bringing her company public. She did not throw something together quickly to take advantage of an Internet boom. She knew what consumers wanted, and she had greater skills in developing product. Second, she was not a one-woman show, and although she herself was a great image for the company, she built in layers of terrific people with top-notch skills. This was true not just in management but also in product creation. She did not do it all herself; her business model was built on teamwork and complementary skill sets.

Next, she had many things to appeal to many people, so she had breadth. Finally, her business was built on a brand: with good management, MSO was made profitable and financially sound.

One part of the BASM was a critical assumption that if people liked what they saw her do in her magazine or on her TV show, they would look at the other things she was doing. So the company spent money on what it calls "cross-promoting." The assumption and strategy and money spent all proved to be right, and were very powerful in developing revenues.

Martha Stewart's customers showed that they were buyers and spenders, not just window-shoppers. Martha Stewart was an uncommon company in a sea of hot stocks of companies that were trying to imitate her in some way. Patience was warranted, and patience paid off.

We tried to meet with the managers of as many of the new Internet companies as we could. Even after taking a hard look, we still we did not know which of them had a winning business model without first seeing them operate. A company like Webvan, which pioneered buying groceries online, looked fabulous in theory, but it took a little while to see how Webvan operated and figure out that its business model was not going to work. Webvan's costs for delivery were too high, and customers were unwilling to pay for it—even though surveys and use showed that they actually loved the service. Webvan's long-term problem was that it cost more to acquire each customer than it cost a grocery store. The company actually did not know that, and neither did we at the very beginning; but as we watched operations build, this started to become clear. It did not take us long to see the flaws in the business model and no clear road to profitability, so we sold.

I was seeing a whole bunch of Internet company managers when the torrent of new public offerings became the centerpiece of the late-1990s stock market. It was tough to know, in the initial stages, which of these companies had a business model that worked and which ones didn't, but there was some sorting out right away. Looking beneath the skin and seeing the obvious from company reports and operations—and sometimes from the cautionary reports of analysts—we soon know, after the excitement of the new offering quiets down, which companies deserve our being patient investors, and which do not. Amazon.com, for instance, did not make money for a while, but it is unique in a number of ways. Its business model and profitability need some improvement, yet both are good, thanks to true differentiation and technological superiority (as with FedEx). Best of all, its customers love it and stay customers; this is really the best feature of all. With its huge customer interest and growth, Amazon earns our patience.

So, even though this may not be true in every instance, the better a company does with its customers—capturing them, keeping them, growing that number, and profiting from them—the more you, as an investor, are going to make. Webvan and iVillage could not retain customers, but Amazon.com could. Almost always, it requires patience to make the big money.

Webvan simply could not grow or retain its customer base because it could not meet its customers' total needs at a cost that company and customer could both afford. To put it bluntly, the service Webvan offered turned out not to be economically worthwhile. iVillage lacked differentiation from the competition.

One company where patience paid off handsomely is Coca-Cola, which incorporated way back in 1892. The largest gains do not usually come from the "blue chips"—established growth companies that seem to have relative predictability. Huge gains generally come from emerging companies on their way to success. We have all heard the legendary stories of those who did not stay with Coke in its early days; some stockholders sold whenever the market got a bit difficult. The sellers did not recognize what Coke really was, did not see the potential, and gave up huge fortunes. But later, when Coke was established and large, there was still a tremendous amount of money to be made. Consider the 1982 downturn.

Those who held on to stocks during the 1982 market downturn, or bought then, could see 5X their money in five years from a large, secure company. The high gains continued until the stock reached its top in the 2000 market, having risen roughly 68X, or 6,700 percent, from the 1982 price. Coke was far from an emerging growth story. This wealth came from Coca-Cola as an established company when it was doing everything right for most of those years.

These events are not uncommon. The story is the same for many, many stocks. Over many years, consumers were using Rubbermaid products and buying Dell computers, but most people who loved the products did not read enough to really get comfortable with these companies over time, losing opportunities to invest, particularly when some temporary events punished the stocks and gave everyone great buying opportunities.

If you love a company and really know it, you get many chances for great stock buys from the volatility and uncertainty of the stock market, and the price swings that occur over time. When you understand that a company is a great company, the downturns are most likely temporary; and when the market gets emotional and sells off, those drops give long-term investors chances to scoop up their favorite companies at very attractive prices.

If a stock has a nice, smooth trajectory upward, people do not sell very often and just enjoy the ride. Almost always, though, the ride is not so smooth, because there are so many instances of various economic, financial, psychological, and political events affecting markets.

There always have been and always will be periods of real pressure on stock prices that worry people, or even scare them. Very often these pressures cause investors to sell their shares. As I noted earlier, the majority of investors do not seem to buy them back. Sometimes this has to do with a lack of knowledge or other tangible investment input, but quite frequently it has to do with human psychology, and the fact that people who sell something, then later see it at a higher price, have a mental block about buying it back. I mention this because it is very, very common.

What is *uncommon* is the commitment of investors who can be patient and hold on to companies that can make them truly wealthy. They do it by "sitting tight," as Jesse Livermore pointed out early in the twentieth century. Having patience and buy/sell discipline and following the rest of the Seven Steps will serve you well because you are very likely to encounter and even own some of these companies.

WHO IS MAKING ALL THE MONEY?

There are three classes of people who hold great stocks for lengthy periods through thick and thin.

First, there are the company executives who feel very optimistic about the future of their enterprise and do not wish to play the market.

The second group is made up of wise investors like Warren Buffett, and others who put much more emphasis on what they own and what it should be worth over time than on the market or other short-term factors. Buffett goes to the extreme and thinks of owning the company and pretty much tries to ignore the piece of paper that is the stock—the value of which can gyrate significantly in the short term. His time horizon is much longer than that of most other professionals. Buffett's long-term investment record is much, much better than that of almost anyone else, individual or professional, and he is considered the second wealthiest person in the world.

Long-term investors are generally considered those with a three- to five-year time horizon for holding stocks and mutual funds when their investments are watched and fundamentally sound, selling only when a sell discipline kicks in (see chapter 4).

The third group is composed of those employees of a company who feel very enthusiastic about the company. This is a whole class of investors that became really wealthy on one stock.

These are the types of people who sit tight.

Naturally, as we decide how to pick and hold stocks, there is always the question that investors ask themselves about what they do if they make mistakes. My approach was to ensure that my mistakes were small—that is, if I doubted that things were going right, I would sell, perhaps because a company was not executing well at the moment. So, yes, I made a bunch of mistakes, but they were almost always small. But you should also do what I do after I sell: watch the company and its stock's performance carefully for a while. If it starts to recover, it could be showing you elements of greatness.

That is when you must buy it back, even if you pay up a few dollars. I did that plenty of times, and it is very helpful and profitable. Being a great company does not mean being perfect, so this is important to incorporate into your investing. I advise keeping a little notebook to help you keep track of significant benchmarks and metrics.

RISKS

You cannot pretend there are no risks in investing, but you can deal with risks and learn to minimize them. Knowledge is the best weapon against risk. Although there are statistical ways to measure risk, they fail to capture the difference between knowing what you own and not knowing. To me, the most important factors are knowledge of your investment and an investor's way of looking at things (BASM).

Ever since the massive fraud at Enron, which destroyed the retirement savings of most Enron employees (most of them had their retirement funds entirely in that one stock), financial counselors have been reminding people constantly that they should not have too much of their money in just one stock.

So how do people get rich from one or two great stocks without having too much money in their stocks? Usually they have bought a bunch of stocks with great potential, watched them, and then bought more of the best corporate performers (in terms of BASM) along the way. Each stock represented only a modest portion of the portfolio, or total assets, at the beginning, and only later became a large chunk of the investor's assets because the investor weeded out the weak stock, flowing the sales proceeds into the best. That approach, coupled with enormous appreciation, means wealth.

Using the methods we describe here, you will minimize your risks and maximize your potential rewards, selling those stocks that do not show great BASM over time and buying more of those that do, just as I did with Cisco and its competitors.

Do

1. Look at all sources of information you might have at your disposal to find names of possible stocks. Friends, employees, your job, news stories, financial publications, and Wall Street are among the sources.

2. Scan these companies to see if you can understand what they do and how they are planning to succeed. Go into depth with the most promising to see if you feel good about the management and what it says in its annual reports and releases. See if you can get a good grip on the business model, which should essentially tell you how the company plans to make money, grow, and do better than its competitors.

3. Own the most promising companies in small amounts. Then, as you gain knowledge and confidence, add to the positions of those that execute the best on their promises. It works. I owned Cisco and several of its competitors at first, weeded out the competitors, and bought more Cisco along the way—and the gains were huge.

4. Think of owning the best growers for years. Build your knowledge and keep those stocks as long as they are delivering on their promises.

Also, buy some established companies that still have exciting prospects (like Coca-Cola in 1982) and expect that you will hold them for yourself or your children for many, many years. Do that in addition to holding mutual funds you like, and in addition to owning small stocks that meet the criteria mentioned above.

Every time there is a big drop in the market, the best companies "go on sale." This is equally true for small and large stocks. People who have little knowledge and confidence, and short time horizons, seem to me to be selling to people who have sufficient knowledge and long time horizons and thus are determined to be consciously patient.

THE PATH TO WEALTH VERSUS THE "CARDINAL SIN"

After the great bear market of 1974, a friend of mine bought some shares for his infant children in what appeared at that time to be great companies. He missed Wal-Mart, which one would have wanted to focus on, since it was not well known—even though in the four years that the company had been public, its stock had already multiplied investors' money more than ten times. That was nothing, really. As it turned out, the Wal-Mart stock story was just beginning.

Anyway, my friend bought a bunch of companies such as General Electric, whose stock price has multiplied by roughly 83 times (8,200 percent) from purchase date to early 2005, even though it is substantially lower than its year 2000 high. He also bought Coca-Cola, which has multiplied his kids' money by almost fifty times. He bought a number of similar blue chips too.

It is easy to find people who held the greatest stocks and mutual funds of all time for some years, but almost impossible to find those who maximized profits by holding these investments long enough to become truly wealthy. Plenty of people missed holding great stocks for even a few years and making 5X or 10X their money; so it is not just those who are unwilling or unable to invest for themselves or their children over the very long term who sell early. Almost everybody sells early.

One of the cardinal sins of investing, I have learned, is treating the greatest companies just like all the other investments you own. It is the single biggest reason why a large number of investors never make the big money.

Here is one more quotation from Jesse Livermore, a great investor who made millions in 1923, when that was an incredible amount of money: "They say you never grow poor taking profits. No, you don't. But neither do you grow rich taking a four-point profit in a bull market."

Livermore talked about how people have to bet against their emotions and continue to have hope when they feel fear, and remember fear when they feel great hope; this means that people naturally feel more comfortable going with the herd whether the herd is extremely bullish or bearish. You have to avoid being one of the herd, and try to know enough to lean against the herd. This is certainly one way of saying "buy low and sell high," since fear is one of the strongest forces that depress stock prices, and lower prices create more fear. Stock prices are at their highest when hope and greed are at their highest.

As I have pointed out, the things that Livermore (for Lefèvre) wrote about in 1923 were true for countless generations before then and are true today because of human nature. That is why people need a method to become patient and to become rich. Whether you do it with disciplines of your own making or not, many, many investors have found that the right path includes knowledge, buy and sell disciplines, time horizons, and more—in other words, what I have collectively called the Seven Steps.

THE SEVEN STEPS: MAKING THINGS POSSIBLE
Nike

So far, we know that knowledge not only creates the basis for understanding what you own but also gives you confidence to weather short-term disruptions, regardless of whether they are from market corrections or from disappointing company earnings reports.

Nike offers us a good practical example of how the Seven Steps were used in a situation that occurs frequently, so it can help you with the stocks in your investing future. Again, the Seven Steps are: knowledge, patience, disciplines, emotions, time horizon, market timing, and benchmarks. When Nike (NKE) earnings dropped in 1986, on the surface it looked like a great sell signal.

However, for those who understood *(knowledge)* that the company had an aggressive strategy and had ramped spending enormously for marketing and promotion, there was a great buying opportunity when the stock became weak. You will see from the buy and sell *disciplines* in chapter 4 that Nike fit the buy disciplines, not those that would trigger a sale, so one would want to avoid being scared by a falling stock or market *(emotions, market timing)* and would instead take full advantage of the drop. Nike stock did experience a scary drop, but whether an investor decided to sell and look again later, or hold because he had at least a three-year time horizon (the minimum time frame for really effective growth-stock investing, I feel), the drop was an incredible opportunity. *Time horizon* and *benchmarks*—in this case knowing what to expect, such as market share gains—are two more steps.

Nike fell by about 50 percent in 1986, as earnings dropped because the company had embarked on an aggressive high-spending strategy to become the leader. Reebok and the other companies in the industry were taken by surprise and never caught up. It is easier to be *patient* when you are also applying knowledge, time horizon, disciplines, and the rest of the Seven Steps.

Dominance is worth a lot in the stock market. This was how and when Nike became "Nike."

There is no question that it is tough to know who will win and how

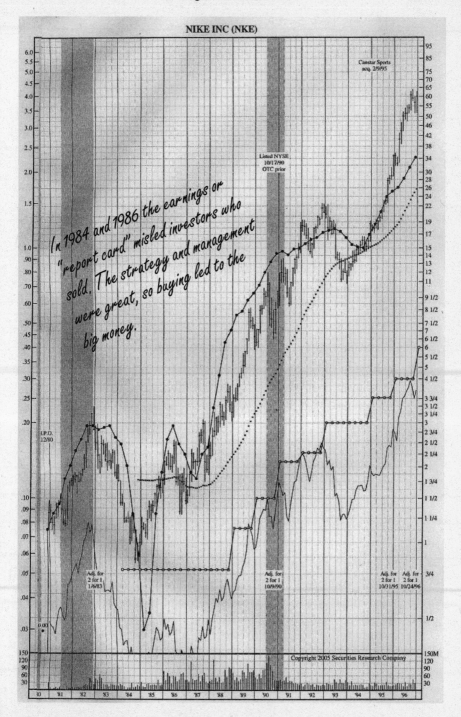

NIKE INC (NKE)

Canstar Sports
acq. 2/9/95

Listed NYSE
10/17/90
OTC prior

In 1984 and 1986 the earnings or "report card" misled investors who sold. The strategy and management were great, so buying led to the big money.

I.P.O.
12/80

0.00

Adj. for
2 for 1
1/6/83

Adj. for
2 for 1
10/9/90

Adj. for
2 for 1
10/31/95

Adj. for
2 for 1
10/24/96

long earnings can stay down. There is no question that if one watches a stock going down, a strong stomach is needed. Most companies that have a couple of down quarters in earnings are not executing well, and many are outright sales. But if one thinks there is any possibility that the company in question is a great company, then the downdraft makes it a buy. BASM once again is the way to know this, and the Seven Steps are the way to capitalize on it and make the money.

WHAT WORKS AND WHAT DOES NOT WORK

Looking at the stocks we have described and the methods we have reviewed, we can arrive at some pithy ways to think about how to view stocks like an investor and understand what works for people.

What Works
- Knowing what a company plans to do to grow and how it plans to accomplish that, so you can track it. This should be clearly stated in its business model, which, for good companies, should be easy to find on their Web sites, in their annual reports, and in other obvious places.

- Knowing that when a company's stock is selling far above or far below its trend line or the valuations of similar companies, it is time to check on a possible buy or sell. Price-earnings ratios are only one way. Price to sales and price to book value are nice additions.

- Knowing if a company has a world-class opportunity in an industry that is going to be growing enormously, as in the early days of biotechnology, electronics retailing, personal computers, and athletic footwear.

- Knowing that world-class opportunity means things like differentiation, business model, and management.

- Most important, knowing that analysis, knowledge, and common sense have to replace emotions when you make decisions.

What Doesn't Work
- Feeling scared when a stock is going down, so you sell.

- Feeling that when a stock is going up rapidly in price, and the press loves it, and so do your friends, you must own it and hold it.

- Not knowing what opportunities a company wants to take advantage of over the next three to five years.

- Timing the market, and not having any sense of how long you should hold the stock, but just thinking that if it goes up nicely, it is a sale.

Nike illustrates a case in which the information was out there for those who wanted it. The risk was whether or not the founder, Phil Knight, could execute well and make good decisions.

The way to find out, of course, is to watch every strategic move, knowing why you are watching it, so that even if you do not catch the stock at the very bottom or absolute best price, you can be there for a great run and a great long-term future.

Nike's earnings turned around very sharply. Because its strategy was working (and because it was becoming a great company), those earnings came out of the doldrums and tripled very quickly, and continued on up for a long time.

If you had knowledge, disciplines, and time horizon—the basic triumvirate of investing tools—you had a chance to make a ton of money. After only a few months, the entire downdraft in Nike had been made up, with the stock back to where it was. More than that, if the knowledgeable and confident investor had bought near the low point, he would have tripled his money in less than twenty-four months, made 10X his money in four and a half years, and made 18X his money in six years.

Doing nothing but holding on as a long-term investor, and not buying or selling during that 1986 period, would still have yielded our investor about 10X his money from early 1986 to the fourth quarter of 1992.

Nike was volatile, and there were other several more opportunities to make a bad sale, live through it, or buy more over just those six years. This is typical, and you can find volatility with Home Depot, Dell, Microsoft, Molex, McDonald's—you name it. It would be very similar if I traced the ups and downs and big moves of other stocks that posted huge long-term gains. Changes in the perception of a company's future, even by a little, will rattle most investors who do not know the situation in depth and who lack a firm time horizon of three years or more.

Time horizon is a framework for patience. The two are almost the same thing, but the first helps with the second. Knowledge and time horizon team up so you can more easily be patient. Without some sense of a time horizon, it is almost impossible to be patient. It is also nearly impossible to overcome emotions just on "faith" alone; knowledge is essential to controlling emotions and steering them toward building wealth.

The stock market is also very volatile, and corrections or surges are much more frequent than people would think. With a firm time horizon, coupled with knowledge of the companies you like the best, you can average down (buying on weakness so your average cost of all shares held is lowered) and make a lot of money as things get back to normal—that is, to the trend line. It is the scary drops and the scary times that very often hand investors golden opportunities if they can substitute three things for emotions: knowledge, disciplines, and a combination of time horizon and patience within that time horizon. You can't just tell yourself not to be emotional. That never works. It can't be just something you intellectually know when you get fearful. You must substitute something. That's the point.

Telling somebody to "buy low and sell high" does not work without further knowledge, because investors need to know what factors lead to low and high prices, as well as what "high" means on a given day. Likewise, just encouraging somebody to be patient does not work in isolation. Investors need to understand what makes a company great and worth waiting for. They also need to understand that time horizons and knowledge lead to an ability to be patient with companies that have the potential to be great.

Home Depot: Small Growth Company with Big Vision

I am now into my fourth decade of investing in small companies, often called *emerging growth.* Some small companies are not classified as growth per se and can be *value stocks*—cheap for a reason; maybe something needs to be fixed. Some small companies are not growth stocks, because they are very much tied to economic cycles or some other external factor completely outside of management's control.

Over the years, the stocks that have made the big money are mostly growth stocks from companies that started their run when they were rather small. In each decade or era, there are new small companies, and some will become great. Home Depot (HD) was such a company when it went public in 1981.

DOUBTS

Sometimes Wall Street talks about a company in glowing terms even before the stock actually comes to market. That was quite true with Bill Gates and Microsoft, it was true with many of the most interesting Internet companies that went public in the late 1990s, and it was true of Google in 2004.

I have already mentioned that you do not know that a company is truly great until you have watched it meet competition and challenges; earlier on, you can know only that a company has great potential. Given that, if there is a "fever" over a new company's stock issue, it can mean trouble. Doubt in such situations is healthy, so you just have to watch whatever the negative stories are.

In the case of Home Depot, there was some degree of excitement over this new type of hardware retailer, which sought to attract a more sophisticated do-it-yourself (DIY) customer with its new store format. There were also a number of doubts, centering on the fact that this was a very small company with very ambitious and aggressive expansion plans. Furthermore, this was a new concept: warehouse stores that would be selling to do-it-yourself buyers and increasing costs by paying better personnel to give customers help and advice. Doubts create fear, a key emotion. People are fearful of risks, and knowledge is the antidote for those fears.

This business model was an opportunity and a risk, given its higher-than-average cost structure. Another risk was that when the company went public, there were only a handful of stores, and most had not been operating very long.

Countering those two risks, in my mind, were the following things: first, I put a huge amount of emphasis on management. Management comes up with the good ideas and the plans to execute and make things happen—not the other way around.

The best new products or ideas sink fairly quickly when management is ordinary, with ordinary strategy and execution. That's why I have devoted chapter 6 to management. There you'll learn how to sort out the best from the mediocre and the incompetent. Naturally, winners are the small number, and losers are the bigger number.

Invest in great management. If you did only two things—use common sense and invest in superior management—you could become rich.

There may be great companies that have made stockholders lots of money over the long term without great management to drive them, but I have never found one.

It raises your odds a lot, though, if you add to those two things above the rest of the Seven Steps.

Bernie Marcus, cofounder of Home Depot, was already known to have very strong management skills. Additionally, the company had told prospective shareholders that it had built-in cost-control systems and that it was going to make training its employees a critical part of its business model. This way its stores could truly introduce customers to DIY projects and ensure that customers were pleased.

What was a bit scary about Marcus's new concept was that he wanted to compete with low prices and yet still pay retail store workers better than competitors while also paying for solid training programs. It was a bet made on vision and brilliance, for Bernie had a business model designed to capture customers, take market share, and keep customers' loyalty virtually forever. Bernie won. Looking into the heart of that business model, one would find the big money.

THE STOCK

With Home Depot, the excitement won over the doubts, of course, and we bought stock on the initial public offering along with a lot of other investors. I think there is a general misconception among investors today, perhaps because of the experiences of the last half of the 1990s, that all IPOs of really good companies rise tremendously the first day and for some time afterward. That is just not the case. Dell Computer's stock fell below the offering price some months later, as did Cisco's, albeit very briefly. Then both stocks soared. This has been true for many companies' IPOs.

Home Depot stock traded in a small range for some months, actually, because some people had hoped to make quick money on the offering, while others were tracking things carefully, trying to figure out if it was all for real. But as results continued to really impress us all, the stock took off, and people made up to 10X their money in less than two years from the time the run in the stock commenced.

When you can recognize an innovative idea—a business model that offers something great—coupled with a great management, you know you should set a longer time frame and be patient. Be patient—not complacent—because you need to watch management execute.

The very first shareholder letter from Bernie Marcus and cofounder Arthur Blank in the annual report made us all feel very good about the assumptions and the attitudes of both Home Depot executives as well as their hardworking employees. I loved the whole letter, because it told me more about Bernie Marcus, not just results. It was a great example of how much investors can derive from the information management disseminates to the public:

Here are a few things that made me more confident:

After the close of the fiscal year ending January 31, 1982, we were pleased to announce . . . sales for the year increased by 131 percent . . . earnings before extraordinary items increased 168 percent.

Results indicate that the Home Depot's do-it-yourself warehouse concept has been positively accepted by our customers, whether they

be novice or veteran do-it-yourselfers, or small contractors and remod-
elers. Despite the economy, customers are coming in record numbers to
our warehouse stores.

There was lots more that would make a shareholder happy, but one thing I
liked in a company that depends upon great customer service was how
much Bernie Marcus and his partner wrote publicly about their employees' terrific efforts to make things so successful. That is something I looked
for; it is not always there, but in this case it was very important.

Here is another remark in the letter that made employees feel good, because Bernie connected their performance to the recognition the whole
company was getting when he mentions "this effort":

This effort has resulted in the Home Depot being voted the 1982 retailer of the year in the home-center industry by *Building Supply News.*

Things were good for the stock until the third calendar quarter of 1983,
when a tech bubble burst, and much of the market that was overvalued began to decline.

Despite how great everything was, I and others began selling because of
the high valuations of the market and, most important, of Home Depot.
Now, one could say (and I have said!) that selling was a terrible idea, because even if great companies are temporarily overvalued, leeway should
be given on the valuation sell discipline, since great companies so often do
surprise us all on the upside with earnings and company performance.

Yes, if you know it is a great company, you might want to take your
lumps and stick with it. After all, employees most often just sit tight, are patient, and ignore short-term market moves. I needed to learn that a bit better, and over time I did.

With stocks like Home Depot, employees who behave this way are
right. Institutional investors have a disadvantage in that we do not want to
underperform similar funds for a year. Yet most of us will buy back a stock
and not be afraid just because the market is not going up.

A MISTAKE IS FIXED

Well, Home Depot did make a mistake. In 1984, it was too aggressive. The company did not turn stupid, but since it was young and in a hurry to make an acquisition, it bought a company that was not really very good. Earnings suffered greatly because of this acquisition for several quarters, and those people who had taken profits were happy. Yet anybody who did not buy back within about a year was not as likely to be happy later on when the stock resumed its strong upward advance—because, in turn, the company showed its willingness to admit its mistakes and then fix them. Anybody in the stock when the next leg of the long advance started at the end of 1985 missed another great run that made people about 54X their money in just the next seven years.

Home Depot recovered and learned from that poor acquisition and became a stronger company as a result. It gave investors even more confidence in its long-term success. It continued to grow earnings at a very fast rate for a couple of decades, becoming what the founders had envisioned and the investors had hoped for.

PATIENCE MEANS RISKS BUT ALSO MEANS A COMPENSATING PAYOFF

This is a classic example of why more patience is warranted with the greatest companies. First, they are more likely to fix mistakes, and so price moves by impatient investors become huge buying opportunities.

Second, while it is always risky to stay with or buy back (if you do sell) companies that are fixing a problem, patience has a far, far bigger payoff with the great companies than with an average stock. The payoff usually means many times your investment at the least, and getting rich at the best.

A sit-tight employee or another investor had many instances when living through downturns brought huge profits over the years. Some investors were happy with triples or quadruples or 10X their money. But for really long-term investors, Home Depot was one of the greatest investments of all time, making people the big money. Investors could see well over 1,000X their money if they were there the whole way, meaning that thousands of dollars became millions.

BENCHMARKS

Benchmarks are simple, yet they are quite important for success.

The first type of benchmark has to do with stocks. You need to establish what you expect at the outset when you invest.

Write down what you anticipate for a growth rate and whether you agree with consensus estimates out there on future earnings. If not, write down the reasons. Have a spiral notebook to jot down your expectations with the date and price, and your sources of the buy idea. Then write down your sources of information to track this company (including phone numbers if the information involves specific people) and the factors that would make you sell (i.e., think about the buy disciplines).

That is one of several reasons why "tips" are dangerous—you do not know when to sell or even have a way to track an investment if you do not have regular information from the source of the tip.

Benchmarks for Your Portfolio

As I said at the beginning of this chapter, the two most important benchmarks are: (1) how your investments—funds or stocks—are tracking over time against similar investments, and (2) having a proper time frame of at least three years, preferably five. Other kinds of benchmarks are metrics by which to measure a company's progress, such as market share gains.

Another benchmark is earnings and a company's performance. Look at a trend line of earnings and sales and use that as a benchmark. It is good if there is acceleration and a company is above the trend line. Seeing it below the trend line does not necessarily mean bad things but should alert you to the need to find out what is going on. Looking at different periods of time and calculating the growth rate over three years, five years, or even ten years creates the trend line. Nike spent a lot of money, temporarily lowering profits, but the spending achieved its goal of taking market share.

Moreover, its trend of revenue growth became better. Profits fell and were below trend, but knowing the other things gave me confidence in great profits to come.

If you have mutual funds, it is important that you use one of the various rating services such as Lipper or Morningstar, or read quality financial publications to know how your funds are doing. Each fund will be matched against other funds in its specific category, so a benchmark is to use the category and look at an appropriate time horizon. One-year time horizons are just too short, as the mutual-fund guru Jack Bogle has always said, along with other experts. Some would argue that five to ten years is best, and you can see from stock examples in this section that if you own the right stocks and mutual funds, this will work in your favor.

Yet there are problems of a practical nature for some people. It is more likely that you can use three to five years. Investors have sold the best mutual funds and stocks in the world because they lacked patience or a decent time frame. In doing so, they gave up the opportunity to become rich.

You need to know what to expect from your company if you are going to be a long-term stockholder. A benchmark helps with expectations.

SITTING TIGHT

Neither Jesse Livermore nor I can merely tell you to "sit tight." This chapter has been about guidelines you can easily exercise so you can own the right companies and not commit that cardinal sin—selling the great ones because you lack knowledge, time horizons, or patience.

The people who have worked for companies such as Wal-Mart over their careers are real people who have their own feelings and reasons for holding the stock. I thought you might be interested in what a retired assistant manager named Al Miles, who got rich from the stock, had to say, as quoted in the book *Sam Walton: Made in America,* by company founder Sam Walton.

When we went on the stock market, it didn't mean anything to some of us country boys. The chairman always said I came across the Red River

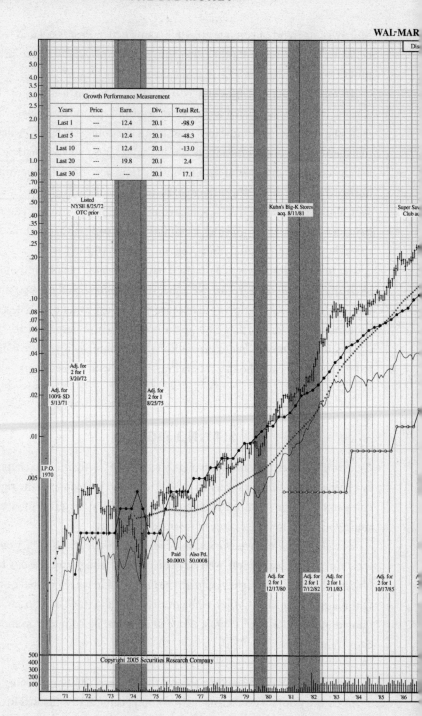

WAL-MAR

Dis...

Growth Performance Measurement				
Years	Price	Earn.	Div.	Total Ret.
Last 1	---	12.4	20.1	-98.9
Last 5	---	12.4	20.1	-48.3
Last 10	---	12.4	20.1	-13.0
Last 20	---	19.8	20.1	2.4
Last 30	---	---	20.1	17.1

Listed
NYSE 8/25/72
OTC prior

Kuhn's Big-K Stores
acq. 8/11/81

Super Sav
Club ac

Adj. for
2 for 1
3/20/72

Adj. for
100% SD
5/13/71

Adj. for
2 for 1
8/25/75

I.P.O.
1970

Paid
$0.0003

Also Pd.
$0.0008

Adj. for
2 for 1
12/17/80

Adj. for
2 for 1
7/12/82

Adj. for
2 for 1
7/11/83

Adj. for
2 for 1
10/17/85

'71 '72 '73 '74 '75 '76 '77 '78 '79 '80 '81 '82 '83 '84 '85 '86

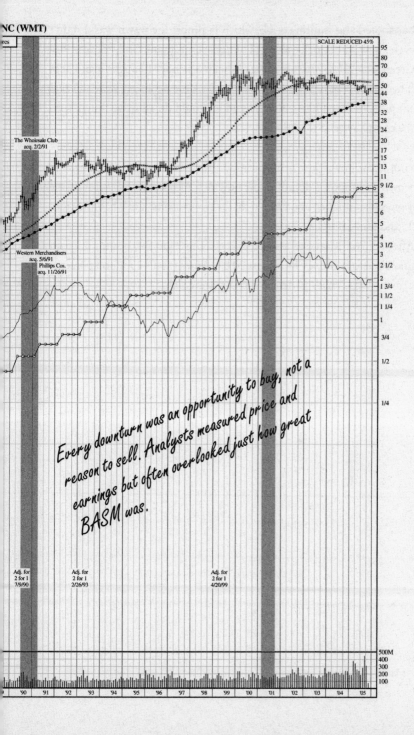

NC (WMT)

SCALE REDUCED 45%

The Wholesale Club
acq. 2/2/91

Western Merchandisers
acq. 5/6/91
Phillips Cos.
acq. 11/26/91

Every downturn was an opportunity to buy, not a reason to sell. Analysts measured price and earnings but often overlooked just how great BASM was.

Adj. for
2 for 1
7/9/90

Adj. for
2 for 1
2/26/93

Adj. for
2 for 1
4/20/99

barefooted and hunting a job, which is almost the way it was. I didn't even know what stock was. But I bought some, thank God, because Phil Green said, "Hey, you buy some of that stock, boy." I bought it and kept it because I believed in Mr. Walton, and I believed in my store. It's real simple. I believed him when he said we could do all these things with the company. And we did.

I do not know how many people can do what Al Miles did, with stocks in their own portfolios. I do not know how rich Al became, but most of the early guys like him became filthy rich, for two reasons: They had the right stock, and they sat tight.

After all, Wal-Mart was a stock worth sitting tight for. It multiplied an original investor's money by almost 20,000 times (that's 2 million percent) over thirty years. That's patience. That's getting rich.

CHAPTER FOUR

BUY AND SELL DISCIPLINES

Understanding Two Key Steps

To expect the unexpected shows a thoroughly modern
intellect.

—OSCAR WILDE

I planned to attend the 1987 A. G. Edwards small-stock-investment conference in St. Louis. So I was very excited when I learned that the city would be
hosting the World Series while I was there. I managed to get two tickets to a
game between the hometown Cardinals and the Minnesota Twins for me
and my son Jacob. We shared a great love of baseball. We would fly out late
on Monday, October 19, attend the conference, and go to the game.

I went to work early that day and was deep in some investment research
by the time the stock market opened for trading at 9:30 A.M. My stock
screen was displaying the opening prices for perhaps three dozen key
stocks that I had programmed into the computer. I looked at the screen
and immediately knew something was very wrong.

Every stock price was shown in glaring red, and every single price was
substantially below its previous close. Every single stock price, without exception, was plunging. Intel was down a few dollars, and would close that
day $10 below the prior close. I had *never* before seen *all* of the stocks that

we owned or tracked plunging like this. Every one of them was dropping like a stone in a pond.

This was Monday morning, October 19, 1987. It was the day of a now-famous stock market crash: *Black Monday.*

A colleague with whom I worked closely had been away for the weekend, and when he landed at Logan Airport in Boston around mid-morning, he called me to see how the market was doing. I told Herb that we seemed to have a crash on our hands and gave him a few sample stock prices that were low enough, even at that hour, to upset the strongest of stomachs.

Herb was a pretty straight guy, a Baptist who did not swear or drink, so he must have been quite upset when he uttered an unprintable epithet. Herb hoped I was kidding, since I often joked around, and he asked me to transfer his call to our head stock trader. I did. Then I slowly walked into our trading room to see how the conversation was going. It was not going well. The bad news was for real, and maybe even worse than we thought just from the prices, since nobody had any idea what was going on or what the causes were. My son and I did not make our trip, and he was extremely understanding and mature about it.

Professionals, even the most seasoned, have the same emotions as everyone else. Learning the ropes professionally does not eliminate human emotion, nor does it eliminate urges to buy or sell emotionally. Nothing makes uncertainty feel any better for any of us. But one can resist the surging tide of emotion if one has a framework of disciplines and knowledge within. Controlling emotions and replacing them with the elements of this framework are the secret.

When the trading day was finally over, the Dow Jones industrials had experienced the single largest point and percentage drop for any day in its history, with many individual stocks falling by far more than the nearly *23* percent drop in the Dow. Investors were left looking at portfolios of stocks that they owned, shaking their heads in disbelief that values had drooped by a quarter, a third, and—in the most volatile stocks—much more.

A CRISIS MENTALITY AMONG INVESTORS

What happened next can only be described as the product of a crisis mentality among investors. Most felt that they had to do something but had no idea what. Buy? Sell? Stick it out? The fact that it was so sudden and traumatic, and such a big blow to every investor's finances, made people afraid or even numb, and did not help any of us try to be decisive.

> When written in Chinese, the word "crisis" is composed of two characters. One represents danger, and the other represents opportunity.
> —JOHN F. KENNEDY

We all struggled with the uncertainty and emotions of the moment but continued to rely on the same buy and sell disciplines that had led us through not only this market year but all previous ones. Senior portfolio managers had some variations in the exact nature of their own disciplines, but we all had a framework that centered on the key elements of good stock selection. In the next few days, we would buy and sell on the basis of our knowledge of companies, coupled with (1) valuations, (2) our confidence in future earnings growth, and how strong our confidence was in (3) the ability of various companies to execute.

In other words, BASM is one thing that comes into play as a means of rescue, as a core tool, and as a way to go on the offensive when the chips are down.

DREAMS, EMOTIONS, REALITY, AND WEALTH

Very often, a funny thing happens to people on the way to turning dreams of great wealth into reality. Emotions and lack of discipline get in the way. No amount of analysis can overcome emotions for some investors, but the way to focus on the reality of what you own is to acquire knowledge guided by BASM and control emotions with the elements of the Seven Steps. You start with buy and sell disciplines, which incorporate valuations and fundamentals.

The combination of BASM and the Seven Steps comes into play not only during a crisis like the crash of 1987 and its aftermath, but during any period of turbulence, uncertainty, or high emotions. Uncertainty is almost always present when you have the hugest opportunities, since these two things go hand in hand.

As you see how we invested during this period, think constantly about where we would have been if we had no buy and sell disciplines, and no fundamental focus using BASM or the Seven Steps.

The three factors mentioned above—valuations, confidence, and execution ability—would help us to avoid apparent bargains in weaker stocks, such as National Semiconductor (NSM), yet buy leaders such as Intel. They were not the only elements of BASM and the Seven Steps that we needed, but they were the place to start. This method of investing would also save us from succumbing to strong emotions (both greed and fear) and, critically, to the common perils of market timing.

Avoiding such mistaken action is one of the Seven Steps, as you now know. Some investors owned great companies and really *did* know what they owned; yet they did not have the patience to hold for the longer term and thus make the big money. Why? Most frequently they failed to take the proper actions because they became highly emotional or attempted to time the market, or both.

Timing is a term that refers to investing by buying everything or selling everything on the basis of the (faulty) assumption that one can predict the market's next move. Attempts to time are common, but academicians and practitioners have concluded that success happens through luck only on occasions that are quickly reversed and very costly.

Emotional investing is very, very common, whether driven by market turbulence or something that happens to a specific stock. Emotional investing is a huge and costly threat to professionals, not just nonprofessionals, and cannot be handled just by gritting one's teeth and trying to be courageous. The emotion of greed seemed very much prevalent during spring 1987, since the stock market was very strong in the face of tepid earnings growth, and many individual share prices were going up strongly. This situation included much of the technology sector, despite the fact that new spending on tech and thus technology company revenues appeared to be lackluster.

Stocks had been quietly declining, off and on, for some few weeks before that incredible October day. But since it had been a very strong year, the general attitude was that this was a normal retrenchment as people took some profits. The last few days before the crash were rather weak, and even after the huge decline on October 19, some stocks fell further. All of this was cause for confusion and alarm. It was also stressful, since most of the great companies had plunged, offering what could be fabulous buying opportunities. Disney, Coca-Cola, Microsoft, IBM, and all the other popular names traded down. It seemed that none was spared.

The stock market, which had been frothy for a good part of the year, had climbed strongly until summer. Then it began to look tired and then started to weaken from summer through fall. On October 19, 1987, the Dow Jones industrial average (DJIA) had already declined about 9 percent from its peak. That day the DJIA plunged over 500 points (this is equivalent to almost 2,500 Dow Jones points in early 2005). It was a scary drop, crushing the value of just this blue-chip index by almost a quarter, while most stocks fared worse on a percentage basis. The NASDAQ index of over-the-counter issues dropped sharply too, and it continued to drop for several more days, since trading in those issues was far less liquid, and investors who wanted to get out needed more trading days to do so.

After a period of emotional ebullience in the market, people did not know what had happened or what to make of it, and this uncertainty tapped their emotions and prompted selling for quite a while afterward. The vast majority of investors who were experiencing feelings of crisis had no investment guidelines to help them.

Over the years, my experience had taught me many things about reasons to buy and reasons to sell. What I did most effectively to realize the biggest gains crystallized in my mind, and in my investing, as three buy disciplines and three sell disciplines. These straightforward disciplines encompassed just about any investing situation one could imagine.

BUY AND SELL DISCIPLINES

To buy a stock, all three disciplines have to be present. To sell a stock, any one of the disciplines should trigger a sale. If you are unsure of how valuations work here, see the section on valuations, earnings, and the economy at the end of this chapter.

BUY DISCIPLINES	SELL DISCIPLINES
Compelling valuations	Target price reached
High earnings growth	Change in management or strategy
Management that can execute	Failure to execute

A management whose reported results are enhanced by fraud or flagrant misrepresentation is a management that fails to execute. Lying and fraud are given special treatment in chapter 9, since there are ways to avoid being victimized by them.

NO YARDSTICK APPROACH

Put away rulers, yardsticks, and calculators, since this is not a quantitative approach meant to replace judgment and analysis with a simplistic numerical formula. For instance, this book concentrates a lot on great companies, great management, and great business plans, and that combination is what creates the best investments for true wealth. Along the way, companies with these characteristics become overvalued at times. Companies with these characteristics also can appear to be overvalued even when they really are not, because they so often beat earnings estimates by virtue of the power of the greatest business models.

Thus, if you own companies that may be truly great companies, my approach is to cut them some slack and not sell so quickly if their share prices go above their valuation trend lines or become valued more highly than those of similar companies for a short time. Watch carefully, though. Use more than one method of valuing a company: price-to-earnings (P/E) ratio, price-to-book (P/B) ratio (value), and price-to-sales P/S ratio. (You can find instructions on how to calculate P/E, P/B, and P/S ratios, plus PEG ratio, on p. 113.)

This "leniency" with what I thought were great companies, coupled with informed scrutiny, saved me from selling my Cisco a number of times, as well as other great stocks. It is okay as long as you do not call all the companies you won on "great" just because they were going up in a bull market and making you happy. "Happy juice" is not a discipline.

Even with a bit of slack extended to the great or potentially great ones, the disciplines will keep you out of trouble, remind you when you do not have enough knowledge about the companies you own, and help you to invest without the unhealthy influence of strong emotions. This is what the Seven Steps are all about: a combination of commonsense factors to allow what you already know to dominate your investing.

Once again, these steps are: (1) knowledge, (2) patience, (3) disciplines, (4) emotions, (5) time horizon, (6) market timing, and (7) benchmarks.

BALANCING FEAR AND GREED IN 1987

The markets were somewhat speculative going through 1987 and failed to differentiate between stocks that deserved expanding valuations by virtue of accelerating growth (corporations like Disney and McDonald's) and those that did not (Digital Equipment and National Semiconductor). But they all went up. I was applying buy and sell disciplines all along the way, to correct for the excessive valuations of stocks in many sectors, so that I would not be caught up in the wrong stocks.

The best investing occurs when there is some balance between fear and greed in the markets, but I did not see this healthy balance in 1987. The markets were quite strong in the face of only modest expansion in the overall economy and corporate earnings. Interest rates were soaring (with many bonds yielding above 10 percent, probably as a result of historically huge debt loads of the U.S. government, the corporate sector, and consumers). Finally, the U.S. dollar was falling, suggesting that foreigners were reacting to these conditions by taking money out of the country.

Market timing simply does not work, so the thing to do is to concentrate especially hard on finding stocks that have a secure growth outlook, are not overvalued, and have good management that can execute well, even in a slow economy. In other words, use the buy disciplines in a practical way (Seven Steps). That is just what I was doing in 1987. I felt very confident about the stocks I owned, thanks to BASM and Seven Steps, let other stocks go up without me, and sold those that were going up but either had become overvalued or were suspect in terms of the fundamental outlook. Sell disciplines are almost the opposite side of the coin from buy disciplines.

When I say to sell because of a change in management or strategy, this does not mean that such changes are doomed to failure. It means that, for the most part, holding would involve an experiment with my fund holders' or clients' money, and I would rather see how things are progressing and buy back later. This would have been the correct move when Hewlett-Packard brought in a new CEO in 1971. Looking at historical changes in the CEO at Hewlett-Packard shows that the early moves were actually excellent. But in 1999 a more troublesome change occurred when the company brought in Carly Fiorina. As much as the press applauded her ambitious speeches and plans, right from the first I, and some others who had history with Hewlett, felt that she was weakening the business model, especially when she acquired Compaq.

The exceptions once again prove the rule, as they say. When IBM brought in Lou Gerstner as CEO in 1993, basically to save the company, I bought some IBM stock for specific reasons, which would go against the rule, just as holding Cisco goes against the rule when it gets overvalued. With Cisco, I did this because it was a great company, and I decided that it might not be statistically overvalued anyway if it did everything right.

In the case of IBM, I knew Lou Gerstner before IBM brought him in, and I thought the world of him. Most important, I felt that he had properly analyzed what was wrong with IBM (the "big half" of the battle) and was the right man for the job. Knowledge, along with common sense and conviction, is what gives you the freedom to occasionally modify or "customize" the general buy and sell disciplines. A lot of people in the business thought his appointment did not make sense. "He's a cookie man," they groused, because he had been running RJR Nabisco, albeit very effectively.

What they forgot was that Lou was a distinguished alum of the management consulting firm McKinsey & Company, where he had studied a wide variety of companies and industry sectors in depth. Even more important, he had proved that he knew how to meet challenges in managing diverse situations.

Managers who truly have great executive ability can translate it from one industry to another. Having specific abilities that fit the challenges and problems of what they face is more important than their company's specific product. Gerstner had true executive ability (I had seen that already at Nabisco) and the requisite skills to solve IBM's problems. I saw this more and more after he went to work at IBM.

Naturally, this is important for investors in two respects. First, business models in one industry have similarities to those in another, but they also have to fit the mission of the company at the moment. You will learn to recognize similar business models more and more as you look at them while doing your investing homework. Second, once investors understand how to identify BASM within any one industry, they can translate that understanding to all other industries.

Selling is as tough for professionals as it is for nonprofessionals. Many of the best growth investors are inherently optimistic about the future. Emotional selling is not what optimistic people like to do. The disciplines are there for just that reason. Digital Equipment (DEC) is a great example of how sell disciplines were used in that period, how they should always be used, and how using them saved me from losing a lot of money.

I had sold most of my Digital Equipment stock almost two months before the October 1987 crash. The stock had been going through the roof as the company came in with stronger earnings quarter after quarter. I had expected the stock to do really well because of DEC's new products and networking breakthroughs, and it did even better than I thought. I hung on a little while longer as it went through what I thought was a reasonable valuation target. It had quadrupled in only twenty-four months, and I sold it at nearly $170. I then watched it go to about $200 without me, until the crash stopped it cold. It was more than fully valued at $170, actually. As I show at the end of this chapter, "absolute" formulas for valuing stocks can be wrong or fooled by changing conditions.

First, I "triangulate," meaning that I look at more than one valuation tool—usually a ratio. So I will measure price against expected earnings (PE) and also PE against the expected growth rate (PEG ratio). Sometimes I use the market capitalization (value of all the company's shares, according to the number in annual reports or recent releases, multiplied by current share price) compared with current revenues. Here's the key: I compare these numbers with those for similar companies and with the *subject company's* (DEC's) *own recent history.*

Giving up the absolute top is all right. It is not easy to do without any disciplines, and it is not the easiest thing in the world even if you *do* have disciplines. Such sales can be difficult emotionally, since you see the stock you sold continue to move higher, even though you fully understand the good reasons for selling. You cannot pick exact tops and bottoms, and stocks trade below and above fair value on market momentum. That is why a discipline can be invaluable. As happened in this instance, it can even save you.

Interestingly enough, if we had all understood how to properly value the stocks of new businesses during the Internet and general technology stock boom of the late 1990s, and if we had used such sale disciplines, there never would been a bubble to burst in March of 2000. Some investors had no interest in fundamentals or disciplines, and many of us who did were plugging the wrong inputs into our valuation decisions. That was because, as you will see in chapter 8, Internet traffic and other indicators of growth were falsely reported and were built on some corporate lies that did not get discovered until later on.

My sale of Digital was mainly based on my judgment that the stock was getting too expensive. Sometimes, in the case of a terrific company, as I've said, I give the valuation a little leeway, since valuations cannot be exact. Valuation is both an art and a science, and we use a few different methods to get as close to accuracy as we can. But I was not sorry that I had sold Digital, since the "terrific company" part was evaporating. My continuing efforts to have current knowledge of my companies had shown me that DEC's great reputation was based on a history of success, the continuation of which was now being threatened by emerging problems.

VALUATION DISCIPLINES MADE ME GET OUT THE SHOVEL; DIGGING UNCOVERED THE REST

One could say that valuation became the sell discipline that alerted me. Then I started to consider how much leeway to give such a great company, at which point the other two sell disciplines applicable to growth and execution began to enter the picture as I gained current knowledge.

The computer sector Digital was operating in, mid-range computers, was showing intense competitive pressures that were affecting earnings and growth for everyone in the industry. My greatest concern, however, was that even though Digital was still the leader, I was starting to worry about its management and strategy for the first time ever.

In the early 1980s, DEC's price-to-earnings ratio was in the mid-teens. Then it crept up to 20. But in late summer 1987, as the stock headed for 30 and reached a twenty-four-month quadruple, it was just too high. Since Digital Equipment was now showing cycles in its earnings, instead of steady growth every single year, this high price indicated a stock market that was paying too much for many stocks simply because they had price momentum.

Steady growth was giving way to cycles, by the way, because DEC was now larger, with customers in almost all industries. As a result, the company had greater exposure to the overall pace of capital spending for technology in the economy.

Greed was more evident than disciplines, for sure, with DEC and many similar growth and technology favorites. I did not know what would happen to the overall market, I just got worried about more and more high stock prices. I was always looking through the market for bargains and scanning lots of stock prices.

Although Digital had pretty much failed in efforts to create a successful PC line in the early 1980s, it was riding high in 1986 and 1987 because it had been so successful in creating a new VAX minicomputer line that could network with other DEC computers, as well as those of many other computer companies. This was a big deal, and the profits were still rising sharply in 1987 because of this success. Yet, as I noted above, I had become a "bug" on management and its strategies and business models. I had earlier chalked up DEC's failure in the personal-computer line entirely to management and now watched management's execution ability a bit more carefully.

Management had been highly successful with an entrepreneurial, comparatively unstructured organization for almost two decades, but around 1984 management had felt pulled in many directions. PCs and new VAX lines were only part of the problem. Fighting over product areas, operating in many geographic areas with territorial disputes in marketing, and other divisive forces were making things inside highly disruptive. So, for those of us who liked to look under the hood, things were getting riskier. Just when the VAX line was pumping profits so well in late 1986, good management, marketing, and technology people were leaving Digital. That was public information, and it alerted me to the risk that the company would not achieve high growth going forward.

You will encounter situations like Digital's many times, as well as stock markets that seem to defy logic, even though those markets will usually be less dramatic and extreme than the one in 1987. If you read and stay current with your companies—maintaining your knowledge base, in other words—you will be fine. Professionals will not have any inside track or edge on you.

I thought it unlikely that Digital could escape its problems forever, unless the organization undertook new initiatives to fix them, so I was watching closely. Consequently, by summer 1987, when the stock was high and DEC's internal problems were at least as intense, there were two reasons to sell: both valuation and future growth prospects increasingly worried me.

Looking at DEC's valuations based on the price divided by the expected earnings for the coming year, as well as dividing the price by the sales (either per share or for all the stock—total shares outstanding times price per share—and the entire company revenues), I saw that this company had become super-expensive compared with other similar companies and with its own price and valuation history.

I use those comparisons a lot and do give leeway to companies with greatness in their BASM or greatness in what we expect their next product cycle to be, so we do not get trapped by mechanical arithmetic. But I recog-

DIGITAL EQUIPMENT CORPORATION (DEC)

Computer systems and peripheral equipment

MOVING AVERAGE
48 Months

RATIO-CATOR
Monthly

When companies accelerate, expensive is okay. But in 1987, emotions and prices ran high, just as strategy and execution weakened. It was over.

Adj. for
2 for 1
5/12/86

Earns. 12 mos.		Earns. 12 mos.		
9/30/90 D .40		3/28/92 D 10.39		
12/29/90 D .73		6/30/92 D 18.50		
3/30/91 .01		9/30/92 D 20.77	Earns. 12
6/30/91 D 5.08		12/31/92 D 20.23	3/31/94	
9/30/91 D 5.06		3/30/93 D 18.10	6/30/94
12/25/91 D 7.09		6/29/93 D 1.99	9/30/94
		9/30/93 D .71	12/31/94
		12/31/93 D .67	3/31/95

1978 1979 1980 1981 1982 1983 1984 1985 1986 1987 1988 1989 1990 1991 1992 1993 1994

nize that great change and improvement do get higher valuations. However, if you refer back to things I have said earlier about valuations, when the differences between the valuation of other companies (and also valuations throughout a company's own history) start to accelerate or perhaps are 25 percent or so above where they "should" be, I tend to think emotions are playing a larger role in driving up the stock price, and things might be out of whack.

BASM and the Seven Steps do tell you what to look at and give you the focus, disciplines, and framework that investors truly need. That fact does not translate, however, into using mechanical approaches. But you do need reference points, and comparisons on a relative basis are far, far more effective in valuing stocks than using an absolute number.

After exercising that sell discipline, I had difficulty finding any new stocks to buy with the cash. My mutual fund, like most, had prospectus rules that said the fund should be almost fully invested in common stocks almost all the time, and it was not supposed to have a cash position above 15 percent of the total assets of the fund. I tried my best to follow the rules but, like all fund managers, I learned that there were times when I found a real abundance of great values to buy, so I might "overdraw" a bit, while at other times just the opposite was true, and it was tough to find things to buy. The latter was the case in this period. I had trouble finding enough stocks to fill the portfolio adequately with equities that I believed satisfied my BASM criteria.

Interestingly enough, years later (1994), when I was the guest on PBS's popular TV program *Wall Street Week with Louis Rukeyser,* Lou mentioned that just prior to the 1987 crash, I had my funds up to 25 percent in cash. This had worked out very well, since I had money to invest after stocks plunged. Then Lou noted that now, in late 1994, during a poor-looking, declining market, I was fully invested, and still my performance had been running better than that of most of the other funds in the aggressive-growth category. Rukeyser wanted to know why I was fully invested and why that was working. I made it clear that it was not market timing but valuation disciplines at work.

My funds did have more cash than normal, just temporarily, in 1987, but not because I was trying to time the market or draw conclusions from the declining dollar or high interest rates. Rather, it was because I could not find enough stocks that had great valuations and still had good management executing well, while offering prospects for strong growth. It seemed to be just the opposite case in 1994.

The stock market's decline had made lots of growth stories look attractive. Investors were somewhat frightened, and fear often goes hand in hand with cheapness (as ebullience does with expensive stocks). But as I told Lou in response to his question, I bought carefully selected individual stocks, not just ones that were cheap. Soon after that television appearance, the market strengthened, and my fund holders were handsomely rewarded.

DIGITAL EQUIPMENT AFTER THE CRASH

I wanted to buy back DEC after the 1987 crash. I had loved owning that company for a long time and had not found it easy to sell. When the crash came on October 19, the stock had spiked on an intraday basis to about $200 per share and fell intraday as low as $110, although it was soon trading in the $120s. The temptation was great, despite the fact that I was worried and scared—scared because of what had happened so quickly, and worried that I would make some wrong moves.

Most people buy tech stocks when companies have great new product introductions and successes, as was the case with DEC. I wanted to buy it. Yet my buy and sell disciplines pointed to problems with departures and management's ability to execute. Emotions said buy, the big drop in price said buy, but the disciplines that had done so well for me, coupled with my new knowledge, said no.

I did not buy it. I *could not* buy it. Very simply, this stock had met my sell disciplines, for very important and "nonmechanical" reasons, and now, as much as I might lean in its favor, I could not see how it met my buy disciplines. It seemed to meet the one on valuation, but it had to meet all three, and it did not meet the second and third. Period.

Before long, management problems did show up in the earnings. First, quarterly earnings continued to move higher but at a slowing pace, which usually lowers a stock's valuation, since it predicts a slower growth future. The stock reacted badly. Then, not long afterward, DEC had an up quarter but it was disappointing to analysts. The stock price had reached its top, and the company began to encounter earnings troubles as a result of both industry problems and management's struggles with its internal problems.

Digital Equipment's stock was a big loser for those who bought it only because it had fallen so far in the crash, and the price continued to decline all the way down to roughly $30 per share.

The disciplines, the leaning against emotions, and the knowledge—the factors that go into the Seven Steps—had saved me on this stock. For that matter, they were a big factor helping me on all my decisions covering the entire portfolio.

It was also BASM, of course, that made the reasons for not buying it back nonmechanical, since this was the tool that made me focus on how management was beginning to slip. We saw it very early. In fact, that post-crash stock decline went on for over two years, with investors buying and selling DEC stock every day, on the basis of their own perceptions of whether it was getting to be a real bargain or a real albatross in their portfolios.

BASM convinced me that Digital was not fixing what truly needed to be fixed, despite some hot products. This is an example of how BASM and the Seven Steps can be a model for you in nearly every market and with every type of company when you decide what you need to look at, how you need to make a decision on buying, holding, or selling—and how likely it is that a stock can make you truly rich.

After all, the other side of this coin is the many, many stocks that have dropped significantly for one reason or another but had great BASM, like Dell, and became terrific buys.

Volatility, fear, and greed are parts of virtually all market environments, and BASM and the Seven Steps are your tools to deal with each of those factors.

WE HAD NO CHOICE; WE HAD TO OWN STOCKS

Along with other professionals who managed other people's money, I had to follow our funds' mandates and continue to own a portfolio of stocks. I owned stocks that I really liked, including restaurants and some good retailers like Dillard's department stores, which was doing exceptionally well. I also had Disney, Nike, Microsoft, and Dell, among others. These last three names had not been public all that long—they were still small, growing fast, and in some ways untested. As usual, I had many stocks that I categorized as emerging growth.

Although I felt a lot of stress and unhappiness about the massive paper losses in the 1987 market and the uncertainly of it all, I did not look out the window with a vacant stare, I did not go to emergency prayer meetings, and I did not wring my hands and remain passive. I had to own stocks, and I had developed buy and sell disciplines to help me in what would be months of uneasy action in an expensive equity market.

> The degree of one's emotion varies inversely with one's knowledge of the facts—the less you know the hotter you get.
> —BERTRAND RUSSELL

One thing I observed in the aftermath of Black Monday was that many investors were completely emotional and didn't bother to discuss or use research, so their knowledge was not being put to work. This meant that there would be a lot of opportunity for others if we could figure out what to buy next. Russell's adage about knowing less and being more emotional was profoundly evident. Just by looking at what I saw in the press over a few days, and listening to the opinions of others, I recognized that people were waiting for something to happen, without knowing what.

Here is what I thought: I knew a lot about many companies. Plenty of them would be great to own at current prices, so it was easy to see how attractive many valuations looked now. There were clear indications that I should enlarge my positions in many of my current holdings and certainly not sell with the herd. Selling did continue in many stocks for days after the crash, so it was still tough to feel good about buying.

After I found good valuations (and there were plenty of them), the knowledge of which companies could meet the next two buy disciplines would be the key to it all.

> One day Alice came to a fork in the road and saw a Cheshire cat in a tree. "Which road do I take?" she asked. "Where do you want to go?" was his response. "I don't know," Alice answered. "Then," said the cat, "it doesn't matter."
> —Lewis Carroll

Our mandate was to compete with all other high-growth funds, and to beat them. To accomplish that, we had to be long-term investors and avoid market timing. The path lay in stock selection along the lines of our disciplines. I *did know* where we wanted to go, despite the fact that I was very nervous and wished I knew a lot more. We always wish we knew a lot more.

TELLING A STORY

A good business plan tells a story about how a company intends to make money, grow, and protect itself against competition. The buy disciplines links a stock to the underlying company. The story is out there in the public domain for those who want to read, use the Internet, and look at the statements about the company's objectives in its annual reports and on its Web site. There are big lessons here for investors. A central one is that those individual investors who read the stories and know about the companies they own, or are considering owning, are always ready to think and to act. So, when markets swing up and down—not just in a big crash, but also in the normal course of events—you do not have to start scrambling. You already know the story, and you are just looking at the price. Knowledge, the first and most important of the Seven Steps, should always be there to tap into, ready to apply to the disciplines.

I knew the stories in my portfolio, meaning I knew what I owned. By adding money to my current holdings, I was increasing the number of shares I owned at lower prices. We all know the old adage "Buy low and sell high," but emotions often make people do exactly the opposite. With those stocks that plunge, it is what we call the *FUD factor*—fear, uncertainty, and doubt, arising from an emotional feeling that the market must know more than we do, while greed seems to increase the more a stock goes up. Fundamentals frequently become pushed aside by emotions without some structure to focus and use knowledge. But BASM and the Seven Steps are very likely to have you follow this useful adage properly (buying low; selling high), and that was what I was doing: selling stocks that were going down.

After the crash, I put more money into my current holdings because I already knew a great deal about my holdings (as one should always know) and had kicked the tires one more time, during the period in which I found it tough to quickly research and buy new names. I immediately added to my positions in Disney and Nike, for pretty much the same reasons. There were lots of stocks that appeared to have good growth going forward, and after the plunge many were statistically attractive on price and earnings. Yet if the overall environment was to be difficult going forward for all stocks, it was more important than ever to ensure that I owned companies with management that could execute. Both these companies had management that I wanted to invest with.

In the case of Disney (DIS), I knew that business was good for both the theme parks and the movies and entertainment areas. Some corporate-raider activity had threatened to take over the company a few years before, and new management had taken over. Since 1984, when Michael Eisner became chairman and Frank Wells had become president, they had embarked on a program to enhance shareholder value. The creation of Touchstone Pictures (1984) to make films for the critical teenage and adult markets was paying off (the first film, *Splash* was very successful). Then, they created a new TV program, *Golden Girls,* which was immensely successful. So was the new *Disney Sunday Night Movie.* Next, some films from the Disney Library were used for TV syndication, which was highly lucrative. Finally, some of the classic animated films were released on videocassette, and a number of them soon reached the top of the all-time bestseller lists.

While these and other initiatives meant better growth going forward, the most important thing was the attitude of the management—it was determined to be more aggressive and creative for the benefit of the shareholders—and management's obvious ability to execute the plans well, without outright failures or even minor slips that could be avoided. I also liked the fact that even though the theme parks were doing well, Disney's senior executives were not resting on their laurels and had started collaborating with the filmmakers George Lucas and Francis Ford Coppola to create great new movies.

Disney's earnings were very strong going forward, with good quarters for more than the next two years. Everybody who invested could understand the story about how Disney generated those earnings. I had no advantage over individual investors, other than using a set of disciplines in an environment in which most investors did not.

The stock, which had fallen from roughly $20 to $11 in the 1987 crash, then advanced to more than $32 over the following twenty-four-month period. It was nearly a triple on a great company and greatly enriched those of us who knew the story and applied the disciplines.

Nike was also great. The company was emerging from a wide field of small companies that were capitalizing on the fitness boom and people's desire to have more interesting athletic shoes. Nike looked like the leader. I met with Phil Knight when the company went public in 1980, had watched him closely, had monitored his company's performance compared with that of other small athletic-shoe companies, and had come to believe in his management drive and expertise. I concluded that Nike was the best-managed company in the industry. I have known Phil and been a fan of his from that early time right up to today.

I knew what mattered most about Nike when the crash took the stock down from about $12 to almost $7 on an intraday basis. First, the company had been able to convince the best and most prominent athletes to wear the shoes in competition. (In 1983 Joan Benoit had set a world women's marathon record wearing Nike.) The shoes were impressive, and so were the marketing and distribution. The members of the management team had all been working together to achieve much faster growth than the industry: i.e., market share gains. In 1985 the Air Jordan line of basketball shoes appeared to great commercial success—it was created in honor of the rookie sensation Michael Jordan—and in 1986 the company passed $1 billion in revenues, and introduced apparel named for Jordan and tennis star John McEnroe.

High spending on marketing and advertising along with a lot of price competition from the countless companies that wanted to maintain industry position and could compete only with price had caused an earnings downturn in the latter months of 1984 and early 1985. Nike had been more aggressive than the prior sports-shoe industry leader, Converse, which had been king of the basketball shoe and sneaker world before this period, so Nike had passed it. Now, though, it was Reebok that was seen as holding the lead in athletic shoes. Nike's big spending and product introductions and promotions made 1986 a watershed year for the company. Reebok was totally taken by surprise as Nike ran past it. Reebok was left in the position of needing to respond and moving to regroup, so it planned to become more aggressive with advertising and products.

In response is the key, of course. Nike had the foresight, the vision, and the plan (plus its excellent management team) that enabled the company to move quickly and not miss a beat. Execution is very tough when new things are being done. Thus, the way I felt about Nike's down quarters in earnings was comparable to my reaction when somebody gets bruised by leaping in the air to catch a pass that wins the Super Bowl. The injury is seen as minor and temporary, and part of an essential move that leads to victory.

Despite short-term softness in Nike's earnings from the high spending, my colleagues and I knew that 1987 would be a strong turnaround year in earnings and the beginning, possibly, of a long period of high growth in earnings. What Phil Knight had accomplished, his credibility and plans and his ability to execute on all fronts made this stock exceptionally attractive, regardless of what the near-term market action might be.

Lesson: Knowing the story—a story anybody could have known—and combining that knowledge with the three buy disciplines were the key to making huge money. The end of the story did come true, as earnings did exactly what Phil Knight intended and what we, in turn, had expected. In fact, the earnings soared for half a decade. One more important thing.

After Nike's IPO, I made a lot of money on a small position, and saw earnings really triple in a little over two years. The uncertainly of the shoe business and countless competitors did mean that as much as I liked Phil Knight from my meetings or equally from what I read, I wanted to watch Nike operate and execute the business model. Aggressive expansion caused earnings and stock volatility along the way, and I took some lumps (stock declines). Yet the keys were: (1) Knight responded well to changing conditions; (2) *critically*, Nike was taking market share—the path to dominance; and (3) I was running five miles per day and loving the shoes and finding—more important—that retailers and running magazines loved Nike. I tried to buy more when the stock went down. Small stocks are volatile but knowledge and BASM helped me and prepared me for 1987. As for Nike stock, it doubled in about a year, and for the five years it multipled investors' money tenfold.

Along the way, we sold various stocks. McDonald's fulfilled a price objective and was sold a couple of years later, but we did not stay out of it indefinitely. Many other stocks were sold, including a bunch of tech stocks, most of which were not truly great companies. Most tech sales were not as interesting or dramatic as that of DEC. Microsoft (MSFT) was held. The number one company that Microsoft was interested in displacing was Lotus Development, which was the largest developer and seller of software in that period. Lotus was the leader, and its spreadsheet program had about 70 percent of the market.

Holding on to my Lotus stock was a mistake.

OF COURSE I MAKE MISTAKES!

I mentioned earlier that I make lots of little mistakes. But by using my buy and sell disciplines, I try to sell if I see a problem, to keep mistakes small. What is really important is that I continue to watch all "sold" stock of companies that have a chance to "be okay" and have potential to "be great," so I can buy them back. I keep a spiral notebook and make little notes all the time about these sold stocks.

In a very few unique situations with stocks like Lotus and Sunglass Hut,

I had become so trusting of management that was making me a lot of money from its great stock performance that I slipped and did not notice soon enough when *management* slipped. That did cost me.

Although Lotus had sold three times as many copies of spreadsheet programs as its nearest competitor, Microsoft's Multiplan, the Microsoft management knew that MSFT was pushing hard to get a whole new spreadsheet program to market, Microsoft Excel. Excel had powerful features not found on the Lotus product. It was definitely better.

Perhaps Lotus's problems resulted from a combination of factors, starting with a poor spending environment in technology and Lotus's efforts to maintain its supremacy using its non-Windows programs despite the handwriting on the wall represented by Microsoft's Windows. Lotus began spending much more on advertising and promotion to maintain market share. The company put a huge push on its development efforts to try to match Excel, but unfortunately for Lotus and those of us who were shareholders, the earnings slipped. So, despite a rebound of over 50 percent from the low price at the time of the crash, I was still holding Lotus when the stock turned down, and I lost some money, though not a huge amount.

I made a variety of little mistakes, of course, but Lotus was the largest, and it pained me that I knew better and still made this mistake. Keeping my mistakes small, admitting them quickly, and selling were keys to maintaining good performance. The examples that I bring up here, such as Lotus, are mistakes that offer the best learning experiences. You can be sure that every year I made some mistakes.

I could chalk up some of my mistakes to being far too busy at times, and to other factors that were not purely investment-related. But with Lotus, it was the mistake of staying loyal too long. I had really liked its business model and management, and was making big profits, so I had blinded myself to the the company's stubbornness and slow reactions. It was kind of dumb, but I learned a lot from it. The key with mistakes is to learn something from them, and then move on.

Perfection is always going to be elusive in this game.

WHEN THE CHIPS ARE DOWN:
A TALE OF TWO SEMIS

Often we are all faced with choices between two different stocks, and we have to decide fairly quickly whether to buy one or the other, or both. The most interesting of these choices is when they involve stocks in the same industry. In October 1987, there were plenty of stressful yet "juicy" choices in front of us. One of the most interesting was whether or not to buy Intel or National Semiconductor, since both had plunged. In an environment where we understood that tech spending was not great, though, could we really justify owning both? Or, for that matter, just one of them?

Intel Versus National Semiconductor

Immediately after the October 19 stock nosedive, some investors extrapolated rather than making a genuine analysis or assessing stock prices and company outlooks at that moment. In other words, they were not using the buy and sell disciplines that we were. They lost. The common foible of extrapolation is actually used a lot, is mistaken for analysis, and is immensely costly. More on this in chapter 5.

Other investors could calmly analyze and put two and two together, and take advantage of opportunities. They won.

Intel and National Semiconductor epitomize stock winners and losers, since they were in the very same semiconductor industry, but with totally opposite fundamental outlooks and stock-price movements in the months and even years following October 19, 1987.

That year Intel was coming out of a semiconductor recession with tremendously accelerated earnings. Intel had dropped to about $18 at its October 19 low. By buying it later in the day, when it had reached its low, both John Neff—star manager of the Vanguard Windsor Fund—and I got a price that proved to be a steal. First of all, in the coming months, with the Dow Jones industrials moving up about 30 percent, Intel made us 100 percent. (Subsequently, it had another decline, but then recovered and went on to hit $51 per share.) Moreover, this was at a time when technology in general was not doing particularly well, and many technology stocks fell further in the weeks and months following the crash.

Many people were buying indiscriminately, though. A crisis can evoke different reactions. Some investors lived in fear and did nothing, or even sold stocks at the bottom. Since nobody really understood what was going on, how much an investor wanted to be exposed to somewhat risky stocks really depended on that investor's risk profile. There have been market declines, including those of 1929 and the early 1930s, as well as others, in which a market plunge was not the end of the trouble. Some investors, however, even in such adverse conditions, became aggressive. That typically worked in instances where they had good knowledge about what they bought, and maintained a multiyear time frame, looking forward.

But indiscriminate buying and selling were widespread after the 1987 crash; investors simply paid no attention to the company information underlying stock-price movements. A great example was those investors who bought shares of National Semiconductor, just at the time when John and I bought Intel shares. While Intel investors were smiling and reaping profits, NSM investors, who lacked knowledge, lost a lot of money. In my opinion, greed overcame knowledge.

National Semiconductor: The Story

NSM was founded in 1959, nine years earlier than Intel Corp., which is actually quite a long time in the world of high technology. Its earliest integrated circuits were aimed at the space program, scientific applications, and consumer markets. In the 1970s, National Semiconductor aggressively went after markets that included calculators, watches, and grocery-checkout machines.

In the next decade, more and more good technologies came out of NSM labs, including speech-synthesis chips and chips for mainframe computers. The company started to go after a share of the personal-computer market, but really became more competitive in this market late in the day, launching construction of three factories in the 1980s.

While lagging behind Intel's aggressive chip development in personal computers, NSM continued to develop and sell a huge number of products for many end users (manufacturing customers and consumers). The company acquired Fairchild Semiconductor in 1987, and also introduced a new product line of graphics chips.

It seemed to me that doing all of these things at once meant that NSM could not have the focus of Intel, which is precisely why Intel got the most product design contracts from the manufacturer of personal computers, the most important market. The Fairchild acquisition came at a time when technology orders and other fundamentals in general were not doing well.

I faulted company management for a business model that lacked focus and for having too many product lines to feed from its research engineers. This is a real problem when you consider that the most important market of all, personal computers, was coming on strong, and National Semiconductor was far from being the leader that Intel was.

NSM stock had come down from over $20 to $15, but earnings going forward were erratic, reflecting these problems. The ups and downs had more downs than ups over the next couple of years. So a buyer saw his shares drop to $9.88 by October 1987, but the stock just continued to melt away until finally bottoming out at around $3 in 1990.

Obviously, buyers had more greed than knowledge. This situation was the reverse of Disney's and Nike's. The story was easy to understand, but it did not have a happy ending. Those who jumped and used only price as a basis for their decision did the wrong thing.

Intel: The Story

In 1980 *Dun's Review* had named Intel (INTC) one of the five best-managed companies in America. In 1986 Andy Grove was named president and chief executive officer (he was chairman from 1997 to 2005, when he retired). Andy was already known as one of the top people in technology, and Intel's management was seen as getting stronger and stronger.

As for technology, Intel appeared to be at the top of the heap. In 1974 the company had come out with a terrific new personal-computer chip:

the Intel 8080. The reviews were glowing. Intel just kept going and by 1980 was widely hailed as having supremacy in the microprocessor market. Another great product, the 286 chip, was launched in 1982; and in 1984 *Fortune* magazine named Andy Grove as one of the "ten toughest bosses in America."

The new products kept coming, and each one actually increased Intel's lead over competitors. By 1987, the company was doing exceptionally well with its 386 chip, and a 486 was under development.

In 1987 earnings were coming out of an industry downturn. Intel had an excellent earnings year and looked as if it was poised for a very good period of strong growth. The stock did well even after the crash. Compared with most technology in a period of mixed results for tech stocks, Intel's was a "star."

John Neff had told the stock traders to buy him all Intel stock trading on any exchange anywhere. John knew the story well, but had stayed away initially, since he felt the stock was too expensive. As soon as the price dropped, he took all he could get, combining the new price with the disciplines on execution and earnings growth. I was not as big or dramatic a buyer, but I was also happy with my purchases.

Knowing how great Intel's story was gave us the knowledge to understand that we had a great price and that the other two buy disciplines were met. The decisions are easier and most often are far more profitable when done within the framework of buy and sell disciplines.

> **We have met the enemy, and he is us.**
> **—POGO**

During the War of 1812, after the United States defeated Great Britain in the crucial naval battle of Lake Erie, the American naval commander Oliver Hazard Perry, said, "We have met the enemy, and they are ours." Walt Kelly, the well-known creator of a very popular comic strip, *Pogo*, had the character Pogo say, "We have met the enemy, and he is us." I wrote a brochure for investors in the late 1990s, designed to give them a framework in which to invest. I used this statement to make the point that you can be your own worst enemy if you don't use the right tools when making an investment.

Knowledge and disciplines are simple things, really, and things that will take you a very long way toward becoming rich. Combining these two can be a powerful formula for wealth.

It is simple to add other things, such as patience. The legendary investor Warren Buffett said in a 1999 interview with *Business Week:* "Success in investing doesn't correlate with I.Q. once you're above the level of twenty-five. Once you have ordinary intelligence, what you need is the temperament to control the urges that get other people into trouble in investing." Most people who take investing seriously have far more intelligence than they need for being successful in their investing. I have maintained throughout my career that investing is not an I.Q. contest.

As for temperament, that may work for the few, but it does not work alone for most people. You need to control emotions to have the right temperament. I do know that Warren Buffett made his vast fortune in the markets (Buffett is the second wealthiest person in the world, after Bill Gates) not only because of his wisdom, knowledge, and skills, but also because he developed a personal style of investing and disciplines that worked for him.

The "rule on the rules" is that they must be easy rules that can be applied consistently time after time, without requiring an investor to do highly complex things that are impractical. You are going to find, when you put the Seven Steps and BASM into practice, that just as you do not think about coordinating your arms and legs while running, these things are going to become second nature to you. *That* is a big reason why they truly work.

Investors struggle against themselves. Their knowledge and intellect are often at odds with their emotions. That is why the Seven Steps really bring out the true investor in you and maximize your chances of becoming rich.

UNDERSTANDING VALUATIONS

To guess is cheap. To guess wrongly is very expensive.
—CHINESE PROVERB

Throughout this book, I emphasize a holistic approach to companies and their stocks—looking at the whole enterprise, not microanalyzing pieces. By using that framework, particularly the business model, you can put earnings growth in context, without trying to be a securities analyst.

Many investors know that to estimate valuations, earnings, and the direction of the economy is for professional investors. Some investors are better at it than others, but nobody has consistently accurate earnings estimates that last a year or more unless we are talking about the great companies that are pretty predictable and help investors with a lot of guidance—and then, you can do this yourself without breathing hard.

Valuations are part science and part art, and a great subject of endless debate among professionals, both as to how to do them, and about what any company is worth at any time. The referee, or judge, is the market, which sets a value on the shares of every stock. For making money, of course, we all debate not what the market says shares are worth at one moment, but what they should really be worth right now and particularly in the future. We can do some things to help estimate that, I believe.

Guessing what the economy will do has cost investors more money perhaps than anything else. All you have to do is go back to old newspaper articles quoting government officials and economists, or research reports, and then look at what happened later. Anybody who does that will stop using the economy as a guide to buy or sell great investments. Sometimes the call on the economy was correct, but since the market had anticipated it early, the market went in the opposite direction than the economic forecast would have made you expect. Sometimes the call was totally wrong. Often, it was just confusing, as represented by one typical set of reports that I saw in the mid-1980s. Half the people analyzing things thought consumer spending had been strong for so long that it was about to slump. The other half cited savings, incomes, and more to believe just the opposite, so they looked for more strength from the consumer. You see it all the time. Harry Truman would have loved that.

As president, Truman used to be anguished by some economists' tendency to hem and haw and give many possible outcomes. Those economists would say things like "On the one hand . . . but on the other hand, it could be something else." Truman then quipped, "What this world needs is a one-handed economist!"

Economist Paul Samuelson, for whom I have had the greatest regard throughout my entire career, wrote the first college economics textbook I used. Samuelson once said that Wall Street indices predicted nine out of the last five recessions. Although he kind of jokes here, most good stock pickers understand that this statement is correct. You cannot forecast the economy with enough accuracy or far enough in advance of events to bet your stock money on it.

I see three reasons why economic forecasts are so often wrong or misleading.

First: Economies are very complex, and this complexity is exaggerated greatly by globalization (an area in which no economists have much experience). Since economics is a social science, in which changes occur as a result of human behavior, behavioral influences are very difficult to know with enough certainty.

Second: Good forecasts, or at least those that appear to be good, are believed and thus change how people behave in their spending and investing and other economic variables. This effect, in turn, can change outcomes so that the forecasts have to be adjusted along the way. Some forecasts may be very good, relatively speaking, and they might then change behavior.

Third: Economists build models from data and use data to discover historical cause-and-effect relationships. Even though computers were around in the late 1940s and 1950s, there was no widespread use of them until the PC era began, and so we have a very short history of data from many sectors and businesses. That undermines the ability of economists to be accurate. For example the recession after the bubble burst in 2000 (there was a stock market bubble and an economic bubble built on business capital spending) was not a consumer recession but only a business recession.

Consumers account for two-thirds of our economy, and classic recessions are consumer recessions. Although people have forecast a consumer recession along the way, we went into 2005 without having had one since the first Gulf War, in 1991. That is a record length of time, and it means that since the PC era began after the 1970s, we have had only three recessions in which to collect modern data, and no recessions since real globalization took hold in the 1990s.

Despite all that I just said about the unpredictability of the economy in the short term, since people are very emotional creatures, when they read that the economy is getting better or worse, they tend to get greedy or fearful and "bet" with their emotions instead of investing with knowledge. Consequently, they are moving their money on things that are uncertain and could easily be totally wrong. You cannot let an economic forecast change how you feel about a great company with a great management and business model—not if you want real wealth.

Many investors avoid great opportunities or sell great companies when they get scared. So in many downturns, including the 1991 Gulf War, the crash of 1987, and the Asian crisis of the late nineties, I was buying companies that had great potential. Who was I was buying them from? Those who lacked knowledge of and conviction about their stocks.

Individuals can beat the pros if they concentrate on a few stocks and really have that knowledge, and some buy and sell disciplines to beat emotions. Live by that and you will live with a lot more money.

Just remember one thing about the economy. Imagine yourself driving home and listening to the stock reports on the radio and hearing the announcer say the following:

> On Wall Street today, news of lower interest rates sent the stock market up, but then the expectation that these rates would be inflationary sent the market down, until the realization that lower rates might stimulate the sluggish economy pushed the market up again, before it ultimately went down on fears that an overheated economy would lead to a reimposition of higher interest rates.

Would you sell a company that could triple your money or perhaps be a "big money winner" over the long term after hearing that? Leave the overall economy alone, but read about what things in the economy influence particular sectors and stocks. Read and read more, and gain understanding of just the few key factors that influence your stocks.

WHAT ABOUT EARNINGS?

Even with the dangers of consensus earnings and what I said about complex analyst models, use them or at least use sales and earnings estimates and discussions of why a company has done better or worse. They do not mean a lot if you do not have a decent knowledge on your own of what the company's objectives and challenges are, but the cases in this book and your own experiences going forward are going to make it very straightforward.

The big stock moves come when a stock surprises on the upside or downside, and I do think that this is a report card of elements that separate the great companies from the good companies from the lousy companies. Being well managed, having a lot of control over your own destiny, and having a good business model indicate companies that will not give you grief in earnings reports.

As I have said, I do respect certain analysts. It is like picking a great surgeon for something very tricky—you would not want an average surgeon, for sure, so why would you want an average analyst to influence your money? Since there are not a lot of great analysts who should be entrusted with your financial future, you have to track them and understand what they are good at.

I talked to a great analyst on the fraud issue. When I worked at Wellington, one of the largest investment management companies in the country, one of its excellent analysts was Tony Cope, a true champion analyst and one of the best I have ever met, let alone worked with. He got promoted to director of research, the boss of the research analysts, but after a while he asked to go back to what he had been doing, since he did not want to manage people and push paper if it took him away from his true professional love: taking apart companies and figuring them out.

When he retired, he was the only analyst ever asked to join the Financial

Accounting Standards Board (FASB), which sets the accounting standards for financial reporting. So, to me, Tony is a true guru. I said to him that I felt that neither professionals nor individuals can ever figure out the toughest fraud and conspiracy cases in accounting. I have felt that such cases are just too complex. Even if somebody uncovers fraud, the discovery usually comes too late for the stock. My choice would be for investors to avoid all companies that do not explain their earnings and accounting well enough, I added, in that most good companies already do explain, and most others would be forced to do so. Tony was in enthusiastic agreement, telling me that he has been emphasizing this theme for some time and is trying to get it known and embraced so that companies will do more, and investors will force those who resist to do more.

Even if you are enthusiastic about by a company where things "look" great, remember that you cannot know how great it is in reality if nobody can explain the numbers in plain English. If that is the case, just walk away. That is your protection.

WHAT ABOUT ACCOUNTING AND TRUE EARNINGS?

Read the cash flow statements and see if they are very, very close to the earnings or not close at all. Earnings are created by operations and accounting, but cash is for real and comes only from operations. If a company defers revenues, makes big investments, or has accounting write-offs, don't strain your brain and don't be intimidated either. Just look at the cash statements.

This is a great tool, but don't ignore earnings. For instance, many companies in certain industries, including technology companies, generate a lot of sales at the end of a year or quarter. The sales count as earnings, but the cash will not normally come in immediately.

There are books that go into great length for investors who want more of this, and they all tell you pretty much the same things. My point here is that the holistic approach will guide you better. Use the numbers as a check on how the business model and strategy are playing out between competitors. Relative health is good to know.

If I gave you a dozen examples, you would hardly remember them; and if you simply go to the Web sites of some companies you are interested in, look at the income statements, and take five minutes just to calculate these simple ratios yourself and then look at them relative to another company, you will learn far more.

I also like to look at growth in revenues, and compare a company with similar companies to see if things are going according to what a company has said it will do. The numbers are useless without an understanding of the company and its plan.

I also sometimes watch growth in total shareholder equity from period to period or else the book value per share, which measures the same thing but on a per share basis. Look at how the company is using capital, and not just the return on capital dividing earnings by total assets. Take the cash earnings and divide by total assets. Remember, you are not trying to do a lot of numerical analysis. You just want to compare a company with similar companies and its own history on certain occasions so that you can see if the best companies and business models are doing what you'd expect: producing the best numbers.

Comparing your company with other similar companies is a great education and better than reading one hundred pages of rules and formulas, frankly. The conclusion that you can also draw from understanding some of these numbers is that you will get more out of analysts' reports and the company's discussions of its operations in the annual and quarterly reports.

VALUATION METHODS

When I was in business school, I read some very interesting articles about how stocks were valued and how some researchers felt valuations could best be done. Since then, there have been many more articles, and some are quite good. Yet this is not how most investors, including professional portfolio managers, spend their time.

We do understand that in the short run, changes in the valuation as expressed by the P/E ratio (price of stock divided by earnings) can cause a much larger price move than do earnings changes. We also know that a stock market index or average or the price of a common stock can detach from reality or fundamentals (earnings) for a year or more, as great investors like Warren Buffett remind us. Emotions drive a lot of short-term price change, and investors who have knowledge—who know not just the price but what they think a company is really worth, even generally, over the long term—take advantage of the short-term volatility.

If you see a stock going in the opposite direction than a formula says it should go, even though some pros might buy more or wait things out, this method is going to put too much emotional pressure on you, and a big part of this book is to get emotions out of the process, not amplify them. So before this method drives you crazy and makes you feel that it is too mysterious or complex, let me outline how many pros deal with it.

There is a short list of simple valuation tools that work, particularly if you use more than one each time; this list is what I call triangulation.

If using arithmetic or simple formulas alone could tell you when to buy and sell, investing in stocks would be very simple, wouldn't it? Keep in mind that commonsense judgments, including judgments about which tools to use and when, are a big part of everything in life. They include deciding when to buy and sell stocks. With that said, here are some helpful tools.

Say that you are unsure about how expensive your stock is. *The Big Money* focuses especially on growth stocks and those with high growth rates, so let's stick to that part of the world. For starters, although this is common, looking at the trailing twelve months' earnings relative to price does not properly measure a growth company's valuation relative to other companies.

So take company A, selling for $20. It earned $1 per share over the past twelve months. It is selling for 20X those earnings. If it is estimated to grow earnings by 20 percent over the next year or more, the estimate would be $1.20 and the P/E, or price-to-earnings ratio—a basic core measure—is the price of $20 over the estimate of $1.20, or 16.67X earnings.

Company B, selling for $25, also earned $1 over the last twelve months. It would be 25X the trailing earnings; a lot more expensive than 20X. But if this company is estimated to grow earnings at 40 percent per year for a while, we can take the $25 price over the estimate of $1.40 and get a forward P/E of only 17.8X. So company B is growing twice as fast as company

A, and is only slightly higher in "price," as we say—price meaning the price-to-earnings ratio.

Here is one way to see how much cheaper this is. I like to use the P/E-compared-with-growth rate, or *PEG ratio*. P/E-to-growth shows you how to compare a company with other similar growth companies and also with its own history—something mentioned in this book a number of times—and then you know if something is getting cheaper or more expensive. The P/E-to-growth of company A is 16.67 divided by 20 (the growth rate), for a PEG ratio of 0.8335. That's kind of cheap. You need to take a bunch of these ratios in any given stock market to see what is cheap and what is expensive, by the way, and only a few minutes of doodling will tell you what you want to know.

Company B, measured the same way, computes a P/E of 17.8X divided by a growth rate of 40, for a PEG ratio of 0.445. That is much, much cheaper, even though the price and the P/E are higher. Using the trailing twelve months' earnings to compare high-growth-rate stocks can be highly misleading, but PEG ratios are a good tool. Also, just compare P/Es with prior periods and other stocks. This comparison tells you a lot.

Here's another trick: take a calculator and see how many years it would take the earnings to reach the current share price of the stock if the company grew at the same rate all the time. For company A, you would need to compound the earnings of $1 at the growth rate of 20 percent per year for seventeen years to reach the share price of $20. For company B it would take only ten years for those earnings to reach the current share price.

This is just an exercise to show you differentials, of course, but it does paint a dramatic picture sometimes. When you do this, also, it reminds you that companies usually do not maintain a high growth rate for seventeen or even ten years. There are changes. There is risk. Use all numbers judiciously and wisely, but this is a starting place. Using BASM is one good way to monitor a company and assess relative risk between companies with similar growth rates, by the way.

Triangulation, or using several tools, is always the best way of using numbers to augment the core principles of analyzing management, business models, assumptions, and strategies. Don't go crazy with numbers, though; they will not do your work for you. Growth-stock investors do not get rich with formulas; they just use formulas as a guide to make comparisons. If one thing is critical, it is that most money flows from what is bad or overvalued to what is good and undervalued, so this is a relative game. That is why I always say that comparing similar growth stocks with each other and with their own histories in different times will do wonders for your understanding of what is cheap and what is expensive.

Keep notes to yourself all in one place, like a notebook, and this will not be difficult at all—even if you hate numbers, as so many people do who still would like to get rich with the right stocks. You can do it.

I will add two more valuation methods to help investors triangulate. One is price-to-book value. Book value per share is the assets of a company minus the liabilities, divided by number of shares. These numbers are found on the company's balance sheet. This asset-base valuation method is not as frequently used as the earnings approaches, but it is a very good benchmark when you look at it relative to other companies, and it is quick and easy.

I like the price-to-sales approach a lot. That is the total market value of a company's stock outstanding (total shares times current price for the equity market capitalization, or *market cap*) divided by the revenues of the company for the current year or Wall Street analysts' estimates. You can also take revenues per share and price per share to do this calculation.

Most money is not coming into or out of the market, but flowing from one security to another. The flow is based on investors' collective feelings about the valuations and prospects for companies, so using relative valuations is very helpful. These simple tools will help you understand the reports you see. Once again we want to focus not on the golden eggs, or earnings, but on the golden goose—the business elements that produce those earnings. Good companies should report-card themselves to you, but looking at analysts' reports and reviewing earnings are another way of confirming to yourself that the company you have invested in is doing what it said it would do.

THE ORACLE WAS NOT AN ORACLE

Last but not least, let me reiterate that looking at companies' discussions of their earnings and brokerage reports on those earnings and comparing them is very useful. For instance, Oracle, the large software company, released its third-fiscal-quarter earnings on March 22, 2005, and immediately there were both bulls and bears in the media with opinions on whether the stock was a buy or a sale. CNBC even had a spot viewers' poll on that question after featuring a little discussion.

Bulls said that the earnings were 1¢ better than expected and that the stock was cheaply valued, since it had not been going up (the stock price had been at about the same level for a couple of years, even though it had some ups and downs).

Bears said that some of the gains were not from operations but from currency. In addition, more of the growth was coming from outside the United States, with domestic results not growing much at all. According to the bears, a big part of Oracle's business, applications software, was in the doldrums.

I looked at the release and found that it was easy to spot the fact that some revenue lines were not growing very much. But I did not see a clear discussion of operations that would make it easy for you. In fact, one could conclude that the release for investors was somewhat misleading. It spoke of strong quarterly results and mentioned great results from the database products. Later it mentioned that Oracle's recent acquisition of PeopleSoft Corporation gave it good opportunities for selling more applications-software products in the future. What was missing, however, was the fact that the current quarterly results were quite disappointing for the applications-software division. This was not in the prominently displayed wording crowing about how good a quarter it was.

You could easily find the details and characterization you would want in brokerage analysts' releases, however. The first two I looked at were from good analysts and made things very clear. Thus, while the stock may be cheap enough to go up and make you some money, at this time it would not fit into the greatest BASM companies, which are discussed and detailed throughout the book, and which can make you the big money.

CHAPTER FIVE

STOCK PICKING

Putting It All Together

Find out where the people are going, and get there first.
—Mark Twain

Grook slowly inched around the huge tree trunk he'd been hiding behind. He could see the enormous saber-toothed tiger he had been stalking. The beast was close now, only a few body lengths away. The tiger was standing at a place where the ground dropped off by roughly the height of a man. Grook had an excellent advantage. He knew that he could swiftly come up behind the beast, drop down on it with the element of surprise, and kill it instantly with a powerful blow to the head, using his heavy stone axe. This would mean a lot of food for his clan, as well as himself.

Grook knew that this would work, since tigers had little peripheral vision and did not see what was behind them. Most important, it had worked exactly this way several times before. This was the way of the hunt for a Neanderthal man in Grook's territory, 34,000 years ago. It was the western Siberian Stone Age.

Grook moved quickly now, covering the distance in a great bound. But as he committed to his final attack, he immediately knew something was terribly wrong. The tiger had already turned, opening its cavernous jaws and baring its deadly eight-inch saber teeth. That was the last thing Grook saw before being devoured by the hungry beast.

Grook, like many, had extrapolated from past experience. Extrapolations are necessary and common in many things in life, including hunting big game or hunting for stocks, but they have to be augmented with some analysis of the current situation. Had Grook understood that this time the wind was coming from behind him, enabling the tiger to smell him, he could have altered his behavior and brought home enough meat for many meals instead of becoming the tiger's meal.

Almost 30,000 years later, around 2500 BC, in the great fertile delta of the Nile River, Amrah, a prince in the family of Pharaoh Khafre, was bestowing praise on one of the priests. The priests were also the scientists. The praise was fully justified. Amrah was watching slaves bring loads of grain from the bountiful harvest into great storehouses. Many countries nearby were having a famine or difficult times, but Egypt was prosperous because the plantings and harvest were always on schedule. Egypt, as well as other ancient societies, had pioneering astronomers who had realized that the heavens were much more than just a collection of points of light.

What the priests had been able to do was several things, actually. First, they recognized that what seemed to many like just a bunch of pretty lights, or stars, made up patterns resembling animals or other complex figures. Next, the priests recognized that these early "constellations" had a cycle, appearing over and over again in certain parts of the night sky. Finally, they used their knowledge about this cycle to predict the droughts, the rains, and the flooding of the great Nile River—the foundation of life in Egypt—and advise farmers when to plant and when to harvest.

Their ability to recognize patterns made by these points of light, something others could not do, made these priests very valuable. Relating patterns to other things is something that many people do in science and business, and it's certainly something done by good analysts and stock pickers.

Lack of knowledge meant the end for Grook (what he didn't know *did* kill him), but knowledge and its practical application meant prosperity for Egyptians. It is the same for investors.

The human tendency to extrapolate, as mentioned in chapter 2, means taking events and assuming they are trends, or taking earnings growth and assuming it is like the bird that flies by the window and keeps going at the same speed in the same direction, indefinitely. It is not limited to investors, but is often as costly for investors as it was to Grook.

There is a spectrum of investors in the markets, with the far left end of that spectrum being the "Neanderthal" investors, who extrapolate only from product cycles, earnings, growth trends, and more, and win a certain number of times before they lose heavily, get wiped out, or get out of the market entirely. At the far right end of the spectrum are those who are able to see relationships between companies' operations, earnings, and business models. Like the ancient Egyptian astronomers, these more thoughtful, knowledgeable investors are *inferential*—they can see that one thing logically follows another. Like the ancients, they typically develop and hone that inferential ability simply from their experiences and their repetitive behavior.

Investors extrapolate frequently, since they often lack a clear idea of how to identify the factors that will make a company great and prosperous. So they take the easy route and just focus on the most recent trends in earnings or stock price.

This is why the simplicity of the Seven Steps and BASM, and building on experience, will make you a real stock picker—someone who knows when and what to buy and sell for maximum profits.

The first thing to know is that an incredible number of analyses and recommendations that you read about are based on extrapolating trends, even though this extrapolation looks and sounds much more sophisticated than what Grook did. This is not a path to the big money. Why? Because stocks quickly *price-in* (reflect in the price) what trends already exist, so opportunities are small when the expected trend continues. Sure, if a company is one of those few that can grow annual earnings year after year on a 20 percent annual trend, and your stock grows with it, after a decade of this each dollar you had in the stock would now be $6. That's really great. But I feel that 6X your money over a decade is not what we are talking about when we focus on the big money and becoming wealthy.

The big money is made when you know something about a great situation that the market has not yet priced-in, and, like the Egyptian astronomers, when you can tell from the business model and the management that this company could be a real winner.

Every potentially great company emerges and experiences a lot of volatility along its path to success. Investors tend to extrapolate the short-term trends, just as I did with my early Nike experience. They buy momentum and sell momentum all too frequently. So when Dell Computer was having short-term problems not long after its public offering, sellers (who overwhelmed buyers and drove the stock lower) extrapolated from the recent results and sold a stock that would go on to become one of the greatest winners of all time and a true wealth stock. The same thing happened when Nike spent a lot of money on promotions, particularly the Michael Jordan line of basketball shoes, in the mid-1980s, and on and on.

It is more common than not that investors act as if the market action is telling them what to do, extrapolating either the company's most recent earnings trends or stock trend (or both) and moving their money on that extrapolation. Those investors have found it easier to extrapolate than to determine the essence of the strategy and business model that would end up making so many people rich. The same thing happens with many hot companies: investors buy the trend and do not connect the points of light in the sky, or in this case the four elements of BASM.

One of the central reasons for this behavior is that investors are unsure of what to look for, how to recognize the right business model when they see it, and how to recognize a great company apart from short-term earnings, good or bad, which is what this book is all about. I have found over the years that information overload has increasingly confused investors. Thus it is extremely difficult, if not impossible, for most investors to pinpoint and use a few simple metrics and analytical factors that will lead to truly understanding a company. Doing that will free them from extrapolation and reliance on stock tips. Until now, that is, since the Seven Steps and BASM have worked to this end for me, and I am convinced they will do the same for you.

BUYING WHAT IS HOT

There is nothing wrong with buying what is hot. Wal-Mart was once a small hot stock that brought in droves of investors simply because it was hot; the same has been true for Home Depot, eBay, Amazon, and many other companies that came before and after them. The problem comes when you do not know whether to hold or sell or buy more as events occur and stock prices fluctuate as they always do. I would buy lots of little companies that looked good, then track them closely. Those that did not live up to the promise of the business model got weeded out. But I bought more shares of those that did, especially when the prices went down.

Investors buy lots of hot companies, then complain that they do not know what to do next, particularly if the stock goes down and makes them fearful. The information age means information overload. Information quantity isn't the point; the point is having a simple process and not rigid metrics. It is extremely difficult if not impossible for most investors to pinpoint and use a few simple metrics and analytical factors that will lead to true understanding of a company and, in doing that, free them from extrapolation or reliance on stock tips.

Once again, Nike serves as an example. One could be mystified by earnings volatility unless an investor took a core management goal, and the business model, and understood that they both focused on gaining market share and achieving dominance. Then revenues, the earnings pattern, and what the company spent its money on all painted a clear picture. Those who extrapolated each quarter, each swing, often missed that picture and thus missed the big opportunity. Some professionals get all hung up on complex models and spend a great deal of time writing reports or making presentations to committees. The one thing an analyst does extremely well, which you should also learn to do, is understand what a company does to make its money. That is a core part of the business model that most investors need to know more about. The most successful investors who served as role models for me always knew a great deal about the companies in which they invested. The big money followed.

I recently reread a great Wall Street investment strategist's report about how professional analysts and money managers overload themselves with information, as do most individual investors. This information overload makes stock picking far more difficult. The real job of individual and professional investors is to select what is relevant—15 percent at most—from all the information available and learn how to use it. Most investors, including the pros, do not do that very well.

What I find so interesting about the report I just mentioned is that it was written in 1982. The strategist had identified an age-old malady of investing, and the situation has not improved but become worse. He wrote that report before our desks grew cluttered with fax machines or computers or e-mail, let alone Internet access. Without a compass and a focus, information overload grows like a weed, fed by our so-called information age, and increasingly undermines investment decisions. Over the years, as investors use more and more tools and information, it would appear that investing has not become one bit better, and the average investor does not find this river of information all that effective in making him or her rich. Think about that for a moment.

While there are many, many metrics that analysts have used for Internet companies, I think we often have a lot of *metric overkill*. This means that—unlike what some people are prone to say—you do not have to know every statistic on your Web page and Web site "hits" (visits). What you do have to know is the key to eBay's brilliant business model and how to track how it is working (the company says this in virtually every quarterly report). This is discussed in chapter 8. Likewise, you want to know how Yahoo's advertising model works to power growth and profits. It is disappointing how many investors in Google ask questions about how expensive it is, and nothing beyond that. You can't understand how expensive something is without understanding its BASM, I feel. And you can't just extrapolate.

Let's look at a company which was not a great company at all, but from which we made a lot of money by avoiding the tendency to go into information overload, by acting with incomplete information, and by focusing on the specific metrics that mattered. It was an early and important part of my training and my becoming a stock picker.

THE WILD RIDE OF AIRLINE STOCKS, AND BIG PROFITS

Right at the moment I started as an analyst, airline stocks were generating a lot of profits and excitement, and were a great training ground for technology and other volatile industries. The airline stocks I was responsible for were making us a lot of money, and the consensus in the marketplace was that they were in the middle of a multiyear cycle that would create huge additional profits. Traffic levels and growth were both quite strong, and profits were expanding.

One day in spring 1972, I visited with the management of American Airlines (AMR), which was still in New York City and some years away from moving its corporate headquarters to Dallas. I was the airline analyst at Wellington and responsible for the fact that our mutual funds and pensions held a massive amount of shares in each of several airlines. At this point, these stocks were benefiting from a bull market for stocks and for airline traffic, and huge money was on the line.

THE CROWD SAYS BUY AND THEN BUY SOME MORE

I had met with a number of Wall Street analysts in my office in Boston and found that most of the estimates in earnings reflected terrific optimism for the rest of the year, as well as for the following year. There was a consensus among the brokerage houses that the airlines would continue to lead the market, and that investors should own maximum position sizes and continue to buy. My friends in the group of top airline analysts on Wall Street helped form this consensus.

I asked American's management some very pertinent questions that day in New York. I could see that American Airlines stock was priced very, very high, at $49, because the expectations were so high. Earnings estimates for the year were only about 25¢ for the current year, but the Street thought that we were early in a multiyear and really huge traffic growth cycle that would lead to enormous earnings at its peak some years away.

So analysts felt that the current year was meaningless, and next year we would see earnings of $2 to $2.75, with an even greater jump the year after. This was an extrapolation (not always a dirty word) of both traffic and capacity trends. Nobody could really know what would happen, so it really was more extrapolation than any other factor, and the high price of the stock was specifically because everybody was thinking the same bullish thoughts.

One has to be mindful of the possibility that stocks will move on future developments when current earnings are weak, since it happens so often in cases like biotechnology, big new product introductions from tech companies, and others. But when you are depending on the economy instead of factors that are almost entirely within a company's own control, it's a whole new ball game. Nobody has been good at predicting the economy well enough to bet a lot of money on it. Therefore a company's control over its own destiny is the key when you decide how much faith to put in predictions, extrapolations, or both. You will get plenty of both as you invest.

The profit jumps that the bulls foresaw for the airlines were so large that many professionals felt that the bullish consensus was still underestimating things—that the consensus should be even more bullish. My job was to find out whether or not that was the case. At this early stage of my career, I was scared enough of failure to have made up some excellent what-if questions. I wanted to do my own work and not rely on brokerage work or estimates or extrapolations of trends. Well, after getting very detailed, thorough answers to all my questions, I left American headquarters and flew to Dallas to see Braniff International Airways, which was headquartered there. Braniff, defunct since 1982, was a great airline, led by the legendary Harding Lawrence, and I was very much looking forward to meeting him for the first time. He had a vision for the company that incorporated buying SSTs—supersonic transports such as the Concorde, which entered service in 1969—and using them to pioneer fast service between the United States and South America. He had a giant painting of an SST in flight behind his massive desk.

On the way to Dallas, I worked on American Airlines' numbers and the answers that management had given me. I reviewed the all-important assumptions that both management and I were making about critical variables such as traffic in the coast-to-coast markets, and the number of seats and planes to be flown—the big cost of operations.

To my astonishment, after doing my very best work, I could not come up with more than 75¢ of earnings to estimate for the following year—supposedly a big earnings year despite my having used a reasonable traffic number based on history and related to growth in the economy. I reworked everything and got the same results. This scared me, because I would be at odds with some of the really great brokerage analysts, including a couple that had been very instrumental in teaching me.

When we landed in Dallas, I called the office and told the director of research, my boss, Bill Hicks, what my results were. "So," Bill asked after hearing my story, "what do you recommend we do about the stocks, particularly American?" Although I was mindful of analysts who hedge on their conclusions, I basically said something like, "We might not want to hold quite so much." Sort of a chicken statement, but I was very unsure, frankly, asking myself how could I be right and others wrong. Bill told me that we would go through everything in depth when I returned to Boston.

In Boston, Bill and another portfolio manager (Bill also comanaged a mutual fund as well as being director of research) went through my work with me in detail. They did not fault what I had done. Yet they also paid attention to what the Street was saying, which was a forecast of more than triple my own earnings forecast for the next year. I was not forceful in recommending that Wellington sell; I just said that cutting back would be prudent. Nothing happened, and we were still holding all our stock when my wife and I left just before Memorial Day weekend for a vacation in Spain and Portugal.

YOU CAN WIN WITHOUT BEING 100 PERCENT SURE

While in Spain, I looked at a newspaper and saw to my horror that the very key metric in the airline industry—Memorial Day traffic—had come in much weaker than expected, and the stocks had all plunged. When I returned, Bill smiled broadly and said, "With you completely out of touch, and your work looking so good, we decided to sell all the airline stocks and take our profits. You did give us direction." We were all subject to the pressures of uncertainty, and I learned right away that in an uncertain situation you rarely get "table-pounding" conviction, so any little pressure will cause some motion. Stocks and markets and people all respond exactly the same way now as then when there is uncertainty. I guess that is where they got the expression, "In the land of the blind, the one-eyed man is king."

Yet individuals sometimes see which way to lean, and it becomes more than a hunch. As investors are involved with more and more stock decisions over time, some people's intuition gets better and better. As I said earlier, an individual investor does not have to prove that his hunch is right to an organization with a couple of million shares that it will not sell quickly and buy back the next day. You can combine your knowledge and intuition more easily. This is one of the many advantages that individual investors have over the pros.

A key point here is that most of the crowd wanted to believe in the bullish extrapolations and did the "Grook-like" thing without doing enough homework. Although I had not yet developed a lot of investment wisdom, I was scared enough at this stage to avoid extrapolations of any kind.

Anyway, on that day, you can imagine my relief to hear my senior colleague, Bill, give me the good news. In those days, we actually could find out who had bought huge institutional blocks of stock, although I do not think that it would be too many years before secrecy veiled that information. We were told that American had been bought by a large, prominent mutual-fund company named Dreyfus (in its heyday at that time), and that the fund had written down almost a million shares of that stock alone, and held large numbers of shares in several others airlines. Dreyfus was a good company, but this was an example of life in the fast lane.

American Airlines stock had been $49 when I left the country. It then moved slightly higher to its all-time high (then) of $49.62. The much anticipated big traffic cycle never materialized, so from there the stock went down, down, finally bottoming out at just over $6 per share.

Earnings were substantially below estimates for the current year and the next two years, and actually were in the red (losses) for some quarters. Earnings were only $0.05 per share at the bottom of that down cycle. The big price move down in the stock was early, as the stock discounted future expectations of poor results—just the opposite of the original expectations that had driven the valuation way up, and the valuation collapsed before the earnings did. Stocks discount (reflect) things fairly quickly.

The top people in my company said that given the incredible level of uncertainty, and given the fact that I had gone against the Street's earnings estimates and buy recommendations, I was to be congratulated for recommending even the sale of some. They told me I was already showing indications that I was a stock picker.

I learned many valuable lessons that day, including the fact that expectations move valuations much more than earnings do. I learned how fallible the pros can be at times and how much they also can go along with a consensus or extrapolations. The biggest lesson for me, and for you now, is that relying on instinct, homework, and knowledge is the best investment strategy you can have, and that an investor should pick carefully what to extrapolate and what not to.

MY BIGGEST LESSON

It was not really the quantitative work, actually, even though my job was to do earnings models. I could have been way off on the earnings, as long as I was correct about which assumptions would turn out to be correct and which would not. It was my assessment, judgment, and commonsense thinking about the airlines' strategy and assumptions that led me to the right conclusions.

Assumptions and common sense were key. I looked at all the capacity that the airlines were adding, and saw that this made it essential that everything go perfectly well with the economy and traffic (load factors). If I had based my thinking only on those assumptions, I would have known that whatever the earnings, there was a real risk that they would come in far below the rosy forecasts. All it takes is a failure of earnings—the amount is not usually the real deal—when a strategy (and sometimes what economists call *externalities*) brings about an earnings collapse. The reverse is also true on the way up.

On that day, I left Grook behind, as all investors who do their home-work will leave him. I also learned some valuable lifelong lessons.

SOME "SEEDY" ANALYSIS

Early in my career, when I was learning everything I could, I discovered there were a few companies that produced the highest quality agricultural seed. One of them had recently gone public. I looked at some information. Some of the brokers who covered agricultural equipment had told me that these companies were small and risky, and that the products and markets were very hard to understand.

Farmers were subject to many unpredictable factors that determined the yield of their crops and the prices they got, so their fortunes would wax and wane with climate and weather, competitive conditions, government policies on subsidies, and factors that were particular to them, such as how old their equipment was getting and how efficient it was.

The key science for those seed companies, which primarily marketed their product in the corn belt, was hybridization. Hybrid seeds were far more expensive than regular seeds but were developed specifically to resist certain blights and diseases, thrive in a broader range of weather condi-tions, and produce much higher yields, or bushels per acre. This meant much better profits in good years, or a higher chance of some profits in poor years. Hybrids also provided some insurance against certain types of crop failure.

But some of the analysts thought the market just wasn't going to grow dynamically, since farmers tended to be very conservative and slow to adopt anything new—particularly if it cost more, as the hybrid seeds did. In reality, the problem was not the price, since seed is a tiny fraction of pro-duction costs, but a fear that the new seeds might not work well in these farmers' soil, and that this would be ruinous.

Some of the analysts looked at the tractor and equipment cycle. Farm-ers could buy equipment only when they had a few very strong years back to back. They had to avoid taking on too much debt in order to have enough money and available credit to purchase really expensive items. So analysts concluded that farmers would not buy the significantly pricier seeds from the hybrid companies or might consider doing so only in their best years. Thus the earnings patterns and fortunes of these companies would be as erratic and unpredictable as the fortunes of the farmers.

Anyway, I was curious, and I saw that the stocks of these seed companies were relatively cheap in valuation. Low expectations for the performance of such companies and their stock meant a lower than average risk of disappointment, but a higher reward if things went well. At a minimum, I felt, I should acquire some relevant information, then call the companies and speak to their management. In those days, there were no Web sites; information sent through the mail by these companies would take a few days or even longer to arrive. This meant that these companies were not able to satisfy stockholders' demand for timely information, in contrast to the nearly instant information we get today.

SHORT AND SWEET

I was really excited by the time I got off the phone with a couple of the top management people at DeKalb AgResearch, in DeKalb, Illinois. They were outgoing and informative. They gave me a simple, quick education and made me anxious to know more, so I accepted their invitation to come out to see for myself what they were doing.

It was an adventure. I loved doing new things. I found myself thinking about how new and strange this world was to me, a "city slicker," as I drove along dirt roads bounded by corn that was higher than the roof of my rental car.

I met and liked the top management and felt that they really knew what they were doing. Not only were they advancing the science of hybridization, they also understood the needs and problems of the farmers. I saw their test fields of corn and their labs, and talked to their scientists. The managers explained the economics of the sale to farmers. The big deal was that the seed cost was less than 1 percent of a farmer's total costs of crop production.

It reminded me of Schlumberger Ltd.; there was the same kind of business model. Schlumberger (SLB) was the leader in employing seismic technology (using underground sound waves) to find oil. Even though SLB's fees for these services were very high, the expenditure represented only a tiny percentage of the total cost of finding and extracting oil. Because Schlumberger was so good at finding oil, its business with the oil companies was growing at a very fast pace.

In a similar fashion, the higher costs of DeKalb's seed would not have a material impact on a farmer's total costs of production. I discovered that the cost of seed was not the determining factor in selling to farmers; it was *trust*.

Farmers, DeKalb's managers told me, were always worried that some new, unknown seed, while promising to protect crops and create better yields, could just outright fail, or be weak in some way, since it was an unknown. Most farmers could not tolerate a ruinous year, and that made them very averse to using a seed that had no track record.

Executives at DeKalb told me about their research, marketing, and farmer-education programs, each of which was designed to overcome the resistance of farmers to trying new products. Management developed great products in its labs and fields, just as a computer technology company might do. Some computer companies only have good research and technology, so they have strong products but weak business models, and thus enjoy only a few successful years.

DeKalb management recognized that the business model had to be built around sales, and that sales had to be built around an understanding of the farmer. This meant spending time and money to develop a strategy for building trust with their customers—the farmers. And they were succeeding. I found this out for myself when I went into town and spoke to people, particularly those who sold agricultural supplies and equipment, and stopped at a couple of farmhouses and talked to farmers. I was able to personally verify that DeKalb's business and business model worked. We made over 400 percent on that stock, and a lot of money on the other seed stocks, so it all worked out very well. In 1982 the company merged with pharmaceutical giant Pfizer to form DeKalb-Pfizer Genetics.

COMING FROM BEHIND: THE SUNW RISES

One day I leaned over a little table in a CEO's office, and realized as we spoke that his company, Sun Microsystems (SUNW), could challenge the leader in the field and perhaps even become great. Reading all that is available today is the equivalent of that little table, since these days, the media report every move of every CEO. This was Scott McNealy, a forceful, dynamic CEO who had no lack of press coverage.

One of the things that can be fun as well as profitable, and that investors who want to be real stock pickers should always do, is to read everything they can find on a company's top management. I mean not just business writings, but general stuff that can tell you who is a great leader or who could have the characteristics to become a great leader. Style, handling past failures and accomplishments, and a way of thinking all contribute to how somebody excels. Scott McNealy, when he was leading Sun Microsystems from a little peanut to a large success story, was one of these great leaders.

There is so much written about who management people are these days that the kind of information I had to glean from meetings can now be found by a diligent, curious reader. It is all there for you. Keep that in mind as you read about my phone calls with great managers and my meetings in these chapters, and as you invest.

A second thing to know is that the majority of great success stories concern companies that came from behind. They saw a need being filled and figured out a way to exploit the market and serve customers in a better way. Those coming from behind included Home Depot, Wal-Mart, Microsoft, and a very long list of other winners, including Sun Microsystems.

It is important to know that investors most often extrapolate the leadership of the original leader for a while, yet there is an opportunity to understand early the BASM of the company on its way to taking over that number one spot—an opportunity to make lots of money. The extrapolation of a current leader's position, and an opportunity with the company that came along later, occurred with Microsoft and Lotus, with Compaq Computer and Dell, and with many others, including Apollo Computer (the leader) and the wannabe, Sun Micro.

When I bought Sun on its public offering, the computer-workstation market that it and Apollo Computer served was exploding in growth as a new, hot sector. I don't think I was actually extrapolating the success of Apollo, but I did think that it would continue to do well, since Apollo seemed well managed and had the lion's share of the market. The company also had great technology. I held on to my Apollo stock, which was making me a lot of money; I also bought Sun, not only because I felt that there was enough juice in this great new market for at least two players but because I saw the potential of great BASM for Sun.

Sun Microsystems had stated its intentions in its prospectus, dated March 4, 1986. A company's own plan was the benchmark I always relied on to track the outfit for results, success, and consistency. It was simply an "open architecture, open systems approach"—just the opposite of Apollo's strategy of building proprietary systems that could work only with its own components and computers. Apollo was like Apple and Wang, whose machines were unique and could not work with anybody else's. Apollo was the original undisputed market leader, and the company felt confident that nobody could challenge it. That is what it told us investors.

Here is the definitive paragraph of Sun's strategy and business model, from the original offering prospectus.

The Company's standards-based open-system architecture offers the advantages of compatibility among Sun products, as well as the ability to interface with other vendors' hardware, adaptability to future hardware advances, and portability of applications programs and availability of numerous third-party software packages. The Company believes that these factors have become increasingly important to end users and OEMs wishing to preserve the value of their applications software in the face of rapid technological change. The Company has shipped more than 12,000 workstations and board-level central-processing units to over 750 customers.

If you never talked to anyone from management but had looked at case experience of other companies, made some notes on the good and bad you saw, and then read this one mission statement, you knew, this was it—a bold, different, commonsense strategy that customers should love, and

WINNING

There are many levels of winning. Sun made it to the gold medal. **Sun Microsystems became the fastest-growing company in America for the five-year period from 1984 to 1989, according to *Forbes* magazine.** Anybody who has invested in highly competitive industries understands what kind of amazing feat this is.

Those who invested in Sun were also big winners. In terms of Sun Microsystems's common stock, the first leg in the late 1980s was about 10X an investor's money. Then there were further solid but more sporadic gains until the early 1990s. But, for a short interlude, patience and knowledge, two of the Seven Steps, were invaluable. Investors such as myself, who recognized a great company when we saw one, realized the gains from the next wave.

An investor could have done another leg through the first half of 2000 before the bursting tech bubble took down the stock. That period from 1993 to 2000 saw stock appreciation of about another 14X an investor's money.

All in all, although it is unlikely that somebody would have held through all the ups and downs, investors who had a lot of faith in Scott McNealy and knew Sun really well could have made a good chunk of the huge returns that Sun generated over fourteen years. I know that my biggest regret was cutting back the size position in my funds when it became large from the appreciation, but then again, this is an area where an individual with the same faith as the professional can keep more stock and actually make more money.

Despite that slow period, returns were much better than an average of 100 percent per year for those fourteen years, with total stock appreciation of roughly 260X the original IPO money invested, or a rise of 25,900 percent. Sun Microsystems, the "Cisco" of its day in terms of company performance and stock returns, was one of the best stocks of all time.

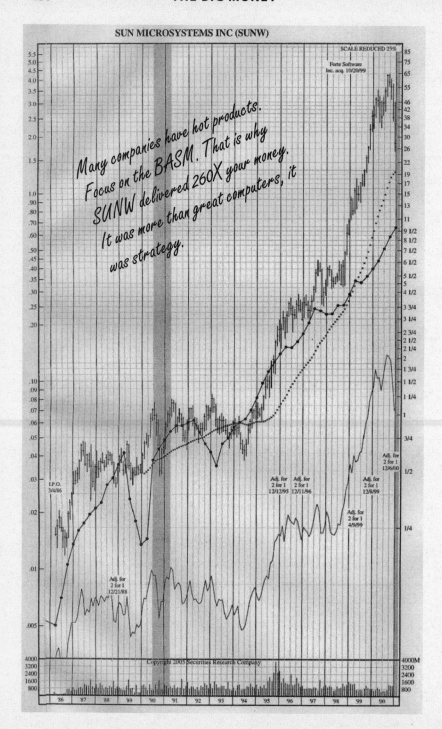

SUN MICROSYSTEMS INC (SUNW)

SCALE REDUCED 25%

Forte Software
Inc. acq. 10/20/99

Many companies have hot products. Focus on the BASM. That is why SUNW delivered 260X your money. It was more than great computers, it was strategy.

I.P.O.
3/4/86

Adj. for
2 for 1
12/21/88

Adj. for
2 for 1
12/12/95

Adj. for
2 for 1
12/11/96

Adj. for
2 for 1
4/9/99

Adj. for
2 for 1
12/8/99

Adj. for
2 for 1
12/6/00

'86 '87 '88 '89 '90 '91 '92 '93 '94 '95 '96 '97 '98 '99 '00

SUN VERSUS APOLLO
How Apollo Led and Lost

It is not the greatest technology that wins, it is the *right* technology, and when a business has the right technology with great or even very good tech, the products go on to make a lot of money for the company and its investors. The central idea of the Sun business model was open architecture to capture the customers, while Apollo concentrated on faster and faster computing speeds. When Apollo began to lose share and brought in a new CEO, things deteriorated further, since Sun had a great culture of development, and Apollo could not compete in that respect.

Apollo's new CEO was as slow and stuffy as the culture he was taking over, according to many on Wall Street. Apollo was not competitive with the better West Coast companies, which believed in making up the rules as they went along and moving really fast.

LIMOS VERSUS GORILLA SUITS: THE METAPHOR

Company founder Bill Poduska Sr. thought he wanted a classic big-company manager, failing to see that it was just this mentality and lack of a real fluid tech culture that was holding Apollo back. The new CEO brought in, I was told, had a limo bring him to work, and employees were required to wear suits and ties, while most West Coast tech companies had no dress codes. Sun threw monthly beer bashes, on Halloween its employees would show up for work in gorilla suits, and so forth. The next thing that happened was that Sun developed a new architecture for its computer chips and ran circles around Apollo.

BASM CREATES REPEATABILITY, WHICH CUSTOMERS LOVE

The coming-from-behind story is one of the biggest stories of all. It has nothing to do with Aesop's fable "The Tortoise and the Hare," which teaches that slow and steady wins the race.

In the corporate world, being right on BASM is better than being first or fast. McDonald's was not first; nor were Staples and Wal-Mart, which won customers away from Sears and Kmart with incredible service, long before they could afford to have incredibly low prices. In the tech world, Dell was well behind IBM and Compaq, but it had a whole different approach to selling into the market that turned out to be far better.

Microsoft came along later than Lotus, which held 70 percent of the market in spreadsheet software. But Bill Gates had drive, perseverance, focus—and BASM. He created repeatability in product cycles, a critical matter for tech companies. Gates made the right choices for the customers and developed a Windows product while Lotus stuck to its DOS product and did not move into Windows until it was hurt by Microsoft. Gates then showed the customers that he could repeat product cycles, so they could depend on him. **Sun had that feature of repeatability, as did Cisco. Repeatability is much more important than speed in terms of coming out with new products.**

THE KNOWLEDGE CAMELS WIN:
BIGGER HUMP = BIGGER POTS OF GOLD

Most of these cases and stories are not unique. They present universal lessons that build on our knowledge and lead to other things, and they help us to more easily recognize the next big opportunity that comes our way—and there are *always* big opportunities going by our noses. The trick is to learn to recognize them and know what to do about them. When you can do that, you are a stock picker and on your way to being rich.

When I took my profits in Apollo in the high teens, I moved that money into Sun Microsystems, enlarging my position. Apollo did what many changing companies did: It came in with earnings that were a country mile different from Wall Street estimates and surprised everybody. A great company with great BASM often surprises us with better earnings; consequently, the stock soars. In this case, Apollo was going to earn $1.35 for the year (this was in the mid-1980s) and came in with earnings of 10¢!

That is what happens when your business model is failing. Apollo eventually began to unravel and finally was acquired by Hewlett-Packard.

First, a central piece of investment knowledge is that most earnings estimates are not "met." Companies doing well exceed them, but companies that do not do well fail to meet estimates. Great companies make you a lot of money by exceeding estimates and expectations because they have characteristics unique to great companies. Poor companies drive you crazy analyzing quarterly earnings and lose you money.

When a company exceeds or fails upon reporting earnings, even for a quarter, if the market thinks it is a trend, the stock moves much more than the change in earnings estimates; valuations expand or collapse, depending on what has happened. Let's say that a stock has a bad quarter, with a 30 percent drop in earnings. Now, that's a lot. *But* you understand the reasons for the short-term slide. And you still think it is a great company because of its BASM. If the stock is down 30 percent, you can buy some, and when it comes back to where it was, you are already up 43 percent. If a company is not a good company, it can drop a lot. Say a company is selling at 20X earnings and is expected to earn $1, so it sells for $20. If quarterly earnings are down by 30 percent, and the market thinks this company is going nowhere, maybe the price earnings multiple drops from 20X to only 14X. That 30 percent drop in earnings and 30 percent drop in valuation (P/E) means that the stock is now 14X an estimate of 70¢ per share, or $9.80, down a whopping 51 percent. Well, Apollo stock collapsed quickly, surprising a lot of people, and it kept going down. Conversely, great companies soar when perceptions change, and you make amazing amounts of money. That is the Sun Microsystems story.

The next truly big thing to know is that extremely often, the BASM signals in advance that companies will do better or fail on earnings estimates. That is how we made tons on Molex, Cisco, and Sun, and a long list of other companies (and knew when to sell many, also). I knew Apollo was in trouble well in advance of its stock collapse, because of the business model and the other things we have just discussed. An investor usually has lots of time to get out or get in, so when the surprises come, you can already be positioned. Many years later, I got out of Krispy Kreme Doughnuts far in advance of its troubles and stock collapse. Patterns repeat.

These are big investment lessons that you should keep in mind all the time. While I cannot actually see the future, I did come close many times by using BASM and then applying the disciplines of the Seven Steps. This was a period in which I was putting together the elements of the Seven Steps. Clearly my experiences led me to recognize that more knowledge created direction, conviction, and confidence in moving money one way or the other. It was not just me; it was all the investors that I respected. The "knowledge camels" were winning and making the most money. It does not happen on the day a company goes public; it happens over time, and you accumulate information just by watching and learning to recognize patterns.

In this case we have seen the big story of coming from behind, while the crowd extrapolates the continuing success of the current leader, and how BASM will win over hot products any day. This story is destined to happen again and again.

The last big lesson is that most companies are not going to have the ability of a marathon runner when it comes to repeatability and extending their success. Perhaps it was enough that Sun created so much wealth over that great fourteen years, yet some companies like Dell and Wal-Mart go on and on. Sun did not. It slipped in the late 1990s and struggled with competitive factors and its own business models as the world changed. The world and competition are *always* changing, and one should never take success for granted. Read about competition, the management, and how the business model and strategy evolve—keep reading articles and annual reports even when you are happy with your big gains.

"REVERSING THE RAZOR"

Occam's razor: One should not increase, beyond what is necessary, the number of entities required to explain anything.

This logical principle, attributed to the medieval philosopher William of Occam, underlies a great deal of all scientific modeling and theory building but does not seem to have gotten through to most investors and analysts these days. All too many analysts (though not all) and other in-

vestors are great at "reversing the razor" and using more and more information rather than focusing on a few key explanations. They sound great,
but most can't pick stocks.

Studies show that adding too many variables can undermine decision-
making ability. Four or five key variables are all you need to understand a
company. The old adage KISS—"Keep it simple, stupid"—actually is the
way to go to be a stock picker.

Identifying and using a few key factors is the secret of stock picking, as
long as one knows which factors. Throwing in more and more variables is
not a substitute for "not knowing" which ones. That is a key reason why
BASM bubbled up from my experiences. It helps you to focus and get away
from the information overload. It works.

The Neanderthal investors often do not identify those few key factors.
They look at lots and lots of stuff—too much stuff, for sure—but then they
go the natural way, which is to extrapolate results until something changes.
If they do not understand the competitive strategy and business model,
then they miss what is really happening and become lost in a maze of earnings reports without having a context in which to place them—the critical
benchmarks of what a company should be doing to fulfill what it earlier
told investors it *would* do. If you do not have those business-model benchmarks to look for, you can be really late in seeing a company change, for
better or worse, and as a result you probably will miss the biggest stock
moves in many cases.

For instance, Compaq Computer was a fabulous stock with great earnings, until it could not compete with Dell's direct-selling model. It took the
Compaq management a very long time to understand that. It did not take
the earnings very long to get very bad, though, once they started to slip.
Analysts who had a style of crunching numbers on every quarter but could
not see the real competitive picture understood too late that one company
was winning at the expense of the other.

The "astronomer-type" analysts put a few key factors together and can
anticipate that the best companies will make or exceed earnings estimates
by virtue of their strategy, model, assumptions, and management. BASM.

I learned quickly that this holistic approach was a better way to go than
focusing only on quarterly-earnings reports, since it meant staying with

the winners. So even though Paychex, Dunkin' Donuts, International Dairy Queen, and many other small companies experienced some volatility in short-term earnings and changes in Wall Street recommendations, their formulas for success did not change, their BASM did not change, and staying with them for these reasons meant huge long-term profits.

For instance, Dairy Queen had a spectacular decade of doing exactly what it set out to do in terms of expansion and profits. Not very many people were told by Wall Street to take the proper view on time horizon (patience) and business model, management, and strategy, and not many people knew how to do that. The stock over ten years or so multiplied investors' money by 100X.

It was far worse with Wal-Mart, since so many analysts and investors were slow to realize what it could become. Various analysts urged people to take profits many times over the years, then later suggested switching to Sears, which was enormously costly advice to anyone who took it. If the BASM stays the same, stick with the stock unless somehow its valuation becomes so excessive that even a reasonable exception cannot be made.

SOME GREAT ANALYSTS

I remember once when John Neff, managing Vanguard Windsor Fund on its way to a world-class performance record, wrote to all the directors of Ford Motor Company about why they should raise the dividend on the common stock. The directors had not done as much work with financial insight as had John. John was a portfolio manager and still was as good an analyst as there was (and still is in semiretirement). He taught me much as I did my analytical work and brought him good stocks to buy.

I have remained an analyst the whole way. Neff was the quintessential analyst, as many of the greatest portfolio managers are. He made us all study for the CFA (Chartered Financial Analyst) exams, three very, very tough exams taken years apart. (In those days, you could not even take the exams in consecutive years, since a good deal of practical experience was an important part of the picture.) I did it, and got my CFA certificate. I owe

John a debt of gratitude for that, and for some good teaching and mentoring in my early days.

John bought *value stocks*—stocks that investors think are cheap and underpriced because something on the surface is wrong, and the crowd does not think it will be fixed. Value investors find bargains that they think will improve results. For most investors, the best way to do this is to buy the best value funds, as it takes a lot of work and financial analysis to be a great value investor. But if anybody ever questioned whether or not great securities analysis could lead to great results, John would be the man to talk to first.

DO YOU REMEMBER THE QUESTION?

In looking back at the top analysts with whom I've worked, I recall one story that shows what an analyst has to go through at times to serve the public with great information. It also serves as an example that if you cannot find answers in plain English in analyst's reports or companies' annual reports—as happens a lot—this can truly mean that there *aren't* any answers or that the company is not going to disclose any. This to me is a surefire sell signal. If an analyst cannot give good enough answers to key questions in just a few pages of a report, writing another sixty pages is a waste. Look at this example, which illustrates what can happen when a company is searching for its own answers:

Dana Telsey has been a star retail analyst with the Wall Street firm Bear Stearns since 1994. While many analysts churn out tons of stuff, there are some analysts, Dana being one, who work very hard and possess great insights into their industries. They truly understand how companies excel.

It was the mid-1990s. The shoe company Nine West, which not only manufactured its own shoes but also had retail outlets, had been making acquisitions to expand. One big acquisition was its purchase of US Shoe. I wondered if Nine West was going to have to deal with some of the weaker aspects of US Shoe.

Dana brought Nine West's chairman and president to some of the best investors she worked with for private meetings, and I was happy that she had included me. In one meeting, I was struggling to get straight answers to solid questions such as how many stores were below average and might be closed, and how Nine West analyzed mistakes and figured out why some stores were better or worse than others. I was getting only evasive, long-winded answers that told me nothing of substance. In other words, the top guy was telling the story he wanted to tell instead of answering questions that would support my figuring things out.

After his response effectively sidestepped another one of my questions (about spinning off or closing stores), I said to the chairman in exasperation, "Excuse me, sir. Do you remember the question I asked you?" He got pink in the face, and then, after an embarrassing moment of silence, admitted, "No."

That "blew up" the meeting. I simply did not care about the company, but I didn't want to undermine Dana's relationship with its management. Walking down the hall to the elevator, Dana and I lagged behind the others. I apologized for doing that. "No, Fred," she said. "You did the right thing and actually did me a favor. They have been doing that to my best clients all day, and that is an embarrassment to me after bringing them around to tell the real story and answer investors' questions."

Nine West was covering up problems. The company went into a steep decline and eventually was acquired.

When managers don't seem to explain things clearly, either in interviews, Wall Street reports, company releases, or annual and quarterly reports, that usually means trouble. Stock pickers need to be ready to sell if they are blocked from the knowledge they need. Get answers or sell.

CONTROLLING DESTINY

Control over destiny is the first punch of the one-two punch, with BASM being the second. Coca-Cola and Nike are much more in control of their own destiny than companies that are subject to the vagaries of demand and commodity pricing, such as Phelps Dodge, the copper company. You want companies whose control over destiny is great so that their business model and management have maximum effectiveness rather than being heavily influenced by factors beyond their control such as weather or commodity prices.

When I saw Gap Stores come along, and Ann Taylor and Pacific Sunwear and lots of other companies that created the right look and clothing for a specific market, there were a bunch of Wall Street analysts who followed each one. Each company had a different approach. Gap Stores (GPS) did well, then struggled a bit to evolve its look to fit an aging customer base. What ultimately made the difference for the Gap were two things: first, the model dictate that the chain would not serve just young people and would thus broaden; and second, having a real talent like CEO Mickey Drexler. Mickey had a great feel for design and what people wanted, and he is credited with the "Gap look." That helped Gap control its destiny.

Like some of the analysts on Wall Street, I knew that Mickey and the model—the two M's—dominated the results. Those of us who did not overly complicate things did very well with the Gap. The gains were huge. Other analysts created very complicated store-expansion and earnings-and-sales models, and wanted every month's sales to fit their model. Many investors who followed the company that more complicated way traded back and forth and lost out on the truly big gains, such as 4X their money in one short move or 18X in another. Yes, some analysis of store openings was helpful, but becoming enmeshed in too many minutiae was counterproductive.

In fact, when Tommy Hilfiger brought his company public in 1992, he concentrated on creating a distinctive look and succeeded. The apparel and fashion industry depends very much on pleasing fickle and demanding customers, and Tommy was good at it. At a dinner we had at the very beginning, I pressed him on how he would sustain early success. He said that he understood customers, responded quickly to the market, and would be able to keep it all going. I asked him if my holding his stock would become "an act of faith." His answer was that the Gap had created a look that made everything else work for it and that he too had created a look. He added, "Fred, when you walk down the street, you can see the Gap look from far away. It is now the same with Tommy. If you're ever walking down the street and don't see that we still have a great Tommy look, sell my stock."

He was right. I did not capture all of the 10X the stock did in the next few years, but I captured a lot of it. Over time, as fashion companies become larger, analysis must evolve and include more on store openings and inventories, but when these companies are small, the keys to their success are design and business model. Eventually, I saw the Hilfiger stock (TOM) getting expensive and the look becoming less distinctive, so I did sell.

Pacific Sunwear (PSUN) went public in the early 1990s and took a couple of years to really get things right, but I could see very simple things evolving there. The key was that young people in its customer base started to buy at an accelerating rate. I watched things carefully. When I could not visit stores, I talked to people who did. I wanted to know how well PSUN merchandised, how much customers liked the look, and how much they bought.

I had bought a little on the public offering and lost a little money as a result of things being somewhat erratic, but I saw the improvement as it unfolded. When I added to my original position, my timing was a bit late, so I missed the earliest part of a big move. Nevertheless, I still captured much of a price run that multiplied shareholders' money by about 35X in only five years. Pacific Sunwear simply had a management and model attuned to testing designs and staying really close to the customers and what they wanted, and the management executed well.

Of course, it is not always that simple. With some companies, there is a real struggle to understand the earnings. Kobrick's Rule says that complexity usually means less reward and more risk.

> Knowledge is, indeed, that which, next to virtue, truly and
> essentially raises one man above another.
> —JOSEPH ADDISON

TWO STOCKS AND COMMON SENSE

When I was in high school, my physics teacher told us something I have never forgotten. It had something to do with physics, but a lot to do with life. He said that you can estimate almost anything in the world you want, even if you know nothing about it, if you have common sense and keep trying to get closer to the answer, writing ideas and estimates on the back of an envelope (or anywhere else).

Many, many envelopes later, I have done rather well doing just that: puzzling over things, making notes. I have made money the easy way doing this. It is not gambling or speculating; it is a commonsense way of figuring on good future earnings to drive the stocks. Here are two examples:

Upjohn was a leading pharmaceutical company and a great stock in many periods. It is now part of a bigger company, Pharmacia and Upjohn. As an independent company in the mid-1980s, Upjohn had developed a drug treatment for male-pattern baldness known as minoxidil, trade name Rogaine. It had been originally used to treat high blood pressure, and this possible additional use was discovered.

There was a huge controversy about this drug, since it could represent a tremendous market opportunity and drive up the stock for a long time. Or it could be a big disappointment. After all, Rogaine was not yet proved. What's more, this kind of treatment for male-pattern baldness had been tried before with other drugs and failed. Many dollars had been lost on the stocks of companies that had previously marketed treatments that ultimately did not work, leaving behind a trail of disappointment. So the bulls and bears were out in force.

I worked out a model on a small piece of paper, factoring in the number of possible patients and a conservative number of those who would try Rogaine. I assumed it might work on one-third of them. Then I estimated how much a dose would cost, and multiplied for a rough estimate of the profit margin per dose. I figured that if this drug had any chance of working, there would be a period of months before there were definitive results both for patients and for the market.

Even though I was an experienced investor with a strong record and lots of financial "stuff" under my belt, I was using some common sense and arithmetic that most of us could have done in high school.

I presented my thoughts and scribbles to our investment committee. Because my model was so clearly arrived at through common sense, everybody figured we had little to lose and a lot to gain; we could make money on this stock, since the stock was not reflecting any kind of success. Nobody really knew a thing about how it would turn out, but I was convinced that my estimates were conservative and that people would want to try the drug.

Well, we bought the stock in all the mutual funds and pensions. Lots of people did try Rogaine, and the stock quickly went up a lot. We still didn't know anything definite about hair growth some months later, but with the stock having more than doubled, we were happy. With the risk of holding now higher, we took our profits.

Another similar stock pick during that era was Radio Shack. The company had actually been a pioneer of the personal-computer age, manufacturing an early model that was very popular. But Radio Shack never formulated a cohesive business strategy; nor did its technology evolve. So the chain went back to its core business of retailing, selling the computer division down the road. At one point, the company decided that since it had a good reputation for marketing electronics at very reasonable prices, it could have an "outbound" sales force. Radio Shack salespeople would go to small businesses and sell them IBM clones, which are personal computers manufactured and backed by Radio Shack.

Out came my envelope. While some people laughed about this method of mine, I believed that if you assumed only a small number of unit sales per salesperson, Radio Shack could generate some tremendous numbers, since it had such a large number of stores and a large sales force. I plodded through the steps and found that the market was missing something. Now, in this case, I did agree to fly down to Texas and visit the company, to see if it was lining up the elements required to execute the plan. Indeed, I found that Radio Shack was doing exactly that. If I had been an individual investor, I would not have flown to Fort Worth, since I was totally convinced. But, as was often the case, since my mutual fund had been performing so well, my colleagues at Wellington asked me to share ideas with them, and I was happy to do that. In this instance, they wanted me to sit down with Radio Shack's management.

Anyway, we bought a ton, and it was better than a double. Over time, though, my confidence waned as I saw that personal computers were just too competitive to support the "padding" of the sales commissions. Furthermore, by then Dell was coming along and selling direct.

Now, both Upjohn and Radio Shack were very good companies, but the markets for these products did not become giant markets, so the outcomes would not have made somebody very rich. The really great companies play to open-ended markets, for the most part. A double or 150 percent gain is always nice, though. Along the road to the big money, there can be many of those. The real point here is that you can start doing things like this almost immediately, reading annual reports and using arithmetic and common sense. This way you will be making some good money on stock picks while you're in the process of looking for the really great ones.

In each case, I thought that the assumptions the management made about its market (bald people, computer buyers) were key, that the business model supported aggressive assumptions, and that each company geared up to sell very effectively to huge markets. Whenever a company can be right on some aggressive assumptions, and follow up and execute well (and I also agree that the market potential is huge) the stock will make you a lot of money—almost regardless of what the numbers work out to be.

You can learn to recognize the proverbial golden goose long before the golden eggs (earnings) appear, and you will want to do that to make the big money.

PREDICTING THE FUTURE: JOE DIMAGGIO

Throughout history, human beings have tried to predict the future. But when predictions turn out to hit the mark, luck seems to be a major factor. This may or may not be the case.

In the early 1990s, I was getting into a cab at LaGuardia Airport to go into Manhattan on business. As the cab was pulling away from the curb, I saw Joe DiMaggio. He was alone and just getting into the taxi behind me. I had missed him by about thirty seconds. Although a lifelong Boston Red Sox fan, I appreciate the greatest all-time baseball players, whether on the New York Yankees or any other team. Joltin' Joe DiMaggio, the "Yankee Clipper," was certainly a hero of mine. I was terribly disappointed. I "knew" that I would never get another chance to see him.

One year later I was on a boat in New York Harbor, at a small party for some investment people and corporate managers, given by the great research firm Sanford Bernstein. All of a sudden, there was Joe DiMaggio, one of the guests. I walked right over and told him how much I had admired him. Then told him that I was actually a real Dom DiMaggio fan. Dom, a star with the Red Sox, was his brother. Joe smiled and said, "Tell me what you thought of the Yankees–Red Sox rivalry back then."

We chatted for more than ninety minutes, and unbeknownst to me, one of the corporate executives took a picture of us together. It was just great. Joe wrote a note to me and signed it, and the executive later sent me the photo he took. Both were framed and hung in my office, and all my New York visitors were wide-eyed and jealous from then on.

I have remembered two things about predicting our own lives. One was from a college professor. "When we awake in the morning, we assume that the floor is there as we get out of bed. That is one of the more 'solid' assumptions" he said, "but they get more 'iffy' after that."

Second, I always remember my disappointment and my real conviction that I had missed my one and only opportunity to say hello to Joe DiMaggio. Yet only twelve months later, I was to spend quite a long time with him, listening to some great baseball stories.

Both experiences taught me a great deal about predicting the future. There is no "system" for predicting our own future, and certainly none for predicting the stock market. The assumptions we make help to define what is most probable and what is under our own control in shaping our destiny in life. The same holds true for companies.

Control over destiny coupled with great BASM is the best predictor of a company's future (and thus the stock's future) that I have ever seen.

ALL INDUSTRIES OFFER LESSONS ABOUT MAKING MONEY

One enduring theme goes back to what I mentioned about analyzing: simple is best. The best business models are clean, easy to understand, and simple to put into operation. Kobrick's Rule says that simplicity is better for management and better for analysts and stock pickers, and almost always better for making big returns.

The more factors there are in the analysis, the greater the risk in the stock, and the less probable in making the big money. This means that less is more. Fewer factors reduce risk and increase chances to make big money.

So, while airline stocks can make you big money, for instance, there are a lot of factors that go into analyzing them, and thus they are all the way at one end of the business spectrum. They are at the complicated end. An example of a business at the other end, the simple end, is a great company that generated uniform results year after year.

QUIET COMPANY, UNIFORM RESULTS, BIG MONEY

The company, which many missed, since it was not as "sexy" as a technology company (or even Home Depot or McDonald's), is the uniform company Cintas (CTAS). It has provided uniforms to companies such as Pepsi, and has done so with efficiency, expertise, and cost-effectiveness for thirty-five straight years of steady earnings growth.

Cintas has done all the right things: developed a clear and understandable business model, paid attention to detail, and managed a large workforce very efficiently by training employees, retaining them, and controlling their costs. A critical factor was that while the company did all these things internally, it also always focused on maintaining quality, which was central in the business plan in order to grow its customer base and business. It may sound easy, but training, retention, and attention to detail are not easy.

I also could see from the simple metrics—consistently high gross margins, great returns on capital, and very steady growth—that Cintas was going to go on for a very long time, a key determinant of a stock that will make the big money. Time and patience have a lot to do with exceptional results and real wealth. Companies that can sustain great results are doing something with repeatability, and not just for a year or two, or for one product cycle, but again and again. When you see a company that has this feature or this potential, it's almost always a company you want to own.

Topps, the baseball and sports trading card company, was a really good company, and we made a lot of money on it. The same thing happened with the best hybrid seed companies, such as Dekalb AgResearch and Pioneer Hybrid, and many more. But as much as we love making triples and quadruples and even five- or six-baggers (5X to 6X your money), when investing in companies like these, always keep in mind that some companies run out of new products and innovative ideas or otherwise do not have repeatability, while others can renew themselves and repeat what they do right for decades. The latter are the true stocks for wealth.

The concept of repeatability is a critical competitive feature that differentiated Microsoft from the pack. This was also very true for McDonald's and Cintas. These three companies are in industries where repeatability is far more difficult than it appears; that is why most of the competition fails to achieve it. Repeatability is a core feature of great business models and great companies, and means big money for their investors.

Cintas went public in 1983. The company provided work uniforms to large corporate customers as well as some medium-size companies. By being specialized, and with a great business model built around execution, it saved customers lots of money and spared them lots of headaches. By providing uniforms more cost-effectively than would have been possible if each company tried to do the job itself, and by achieving repeatability, Cintas did what all companies aspire to do. It created customer confidence and loyalty, while growing the customer base rapidly and taking lots of market share on its way to being number one.

The beauty of Cintas's BASM was a management that aggressively marketed to new customers, but not without ensuring that it could deliver the quality and consistency it promised. This is never easy to do. Cintas was a company that any focused investor could understand, but what looked simple was difficult for the management to execute. It was, as we say, an execution business. Not everyone could recognize the need to have fail-safe detailed systems to ensure delivery schedules, replacements, cleaning, and so forth. Because it looked so simple and transparent, some investors thought that any company could do the same thing, so competition would be too ferocious for Cintas to become a great growth company and leader.

Cintas fooled the bears. The stock delivered: after the first fifteen years it was worth over 40X the price at which it went public.

Today Cintas is still going strong. The company has 700,000 customers and has good reason to believe that it could one day serve all 14 million businesses in the United States and Canada that need employee uniforms. Not long ago, the company was selected as one of America's best-managed companies, and in 2005 Cintas was selected by *Fortune* magazine as one of the most admired companies in America for the fifth year in a row. It is now proud to be the uniform supplier to NASCAR.

Knowledge. Reading. Understanding. Once you realize the value of looking for what type of company any entity is, and what its business model is, stock picking gets easier and easier. That is the road to being a stock picker—the road to being rich.

CHAPTER SIX

MANAGEMENT

The Best Management Means the Best Stocks

THE GOOD, THE BAD, AND THE UGLY

Management means, in the last analysis, the substitution of
thought for brawn and muscle, of knowledge for folkways
and superstition, and of cooperation for force. It means the
substitution of responsibility for obedience to rank, and of
authority of performance for the authority of rank.

—PETER DRUCKER, MANAGEMENT GURU

This is one of the most important chapters in this book, and for some
people it will be the most important.

For some, picking stocks on the basis of management will be all they
need to do. Experienced investors who are used to using BASM sometimes
come across a great or even potentially great management and recognize
very early that it could be a big winner. People do run into or watch great
leaders and visionaries like Bernie Marcus, Bill Gates, or Michael Dell in
their early days; and when they see someone who may became the next
Marcus and Gates today, can they know and recognize what they are seeing? Some do—those who have made the most of their investing experiences using BASM and know the case histories of the past winners. These

are opportunities to become very wealthy, and you do want to know them when you see them.

Naturally, buying a company on the basis of management alone is not the goal. You must continue to watch carefully, and as you make money you still monitor to see that each element of great BASM pans out. But remember, great business models do not exist without great management. Great management creates the great models and also creates the great assumptions, execution, and the rest. It all flows from management.

Over time, some business models need adjustments for competitive conditions. A business model cannot live on by itself, in isolation; it has to be managed by a great management. Jeff Bezos has made great evolutionary changes in the business model of Amazon.com over time, Steve Jobs greatly improved the Apple business model in 2004 and 2005 (Apple never had a decent business model in its early days; it just had the best desktop computer anyone had ever seen), and Lou Gerstner came into a failing IBM and saved that company by realizing that although IBM's business model had been great in the past, it needed big changes. The examples are almost endless.

As you use BASM, you will become ever more skillful. I have always asked investors, "How are you going to recognize the next Bill Gates if you do not truly see how the great companies of recent times became what they are today by getting BASM right in their earliest days?" That is a big reason why a case history is so valuable, and why it teaches you to recognize the "big game" in a jungle of countless companies early on.

"WHAT TO DO WHEN A SECURITIES ANALYST CALLS"

One day in 1969, while working in my college library, I came across a magazine cover that intrigued me. It was a magazine for corporate treasurers, and the cover picture depicted a young man—supposedly a securities analyst—coming through a door into the office of a corporate treasurer.

This was a time when the profession of modern securities analysis was just becoming known and respected. The number of analysts was increasing rapidly, but they were still a small band.

It was obvious that many corporate treasurers had never seen or met with an analyst. The article talked about being prepared to answer lots of questions about operations while not giving away information that might give competitors an advantage. The article gave some examples of the types of questions and information that analysts were after, so that they could make their predictions about the stock.

For those of us with training as analysts, the rapid evolution of securities analysis has been like watching aviation progress from the Wright brothers to the jet age in virtually no time at all. Many of my friends and I would love to find this old magazine now—it is a great piece of modern history.

A couple of generations ago, there really wasn't any securities analysis, or a profession of securities analysts. Good investors were people who knew how to pick stocks from knowing businesses, knowing who was running the companies, or just having a great feel for the markets, trading on momentum, and other similar factors.

THE BASICS REMAIN THE SAME
Picking Winning Management Means Picking Winning Stocks

Although the process today is characterized by information overload, the essentials and basics are still exactly the same as they were when that magazine was published, and keys to identifying the great investments are also the same today as they were generations before then, for that matter.

As I said earlier, as a generality, a professional has no advantage over any individual investor in picking winning managements. In fact, often the professional cannot put his or her "hunches" into reports or even make them a part of a stock recommendation because it is so hard to document a very early call on a great management, even if the analyst can see that the potential for greatness is there.

The earlier you pick great management, the less information you have and the greater the uncertainty, but that also means the more money you make—sometimes by a very huge amount. This is one of the great axioms of investing. Those who need unlimited information are often too late and buy after the stock has gone up. Stocks get driven early by those investors who have a compass, focus on just the right information, and gain confidence from their information and from their know-how (focusing on BASM). That is where the big money is—if you are patient and hold on.

So companies that have potentially great management can be bought in small amounts. As you see them operate, you sell some and enlarge positions in the best of them, even if at higher prices. This works for me, and it will work for you.

The are no cookie-cutter formulas. If there were, everybody would be able to do this perfectly. But I have developed a method to concentrate on certain things, coupled with common sense and powers of observation

Common Traits of Great Management

First, the best management demonstrates immediately that it can envision a great future for the company and articulate a cohesive and logical strategy to get there. The strategy cannot be pie in the sky; it has to be based on resources—human, financial, technological—within the grasp of the company.

What Ray Kroc did to make McDonald's the largest restaurant chain in the world would fit this description. What Michael Dell and Bill Gates did with their companies would too. It is not true of most airline management, historically, but it was true of Howard Schultz of Starbucks and Tom Stemberg of Staples.

Next, management has show that it can execute the details, so you watch carefully. If you are fortunate, you get management that really takes vision into execution seamlessly, as Fred Smith did with Federal Express.

Great managers make promises and projections to you, the stockholder, that they can deliver on. They are driven to stay ahead of the pack and understand how to lead. They truly want to win, and they have a passion for the competitive game, but at the same time, they are realists in terms of the goals they can actually execute well and they do not disappoint investors or mess up their own game plan. I get excited whenever I find these qualities.

MY FAVORITE SPECIFIC CRITERIA

Consistency, repeatability, vision, execution excellence, perseverance, admitting mistakes early and moving aggressively to fix them, and showing common sense. Managers who meet these criteria are the ones who most often create and manage best their assumptions, business models, and strategies, which after management, are the other three factors of BASM.

Repeatability of great product cycles, market-share gains, execution of the core elements of the business model, and the earnings and other key results is really tough, but it's the thing that companies like Microsoft and Staples could do with new products and new stores, while most could not.

McDonald's shows the most visible model of repeatability. The company structured complex, expensive systems so that it could exactly duplicate taste and all other customer elements of its business, including waiting time. Microsoft had to repeat the ability to anticipate customer's needs and roll out products that met those needs closely. The company failed some of the time, since debugging software is just so problematic, but not often, and it did what one has to do—repeated much better and more often than its competitors—and won.

Retailers like McDonald's and Staples have to be able to repeat the very complicated methods they use to pick their store locations, and repeat the arduous and expensive process of opening lots of new stores and bringing them to profitability on schedule, and this is done really well only by the retailers we see as excellent, since most of the others are just not good enough to devise systems to repeat very well. There are many instances of repeatability that consumers take for granted, ones that you as an investor will start to scrutinize; and you will very quickly find that such scrutiny becomes second nature for you.

As you know by now, BASM is my abbreviation for business model, assumptions, strategy, and management. I am going to continue to stress this in the remaining chapters, since using it as your prime set of criteria is a great way to think about companies and their stocks, and will simplify life while making your investing better. Assumptions are the set of assumptions, or projections, about how big a market is for a company or a product, as well as the anticipated competition and demand over the next year to three years. Good management makes good assumptions, since those are what determine much of what a company tries to achieve through its strategies.

The important things about BASM is that all these factors should be consistent with one another in a very commonsense way. You do not look at these things and make a decision to act instantly—you look at them and watch how a company uses them. Then you easily reach a conclusion.

As discussed earlier, the metrics you use in evaluating a company include gross margin (sales less direct product costs divided by sales); rate of earnings growth, and whether that rate is decelerating or accelerating, and if it is at least on trend; net margin after taxes; and also profit after taxes divided by total assets, or return on capital (ROC). These tell you a lot about competitive position and how well the company is managed. Just keep in mind that these are report-card issues. While you do learn something about management from them, the report card does not tell you about vision and fixing problems. Listening, looking, and acquiring relevant information will.

All industries have some kind of metrics by which performance can be measured. Retailers, for example, are measured primarily by comparable store sales each month or quarter to see how healthy they are.

I developed the following simple metrics for Internet companies, and they fit well with BASM. I call them the *five M's* over time, I can see that they are useful on a broader basis for various companies beyond the Internet sector.

1. Mass: enough size and presence and customers to be competitive. Around long enough to show that it can acquire new customers at a good pace and at an affordable cost.
2. Model: a business model that is strong and shows the path to growth and profits very clearly.

3. Momentum: a high growth rate, and one that is steady or accelerating.
4. Market share: taking market share from similar companies. In other words, growing faster than competitors, but not by doing things that are unsustainable.
5. Management: good, perhaps great management. This and other factors about company health and great business models are found throughout this book.

A really good metric, which could be moved to the top of my list, is market share. The best companies normally grow faster than competitors and thus take market share. Many CEOs use that as a key objective in managing their business.

You will use only some of these metrics, and only some of the time. You learn to use them by trying them out as you learn from the cases in this book and from your experiences, and see what you need to monitor in "report carding" the management.

SOME EXAMPLES

Betting on management is a core concept of the greatest and most profitable investing. The earlier the better, since you make much more money that way, and if you learn the techniques, you will do so with controlled risk—not zero risk, but controlled risk. For instance, although I do not advocate sidestepping analysis, let's suppose all you did in the early years when Wal-Mart was growing its fastest was to read about Sam Walton. You would have a good sense of him and his business model and execution. If you were a student of BASM, you would see how he stood out. I think it is likely that you would buy and hold and capture at least a big, juicy piece of that thirty-year stock run that made people *2 million* percent on the original IPO investment (20,000X).

You do not get a general rule or crystal ball to tell you when you have a major winner as you buy and hold a young company that has recently gone public and has little or no track record. There are two ways that I see to do this.

First, it is very common to buy companies that boast exciting new products and seem to have lots of buzz or accolades that will help the stock initially. Most people who buy for this reason "flip" the stock, or sell it immediately after it registers a nice trading profit for them. They make some quick, usually taxable gain on a small number of shares, since hot company offerings allocate shares to investors and nobody gets a lot. Google roughly quadrupled in about a year from the IPO, but all the press attention and talk meant that even people who knew little could feel that this would be a good stock, initially. In all these cases, with demand for shares much higher than supply, there was a form of auction to allocate. Most of the time, brokers allocate to clients according to how much business they do. Nobody gets much. So, to make a lot of money, investors had to understand—to have knowledge—so they could buy more after the IPO and have a larger number of shares, or want to hold on for more than a quick 50 percent or double. This is the same thing we saw with Cisco, Microsoft, and all the others that showed signs of success even on IPO day. With virtually every one, I needed to watch it operate, and for those I liked, I enlarged my tiny original position from time to time. Most investors who do this do not track the companies they have flipped; so if the company turns out to be great, they notice this somewhere down the road and buy back in at prices much higher than if they had been following the company's results from the first day it went public.

The second way to buy IPOs is to use BASM. No surprise there. When a company has little operating record, keep in mind the three most important elements of a good business model that we have discussed. A good or great business plan specifically lays out in clear, simple terms what the company will do to become profitable, grow, and protect itself against competition. In addition to judging those things, you can also ask a broker, an analyst, or the company, or read in the prospectus (a detailed public-offering document chock-full of fabulous information that many people simply do not take advantage of) what key metrics you need to follow to know how the company is doing.

For instance, when Staples, Home Depot, and Starbucks each went public, you wanted to know how new stores were doing in terms of profitability and the time those stores needed to reach a certain level, usually equal to the achievement level of the rest of the company. The best management is the best at tracking itself and giving you a sense of how to track it. I explain this with Staples, below.

Without profits to guide you, you can still track sales, market share, and other key but simple things.

You would almost think that BASM was tailor-made for IPOs. I just do not understand how people can buy IPOs and expect to make big money if they do not use BASM or something similar that has the same elements to direct their focus. I cannot count how many business models I was attracted to over the years when I read the offering prospectus on an IPO, but I was able to focus on a lot of them that worked out to make us big money. These were companies that started with a clear description of how they would be very profitable and grow and be unique or otherwise protect themselves from competition, and then went on to execute; so as I watched, the other elements of BASM fell into place. Microsoft and Dell had critical *assumptions* about their customers. Bernie Marcus (HD) knew how to train a different kind of salesperson for a new market opportunity. I quote from his first shareholder letter (chapter 3) and from the prospectuses of Dell and Sun Microsystems (chapter 8), since these are the best examples for you to quickly learn these things.

This chapter has some really short examples, and some longer cases, and tries to approach the question from different angles, since picking any one stock from a great management may differ from instance to instance. Management does not differ from industry to industry as much as it differs in management styles. That is a good thing. There are at least sixty or seventy industries with differing product or business approaches, and that is too much to absorb. But there are only a few major management styles that I have found in the biggest winners, and these styles apply to all industries, regardless of whether they are biotechnology, cable TV, hardware stores, semiconductors, retailers, and so on.

BUYING STAPLES, STARBUCKS,
HOME DEPOT, AND MORE

The number one thing that investors always ask about is how they could identify the next Bill Gates or Michael Dell, or the next Cisco, Home Depot, or Staples. I successfully bet on every one of the above managers and companies (and many, many more) starting the day they went public. I tracked what they said and did carefully, and when I did not find consistency or execution ability, I had to sell lots of small companies. But I sold early and made the losses small. At the same time, I built up the original, small positions of the good ones. I used the Seven Steps and the disciplines stressed repeatedly in this book.

First: With Microsoft, Dell, Home Depot, Cisco, and Staples, I knew several key things when they went public. (A) The top guy had vision and could translate that vision into a strategy to make his company a long-term winner, not just a good story for a year or two. (B) The person at the top was very competitive, but not someone who would take ridiculous risks, and he showed investors a solid plan to dominate his industry and become number one. (C) Each company had already done something right and seemed to have what looked to me like a solid business model that described how it would excel in the industry, compete and grow well, and be profitable. (D) Each company was in an industry that was just taking off, and looked as though it would be huge—an industry opportunity for the future. (E) Each one either already had, or looked as if it would have, a lot of competitors who wanted a piece of that exciting industry.

The business plan had to be logical, show common sense, and be presented in a way that made it possible for every nonprofessional investor to easily understand it.

Second: I asked each company, or read in its documents and reports, what its industry outlook was, what the general secrets of success would be in its industry, and what specifically the company would find most challenging as it looked ahead.

Third: I observed, tracked, and looked for (A) execution; (B) growth rates and market share as the key metric; (C) gross margins and bottom-line profits, just to make sure that the high growth and market-share gains were not being achieved with low prices that would undermine profitability. Also, (D) I wanted to be sure that the company did what it said and said what it did.

Fourth: Some small companies, including those I bought in initial public offerings, did not live up to expectations. I could see quickly that margins or market share or inconsistencies between stated goals and operations were not good. So I would take a small loss and get out quickly. The losses were small because that was just a discipline—when I had my doubts about a company with little operating experience, I would get out. But if I was unsure, and there was still some hope or promise, I would monitor it even after I sold. Sometimes I would buy back the stock even if it was at a higher price. I did this early in the public life of Dell, and that worked.

When companies were tracking well, I bought more shares along the way. I even did that after Cisco had doubled from the price I bought it at when it went public, because the company had proved itself. Obviously, it was still a huge stock going forward. (I did another 18X my investors' money after it doubled over the following four or five years, and then made even more.)

Bill Gates was exciting because the public validated his vision of where programming-language development and PC operating systems were headed. Of course, he was helping this happen. He naturally had exciting visions of what would come next and specific plans for what he would do at each stage to exploit new opportunities.

In the case of each company, every one of the managers who proved to be winners could articulate a clear vision, and it did not sound like a fantasy or a marketing speech. Each one could define things in discussion or in annual reports and prospectuses, and explain how the organization would get there.

STAPLES
Marathon Man: Tom Stemberg of Staples

Most growth stock stories take time to develop and make you the big money. Although I have made very high gains with high-tech stocks, often in short periods of time, typically you need some patience to make huge gains. Sure, you can buy what will become great companies when they go public and make three or four times your money before long if they operate well. But the rest will take a little bit of time.

I have known Tom Stemberg, founder and chairman of Staples (SPLS), since the late 1980s. He is one of the most consistent businessmen and business strategists today. That consistency came through to me very early in my relationship with him, and equally well in Staples's prospectus, annual reports, and operations over time. Staples, headquartered outside Boston, went public on April 27, 1989.

Office Depot (ODP), headquartered in Fort Lauderdale, Florida, had gone public one year earlier. Each company opened stores rapidly in its own immediate area but had visions of being the biggest national office-products superstore. Many more competitors would join these two over the next few years. Few survive today, as this has always been a very competitive battleground.

Stemberg impressed me with his supermarket experience and how it would directly translate to success in developing and growing a big chain of office superstores. This was a new business category for the country, and one that looked very promising. I owned stock both in Office Depot, since its chairman, David Fuentes, was a good CEO, and in Staples, where Tom Stemberg seemed likely to hit a home run.

His vision was clear, his business plan was detailed but simple and straightforward, and he wanted to be number one. I had learned early with Molex—and this learning was reinforced by experiences with many other companies (including Dell)—that knowledge of the customer and working with that knowledge were keys to big success. Stemberg prided himself on the fact that Staples cards were in the hands of over 150,000 small businesses and organizations, which provided a lot of customer information. This was a very big deal to me; it demonstrated how Tom Stemberg thought and what his chances were.

He said what he did and did what he said, and he and his team could execute expertly. On average, Staples opened a store every eight days for the next few years.

His first annual report stated six key elements of the business strategy, including the goal to dominate the Northeast market, and the goal to become the market-share leader in every market entered. Those were magic words to me. Coupled with execution ability, these elements would give Staples a chance of being a huge winner, and that is exactly what happened.

Staples did a good job of report carding itself. Along the way, annuals and other reports would say what the company intended to do, and subsequent reports would tell us how it did. This may seem all too simple, but not a lot of companies are so good at the doing part or the telling part— stating their plans, objectives, and report card in plain English. You just have to take a little time to read reports, read about CEOs, and jot a few notes in a notebook, so you can look to see if things are tracking. Then you sit back and watch your stock become a Staples, a Home Depot, a Cisco, or whatever, and get rich. But never forget to read each successive report card carefully.

The best companies are always beating expectations, and you usually do not have grief over their numbers. When they do have the occasional slip, you have confidence in them and stick with them. The bad companies dish out regular grief, and you feel as if you have to crunch numbers all the time. This alone should tell you that the stocks of such companies are not going to make you rich.

All of the key elements were there in Staples, and they did not come from a book or a product; they came from Tom Stemberg. He did what he should, and the company and stock were huge successes. He became number one the slow way: consistently delivering on his promises and persevering. The first time investors met with Tom, or read his prospectus describing the customer information and his business plan, they knew they had to at least give the stock a chance.

Lesson

If you want to buy early (and even if you buy in later), look for a clear, easy-to-understand business model in a prospectus or annual report, look for the management's objectives and see that they are clearly stated, and finally, look to see if the company consistently comes back in its releases and tells you how it is doing.

Staples met all of these criteria, and you will find lots of companies that do, and countless companies that do not. This is the best way to assess managements before they have a top-notch track record. When they have that, you have the report card.

Last but not least, when you do look at numbers, the two to watch most carefully are market share and profit margins (profit before tax and/or profit after tax—just to ensure tax-rate changes do not confuse you— divided by sales). What I did with Staples was to look at the level of sales in its financial releases or quarterly and annual report. You don't need to dig out "industry" numbers, which can take some time. I just looked at the two head-on important competitors to Staples, Office Depot and Office Max, to see how much their sales had grown in the latest quarter (or year). The fact that Staples so frequently grew faster meant it was taking share against its key competition. That did it for me, combined with the fact that SPLS profit margins did not decline. Thus, Staples was not "buying share" by cutting prices.

I always worked at having meetings to get information, but today there is far too much information flowing out to investors. Almost always these days, if you are looking for specifics, you have what the pros have, thanks to Regulation FD (a full-disclosure rule from the SEC mandating that anything a company tells any analyst or any other individual in any capacity, it must tell the public at the same time).

The Internet has made it simple and quick to get current information in between those quarterly reports. Just go to the company Web site and look at all the corporate and financial releases from its investor relations department. The Internet also makes it easy to see who has written articles about a company or CEO so you can stay current and build deeper knowledge. You can look at a company on a financial Web site (Yahoo Finance is one of many) to check SEC filings and learn who "star" analysts are (brokerage reports), whether insiders (management) are buying or selling their own company's stock, and more.

When you go to a company Web site, you can quickly see if the quarterly reports or news releases on the site answer your questions or only prompt more questions. Anytime developments arise that seem to affect your company, check its Web site to see if it has issued statements or put out a news release. But do not stop there: Check some competitors' information, too, and try to find some brokerage reports. That most analysts are not the world's greatest stock pickers does not belie the fact that many are real experts in industry and competitive conditions, and you can learn a lot by reading what they write. If you do not have a good broker or do not want one, put a little money into one or more of the discount brokerage operations that offer analyst's reports.

An investor aims to identify the key drivers of growth, the competitive advantages a company enjoys, and, equally important, how it intends to preserve its lead and advantages. Great management lays out those things for you. This is true of Staples, and true of the other great stocks, whether they are included in this book or not.

Often, you will be in a stock that is doing well, and you might become a bit lazy about looking at things from time to time, because you feel you have a good company, and it is going up and making you money. But in this competitive world, things change, and you need to keep checking in and tracking.

Here are two common examples of a situation in which you hold a stock that has made you a lot of money, so you love it, but things happen that tell you it is time to sell.

In the late 1980s, I made a huge hit on U.S. Surgical Corp. I had been investing in medical technology and medical-products companies, since this was a dynamic area, with some very good innovations and developments, and fast-growing companies. I had read that one surgical-products company, U.S. Surgical, was pioneering a new technique called laparoscopy, for gallbladder surgery. It was the dawn of less invasive surgery. Laparoscopy allows doctors to operate through slender fiber-optic tubes, which they insert through far smaller incisions than are required for traditional "open" surgery. A tiny camera at one end of the laparoscope transmits images from inside the body onto a TV monitor, so the surgeons can see exactly what they are doing. Laparoscopy was designed to be less expensive and safer, involving significantly shorter hospitalizations and recovery times.

I immediately jumped onto this, getting all the company's information. Then I drove to Norwalk, Connecticut, to meet with all the key people. I was very impressed with everything, and even went through the plant that manufactured the instruments. The stock was starting to move up, so I quickly bought some. Then I called doctors to ask their opinions, got more confidence, and added more stock. Soon I had a really big position.

This stock went up by about 15X in only two years because of the huge excitement over not only the success with gallbladders, but also the fact that instruments and training were developed for other surgeries. Less-invasive surgery was very attractive both to surgeons and to patients.

But I was troubled. The best medical-product companies always had a good pipeline of promising products coming along from research and development in order to be balanced multiproduct companies. This is a core job for management; the best CEOs are managing a total company for the long term; they don't just oversee a hot product that wows investors. A total company has a portfolio of products in different stages of development.

The expectations were very high for USS. The growth was very high, the stock and its market valuation were very high, but good old common sense was telling me that I could not and should not extrapolate a long way out from the early-stage explosive growth of these new products. A company is just not likely to grow at 50 percent rates for very long, if it is a good-sized company and not a little company starting out—unless it comes up with more great ideas and products. At a 50 percent rate, a company would triple in size every three years. Common sense alone would make one suspicious, unless greed gets in the way.

Yes, growth would continue nicely, but the stock was priced for huge growth, as is always the case. Common sense is one of the two best tools in investing, along with curiosity.

I started to ask the company and brokerage analysts about new products coming along. There were some, but nothing that could support this kind of corporate growth rate and thus this kind of stock price. To me, repeatability was in question. Thus, it was a risk, and I had to dig deeper. The very first of the Seven Steps, knowledge, came into play, followed by buy and sell disciplines, with the accent on a management that could execute. Was U.S. Surgical good enough in product development to repeat? It was clear to me that the stock valuation was high, and far above its own historical trend and the valuation of other hospital-supplies companies. If we

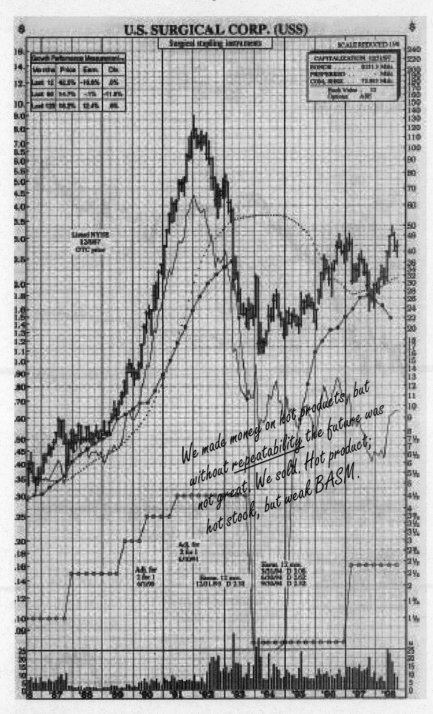

U.S. SURGICAL CORP. (USS)

Surgical stapling instruments

We made money on hot products, but without repeatability the future was not great. We sold. Hot product, hot stock, but weak BASM.

had to depend entirely on more growth from U.S. Surgical's current product line and nothing else, I felt that the stock had gone far enough and was at risk.

Now, anybody could have come to this point and looked at the difference between extrapolation and finding out what is next for a highflier that has had a big run and is expensive. I could find too little to support the stock, since I saw nothing that would add to sales beyond what the company was currently doing. Yet sales continued strongly, and I heard many investors saying that this was going to go on for a long time.

When in doubt, sell, then figure it all out. So I sold. My buy and sell disciplines kicked in; U.S. Surgical looked like an overvalued stock with no assurance of repeatability on the product stream.

This discipline prevented me from falling prey to too much extrapolation and too much emotion. If the stock had a decent correction and backed off a bit, it might look like a buy to me again if I found no problems.

After a little time passed, I saw that sales had slowed a bit. Then the stock started to come down. U.S. Surgical defended its growth rate and started to give forecasts that didn't seem realistic to me. I stayed away, and eventually the stock came down more. Here's what happened next: It was found that the company had cheated by telling hospitals (falsely) that there would be future product shortages, so they would stock up in advance. I do not know what company executives were thinking: how would they make up the sales void down the line when hospitals could not keep buying? Anyway, this "stuffing the channel" trick made the stock crash, and U.S. Surgical irreparably lost its credibility. Eventually it was acquired by Tyco.

The Lesson

When a company is doing exceptionally well, do not get complacent; just assure yourself that the higher the growth rate, the better the company's engine of growth, whether it be products, or expansion geographically, or new customers. USS had a huge growth rate, but I could not find the big engine to follow on after the current product strength. Ultimately the market could not find it either.

Management was at fault entirely. The top guys could not figure out what else to do. They had invented something great but were not managing the company for repeatiblity, the very thing that Microsoft, Cisco, and others had as a cornerstone of success. For instance, Johnson & Johnson, Biomet, and Medtronic were structured and managed for continuous product development; all enjoyed long-term, sustainable growth. Medtronic, the leader in cardiac pacemakers and related products, calls itself, with some justification, the leading medical-technology company in the world.

Medtronic's management understands repeatability and can execute and achieve that goal. It has performed well over decades: for the 1980s and 1990s combined, the stock multiplied shareholders' money by roughly 100X. That is what management is all about.

Management creates the big stocks by creating the products, the business plans, and the repeatability.

A Common Lesson

You are going to find short-term wonders like USS and marathoners like Medtronic very, very frequently in your investing life. The story is management more than product. Always remember that. Do not ignore technology, since customers demand great technology. But tech is only a starting point for becoming a great company and making customers happy and loyal while establishing repeatability. (You will see this is particularly applicable to buying tech stocks, which is discussed in chapter 8.)

YOU OWN A GREAT COMPANY, GROWTH SLOWS DOWN—NOW WHAT?

Over the last few years, one of the greatest companies in the history of technology, Hewlett-Packard, has performed poorly relative to its own history and the promises of Carly Fiorina, its CEO who was fired in 2005. Many did not catch on to the CEO's inconsistencies until they tired of the crummy stock performance, but you could have easily known better before the stock had suffered as much.

Now, I have a sell discipline that says sell anytime there is a change of management. This does not apply, however, when a stock is already down because of poor management, and new management has been brought in to turn things around. Thus, I did not sell when Carly came in; I hoped it would be like buying Chrysler or Bank of America when new management quickly fixed the mess that the prior team had left. Yet HP's overreliance on its printer for nearly all its earnings only worsened, and promises to diversify and improve things all fell flat.

Soon Fiorina stopped talking innovation and turned to acquisitions— notably a giant one, Compaq Computer. I have known for a long time that most big acquisitions fail, particularly in technology, and that they are done mostly when management runs out of innovations and good growth ideas. When Carly announced intentions to buy Compaq, I felt immediately that she and the company had failed at the B in BASM, and Carly had failed at the M. There was no way I could give HP decent grades for business model and management at that point.

Given all this, I was able to sell early. Almost three years before Carly's firing, I told my peers and friends that the CEO was pulling the wool over their eyes. You can avoid being bamboozled if you make sure that when management makes statements that conflict with great BASM and the Seven Steps, you walk away.

By the way, for those who did not use BASM or see these things early, there was also the big failure of the Compaq acquisition. HP annual reports gave the specific metrics that management forecast would be achieved by buying Compaq Computer, such as raising operating margins and taking more market share. It was in all company documents in 2002. But Hewlett-Packard not only failed to meet any of the key metrics but also lost more market share to Dell. You can do better. Use BASM and the Seven Steps and company documents, and you will be amazed at how much these kinds of things are just plain obvious.

RECOGNIZING WINNERS

So, how does one recognize winners? Well, first of all, we all want seven neat little rules for everything, which is why so many people who have

spent their lives reading books with six or eight or ten rules about everything from relationships to investing come away shaking their heads and
ending up where they started. The Seven Steps are not rules; they are a
process for acquiring and applying knowledge and combining that with
disciplines to overcome your own emotions. The paths to success are not in
rules; they are within *you,* as are the emotions that tend to block success.

Looking for great business models and great management—normally
meaning a great stock—does not take formal training or require genius. It
merely requires that you recognize things for what they are when you see
them. You do that by getting your hands dirty, immersing yourself in relevant information. Experience comes quickly through using cases. By applying what you have learned, a little bit each week, you will find that in a short
time you will be able to distinguish the ordinary from the great, as I did with
Staples and other companies. It is like catching fly balls, riding a bike, or
anything else. Almost all investors can do it if they are willing to practice.

> The answer is out there, Neo, and it's looking for you, and it
> will find you if you want it to.
> —Trinity to Neo in *The Matrix*

The good stocks are often right in front of you, and knowing the correct
and simple techniques to identify them will open your eyes.

MANAGEMENT LIFTS THE FALLEN COMPANIES

The concepts in this chapter are key to making maximum money from
your investing, and the cases and concepts of this whole book are given to
help you do that regardless of whether you buy growth stocks or what are
called value stocks. Shares of the latter are statistically very cheap. These
companies or their industry may have a lackluster outlook, or be out of favor for other reasons, or be "broken" and in need of fixing by good management. Whatever situation a company is in, there is one commonality,
and that is a "cheap" salvation for an ailing company, where management
can do things to make it better.

BET ON MANAGEMENT: IT CREATES THE PRODUCTS; IT GETS THE CUSTOMERS
Chrysler

At the beginning of the 1990s, Chrysler Corporation was trying to turn around, struggling with unpopular cars and a lack of money. It had already pulled back from the brink of bankruptcy once, almost a decade earlier under Lee Iacocca and others, and now it was struggling again for the second time. Cars are a mature, tough, global business these days, and it takes unusually good management to create even "decent" growth.

I sat with Lee Iacocca at a dinner, I met with the top management people, and I met Chrysler's chief designer. It was a time when the carmaker was going to bet what little cash it had on creating new lines of Jeeps and a number of minivans, expecting to combine a good feel for what the public really wanted with some exciting designs and engineering.

What I looked for was the following:

Was the consumer research logical, and did it sound as though Chrysler really had done enough homework to bet the ranch on these cars?

Did the plan itself sound well conceived and logical, and did it pass the commonsense test, from the timing of introducing new models to the platform engineering techniques intended to lower costs and make pricing more competitive?

Most of all, I wanted to know the backgrounds of the various top management people, and find out if Chrysler was applying the right people and skills to the list of what had to be done for the entire team to win. What I found out quickly was that it wasn't just the famous Lee Iacocca who had a winning track record. Each of the top management people as well as the designer could point to past successes in the auto business. It was a management team to bet on.

I made the investment and presented the facts to our investment committee. A lot of Wellington's mutual funds and pension funds did make that investment. On the surface, and just by the numbers, it appeared to be a high risk. Yet the bold, exciting car designs looked great, and Chrysler's plan was not a one-shot deal but thought through and intended for a number of consecutive product cycles. That did happen.

Lesson

Management made the difference. You could have read it all in many places even without questioning the members of the management team. As for the plan, it worked just as management had predicted. Chrysler's people did a great job. The cars were in the showroom when expected, and the public loved them. The stock tripled in one year, went sideways for a while, then tripled again for 9X our investment.

This was the reverse of selling when a new management comes in (per one of my three sell disciplines). That is because I could see that the company had already gone through its devastating fundamental fall, the stock reflected it, and now it had a very solid experienced "rescue" management—not an unknown crew—with a solid rescue plan.

Another Lesson

Chrysler is a wonderful example that demonstrates the key reasons why investors who concentrate on management, assumptions, strategies, and business models have the real advantage. It is those factors that make the products or services and the numbers work out. Management is often the most critical factor for you to understand.

It may seem as if just concentrating on a company's management to help you make your buy or sell decision is too easy. With technology stocks, and some other situations, the decision can be much harder. But often it is the experience and philosophy of the managers involved that can make all the difference.

What if you do not know whether the new people have the experience—it is just muddy, and unclear at best? You do not buy the stock. Period.

The background of a manager can be helpful but misleading if you rely too much on it. I commented earlier that Lou Gerstner came to IBM after running RJR Nabisco. He is a great example of somebody who had proved that he understood business models and had broad executive skills. This is far more important than what kind of industry skills somebody has, although I do not discount that element entirely. John Sculley came to run

Apple Computer in its early days. Like Gerstner, he came from a consumer products business: the Frito-Lay division of PepsiCo. Yet, unlike Gerstner, Sculley tried to apply his preconceived notions of what he knew from the corn-chip business to the computer business, and failed miserably. Gerstner realized he had a business-model problem at IBM, but he also did not come in with preconceived notions. (Apple had a huge business-model problem too, but Sculley quickly showed that he had no clue.)

Two big things made me feel good about Gerstner's chances for success. The first was that I knew his style, his open-minded approach, and his executive ability, and I respected him. Any investor could also have read about Gerstner's history and abilities. The second was that he came into IBM with no prior mind-set and wanted to learn. What is critical here is that he aggressively entered a process to define the basic reasons for IBM's ills. All too often I have seen lesser executives extrapolate from the past, make assumptions too quickly, or just proceed to "try harder" at the same old stuff, such as cutting costs (and firing people) and beating harder on the sales force. Lew wanted some education on the deep-seated problems of IBM, and this became the key to solving them. Naturally, this relates to the first thing and is a mark of a great executive, which I had already decided Lou was. I found out about Gerstner's open mind at IBM fairly soon, but people could also watch and read and find that out—not as quickly as I did, but quickly enough, since this was not an overnight story.

Sculley was not a management expert but a "marketing star" who did just what I said many executives do: he was the opposite of Gerstner—in that Sculley was a know-it-all who proceeded *before* he knew anything. Quickly, investors saw the lack of any results. Sculley was the "anti-Gerstner." *It was not the résumé, it was the person.* Always focus on that. A valuable lesson.

GREAT IDEA, GREAT CEO, BUT POORLY MANAGED: CALLING MCI

You may often run into a floundering company that has a famous CEO at the helm. Perhaps he's known for his past performance, or because he's a well-known entrepreneur who started one or more companies. Most often, it is because the entrepreneur is just that, and not a great hands-on manager. Is this bad management? Yes, but it can be fixed, and when it does get fixed, as frequently happens, stockholders make a barrel of money.

This situation presented itself in the early days of MCI, around 1986. This was long before it joined with what became WorldCom. MCI was having a bad time of it, and the stock was in the cellar. The founder William McGowan and others had made a risky bet by making a giant acquisition of a satellite company just when AT&T and others were forging ahead with optical cable, the better path.

I met with McGowan and was immediately convinced that this pioneer and man of vision was intent on putting in the right people and strategies needed to turn the company around. And he did. McGowan changed the face of telecommunications by bringing low-cost long-distance phone service to the masses and leading the fight to break up AT&T's monopoly. He articulated a vision that we all could understand and applaud. On top of this, McGowan entrusted his plan to solid operating managers.

In cases like this, I always recall the pithy words of Peter Drucker: "Management is doing things right; leadership is doing the right things." In other words, if somebody has a vision and can point the ship in the right direction, and if he also has enough common sense to build the right operating team, you won't have to second-guess management every step of the way. The odds are in your favor. Buy the stock.

McGowan needed help, perseverance, and direction to get through a tough period and realize his dream. He realized what had to be done and then moved to do it. My MCI stock was bought at what would be pennies today, split-adjusted. After my purchase, the stock went up by close to 10X in about twenty-six months.

Lesson

MCI's creation of a winning long-distance communications strategy was a good idea, a good management story. So often, great ideas lure investors into a stock, and they find out the hard way that there was no great management to translate the ideas into earnings and growth. In MCI's case, a deficiency of management and direction was corrected, and the great idea became great earnings, driving the stock.

Most of the time the reason people have a problem seeing this as straightforward is that they have the mind-set of analyzing a lot of numbers and specific aspects of operations, which make them overlook the importance of the people who make the operations and numbers happen. People make the numbers grow.

The average investor is capable of paying careful attention to companies' forecasts, statements, and reported performance in order to identify the best management and even many of the stars. These are the central elements in identifying the most rewarding investments.

Obviously, nobody wants an average lawyer, brain surgeon, auto mechanic, or just about anything else. When it comes to your health, it is more critical to avoid an average (or worse) surgeon than when you are putting in new kitchen cabinets. When it comes to your financial health, you do not want an average money manager; nor do you want to invest in companies that have only average management teams. In this day of intense domestic and global competition, the average management may make glowing remarks about some sexy new products or good quarterly sales numbers, but over time it will get eaten by the tough guys out there in the industry like John Chambers of Cisco, Bill Gates of Microsoft, Bernie Marcus of Home Depot, and plenty more you may never have heard of.

FIFTEEN MINUTES EACH DAY

The best management builds the most wealth for stockholders. You, the investor, then, need to know how to identify the best management, and you need to have enough knowledge to hold on to the winners even when they have a slow quarter.

You may not have fifteen minutes to review the news and company releases of your five most important stock investments on a given day. Nevertheless, you should average fifteen minutes a day, so you can be armed with current information, jot down information in a notebook, and look for consistencies versus inconsistencies. You will be surprised at how quickly patterns appear. Some companies are always explaining why things did not work according to their forecasts. Others tell their investors that things have worked very well; then they go on to explain how they will capitalize on their successes.

Think about our story of the 1987 crash. First of all, fifteen minutes a day would have given you a sense that stocks like Digital Equipment were soaring at a pace that made no sense when compared with the reported numbers, and were becoming ever more expensive. You would have seen disturbing market patterns and you would have translated that fifteen minutes a day into some deeper digging. The whole market was going up at a much faster pace than corporate earnings, but some stocks were just crazy.

At the same time, you would have been reading about rising and high interest rates and soaring debt levels for corporations, individuals, the federal government, and state governments. As I said before, you should not play economist and try to figure out the direction of the economy. But whether it is rising valuations or economic news that journalists tell you is unsettling and could be bad for stocks, there is only one thing to do: be sure of what you own. These are the times that those fifteen minutes a day become most important, so that you don't get emotional and violate buy and sell disciplines because of insufficient knowledge.

BE SURE OF WHAT YOU OWN

National Semiconductor was a good company founded nine years before Intel. Nine years is a lot in the world of high technology. Yet Intel went on to become the industry leader in the most important product line of that era: the microprocessor. Do not make the mistake of thinking that Intel was lucky or had better scientists. Intel's management—Bob Noyce, Gordon Moore, and Andy Grove—became some of the best corporate managers in America and distinguished themselves with their vision, strategy, and execution.

While National Semiconductor did an outstanding job in creating a wide array of terrific products—semiconductors that ended up in everything from wristwatches to moon rockets—their scientists were spread over many end-product areas and did not have leadership with a burning sense of focus and drive. Their leaders had not made these capable scientists focus all their energy and talent on the personal-computer end market until after Intel had surged ahead. Even then, management did not throw all of NSM's research talent into that mission.

If you were going from fifteen minutes a day to digging deeper, you could have retained Intel and sold National Semiconductor during a nervous time, on the basis of the fact that you could see a big divergence in the two companies' momentum and executive decision making. Also, you would have known enough that if, after the crash, you bought into semiconductors, it would have been with Intel, not National Semiconductor, where bad decisions sent the stock spiraling downward for a long time.

APPLE: GREAT PRODUCT, WEAK MANAGEMENT

You will now fully appreciate the difference between John Sculley at Apple in the 1980s and Louis Gerstner at IBM in the 1990s. Neither came from a technology background, but the first failed and the second succeeded, since management is management, and the principles at the beginning of this chapter were applied well by one and not the other.

Dell Computer had plenty of problems in its early years, but time and time again, Michael Dell found solutions, and moved forward toward his perennial goal of being biggest and best. Apple's personal-computer products have always been viewed by many in the industry as the best in the world. Even so, the company could not capitalize on that product supremacy to realize its potential. After the early years Apple stock did not perform as well as stocks of the best companies. The difference was that Dell had a great management and business plan, while Apple had neither, so its technological greatness was wasted.

Often, investors center more on exciting products than on the characteristics of a company, when the latter is what creates renewed vigor for everything from technology to retail and ultimately powers great stock appreciation.

At the beginning of the 1980s, a few companies had begun to manufacture personal computers. Estimates of the growth for that sector were good, yet nowhere near the huge demand that ultimately developed. At that time, Texas Instruments, Timex (yes, really!), Commodore, and Atari dominated the low end, while Apple, IBM, and Tandy made the more expensive machines. People largely regarded them as rather primitive gadgets that could be employed for playing computer games at home or for experimental use in the office. At this early stage, very little software, with few applications, was available—and it was expensive. Michael Dell was about sixteen years old, so he had not yet appeared on the scene.

Apple was initially seen, like a few similar personal-computer companies, as a small, speculative outfit selling very few units and without any assurance that it could be competitive. Then the products started to get very appealing.

One day, our director of research at Wellington Management, Bill Hicks, bought an Apple computer with the original primitive spreadsheet program and put it outside the door of his office. Bill, like many investors, was a curious person and always strived to do better. He said to us analysts, "Why don't you try to see what a spreadsheet will do and if any of you thinks this is any good?" At the same time, many other investment firms had not even gone that far. Anyway, a lot of us research analysts tried the computer. A few of my colleagues, one in particular, scoffed at it, and gave reasons why it was a dumb idea. Sticking to "pencil and paper work" was the way to go, he declared.

Some of the users liked the calculations they produced with the spreadsheet and pushed on, trying different things. Usage became more frequent. One day Bill observed that the line of analysts waiting to use the machine was growing kind of long and that he was going to buy a second one. I immediately bought a plane ticket to Silicon Valley to meet with people at Apple. I had already used the computer and had listened to my colleagues' positive and negative comments. On that basis alone, I already wanted to buy the stock—not that I fully appreciated the magnitude of what was to come. I don't know that anybody did.

I had no feel for whether the Apple management was any good. Steve Jobs was an impressive genius type with lots of vision and ideas, but no real business plan. He was not yet the great, mature genius-businessman that I had the pleasure of talking to years later.

I met others at Apple, but they lacked a core plan, since none had been created by Jobs. Consequently, they were all concentrating on a great product and a great market opportunity. I agreed with those two things, and just expected that these guys would develop better plans before long, so I went back to Boston to recommended purchase.

How could I do that, you ask, given my emphasis on the importance of great management?

I felt that there were four huge things going for Apple, even though I saw no great company yet: (1) a visionary had created a truly great product; (2) a rapidly growing customer base loved using the Apple computer; (3) an enormous market opportunity was beginning to take shape in the whole personal-computer industry; and (4) Apple's management was developing new products (i.e., repeatability) and not depending on just the one hot computer.

My first visit made me feel good, but I didn't come away feeling positive that this company had the leadership to be a great force, as I had with McDonald's and Molex. I hoped that I would become more confident over time, watching management operate. Such patience is necessary to determine whether any company is going to be great, regardless of whether you think the management appears to be terrific, or it is untested. You must see how the team is going to contend with competition and other obstacles that cross its path. It takes some time to see if the CEO and the product development and the business plan are going to be big winners over the long term.

I am not going to tell you that you should buy only the world's greatest companies for the rest of your investing life. Spend your time looking for them, since that is how you can get very rich. If, along the way, there are companies with great products and potential, but you are unsure of the management element, just know the risks involved with Apple. I did know, and I did not want to pass on this opportunity.

The Bending-the-Rules Lesson

Apple is a great lesson in how to bend the rules. If I had not learned this lesson from Apple, years later I probably would have sold Cisco and Sun way before their stocks mushroomed and made the really big money. This is even far more true for Dell, which beat both these stocks by a lot, but which I would not have owned after the early days when Michael Dell was not executing well.

Common sense, as well as a bit of history, showed me that sometimes a company takes time to get its act together. Just as we sometimes think a company is going to be great, watch it operate, and see that we were wrong—it cannot muster repeatability and the rest of what it needs—the reverse can also be true. With Apple, I needed to see if the nuts-and-bolts management could augment its great products, market opportunity, marketing, customer satisfaction, and loyalty. Those things were a good start.

It was no small matter that the market demand was soaring, and the product was awesome. The press and the business analysis done all over Wall Street forecast that personal computers could be one of the most exciting growth stories of all time. It all turned out better than any of us thought, with computer sales going from a few hundred thousand annually to more than 20 million units annually in under a decade. Anyway, I was an optimist and thought that we had to give every chance to a company in an industry like this, especially one with such amazing product features.

This raises the point of how to treat forecasts and how much stock to own. Not all stock positions have to be the same size. You can sometimes buy small amounts and watch, then move money on the basis of both your conviction level and new developments.

If you own a little of something, you will watch the forecasts much more carefully. This way you can be more likely to move more money into the stock as things get rosier, and thus make far more money in the long run.

My "rule" on management execution is mostly for the 99 percent of companies that are not brand-new, whereas Apple was brand-new in a brand-new industry. This is why learning from the case method and experience takes precedence over a rule book. You need disciplines, but you cannot apply them blindly. This was the beginning of the PC era; then other great growth stocks came along (e.g., Nike), and then biotechnology. I had to understand that if a company was going to grow well for five years, ten years, or more, valuations applied only on a one- to three-year time horizon would have you selling the greatest long-term companies much too early.

Apple helped me to work this through in my mind, as did others to come, and that is why I gave valuation leeway to Apple, and later to Sun and Cisco. By the time Dell appeared, I was very much into the workings of many of the greatest business models ever, and it was the business model that made me stay there even though Dell broke my "execution" rule. Dell's business model, by the time the company went public, was even more exciting to me than Apple's products had been.

Apple's stock went up a lot, and was great. Then, after we sold and took our profits, I watched the lack of consistency in operations at Apple. Soon, neither Jobs nor his friend and cofounder, Steve Wozniak, wanted to do the corporate CEO task—they were pure geeks, and came to hate the business end. Thus in 1983 they brought in new management from PepsiCo, John Sculley. He was a marketing star who had made Frito-Lay (corn chips and snacks) a huge grower as he headed up Pepsi Cola, USA.

Earnings were growing very strongly, so the profitability and high net-income growth were strong underlying pillars. I figured that if I sat around watching Sculley operate for a while, the stock would go out of sight, since earnings growth, industry growth, and Apple products were all running hot. Buying back, watching operations carefully, and visiting with Sculley seemed to be the best plan of action. I visited him to establish what he would show me about his operating style and plans, so I would have the benchmarks required to monitor him over time. Today you would get those benchmarks and the outlook quickly from company statements and reports, and probably just as quickly from the company Web site.

Just buying the hot sales and earnings would be too risky if that was all that we had in mind. We had not determined that Apple was a long-term winner; we had decided to watch it as things unfolded.

For that matter, Cisco went through a couple of rounds of management changes, and the founders (husband and wife) left completely; and then John Chambers came in, becoming the third CEO, and created the best part of the long-term growth story. At the beginning, Cisco was what Apple was—a really great product in a market destined to be huge. I am often suspicious of management changes because they usually mean something is not working, and they often go badly, as the Apple case demonstrates. Yet, I look carefully, since there are times when such change is terrific. I have always felt that if John Chambers had not joined Cisco early, Cisco would not have been as great as it became.

Sculley and Jobs became known as the "dynamic duo" for a while, and we all felt good about Apple management and liked the fact that we were making very good money on the stock. But in many ways, we were fortunate. Contrary to the perceptions of many investors, particularly those with memories that go back only to the euphoria of the late 1990s, most initial public offerings of risky, untested companies do not work well.

CORN CHIPS ARE NOT COMPUTER CHIPS

Jobs (and his board, and the market) had ultimately seen the need to put Apple's house in order and bring in professional management. While John Sculley was seen from both inside and outside as a marketing genius, he had no experience in this kind of world. The biggest differences in this new role for him were not in technology per se. The critical elements and challenges had to do with a company culture, which must support innovation, and understanding the current and future needs of the developing marketplace for personal computers.

I returned to Wellington disappointed by Sculley's ego, arrogance, and lack of knowledge about the PC industry, and told my colleagues, "John Sculley is a very impressive corporate guy, but he doesn't know the difference between a corn chip and a computer chip." I was most disappointed in his attitude. Instead of being there to learn at first, he felt he already knew it all. That was the worst. My colleagues, particularly some of the more senior ones, felt we should give him a chance, since this was such a terrific situation. I agreed.

We made more money on the stock. Over time, I watched carefully, observing Apple's inconsistency in results and the failings of Sculley. Thus I did get to use my buy and sell disciplines in a regular way later, and we did three great cycles in Apple's stock and made a ton of money from the early 1980s into 1987, when most tech was getting very overpriced, and I was selling things regularly.

THE END OF OUR APPLE STORY

Apple was a good company because it did have a happy and loyal customer base, but Sculley never understood the essence of the industry enough to develop a true business model; nor did he understand that he should have followed up on Bill Gates's overtures to work together on Windows for the sake of both their companies.

Apple never did achieve greatness, but with a combination of rules and bent rules for specific reasons, not just for a hot product, we made a lot of money, and I learned a number of valuable lessons.

Apple is a great saga, but this is the end of it for us, for now. Apple does teach us that you should try to give a company a chance to achieve greatness, while observing signs of whether or not it is delivering. The story also relates to other company experiences, before and after those early days of Apple. You should continually learn from all company experiences and try to relate them to your other investments, since so many links and comparisons do exist and will help you to recognize the good, the bad, and the ugly at earlier stages. Your little notebook will prove an invaluable asset to you.

The Final Lesson

Even though Apple continued to consistently create, develop, and market the best technology and the best products in the industry, it could not become a great company and a great stock because its management never formulated a great business plan. Apple continued to have problems that required additional CEO changes until recent times, when Steve Jobs returned.

IBM: JUST THE OPPOSITE STORY

Some professionals or otherwise experienced investors might be thinking about the IBM story in the early 1990s, and how Louis Gerstner, another star of the consumer-products world, came in and totally fixed the company. This was just the opposite of Sculley and Apple—at least on the surface.

Gerstner was a very talented corporate manager without any background in technology. His experiences at American Express, and then as chairman of RJR Nabisco, were mainly in the consumer area. Thus one might wonder if he was being miscast when he took on the role of fixing IBM, a company terribly mismanaged and in trouble when Lou accepted the job of IBM chairman in 1993.

On one occasion, when Gerstner was in our offices at State Street Research, he told me with pride how he had raised the Nabisco profit margins by making the crackers a tiny bit smaller. I recalled that remark when I first saw him in his new role as chief of IBM Corporation. One of the things that IBM does is to manufacture semiconductors, on silicon wafers. I was a bit cynical and said, "Lou, I don't think you can raise profit margins at IBM by making the wafers smaller." He laughed and told me specifically what was wrong with IBM and what he would do about it.

What was wrong? Lou actually was not naive about technology, since he had received a bachelor's degree in engineering from Dartmouth College. He knew that the central problem at IBM was not technology, but that this company had been very poorly managed for years. IBM management was risk-averse and could not figure out how to competitively price mainframes to compete with the likes of Hitachi. The result was a culture that could not accept change or adapt to it, in a world of increasingly rapid change. Almost as important as the cultural problem was that IBM distanced itself from customers' needs. This even included the incorrect pricing of mainframe computer processing power. The company needed a balance so as not to destroy profitability while developing new generations of products, and also not allowing Hitachi to hijack its market. IBM was floundering so badly that it was losing money at an accelerating pace in the early 1990s. The stock was in the cellar, but the bigger problem was that outside analysts were starting to predict bankruptcy and the end of this former star company. The dire forecasts looked quite reasonable in light of the facts.

So, in contrast to companies such as Home Depot and Cisco that had a great deal of their success flow from the importance of being close to customers and their needs, IBM had a hothouse culture of isolation from market changes, and customers felt totally ignored. Technology was not the real problem at IBM, Gerstner concluded. Instead, it was a group of issues, such as overwhelming bureaucracy and lack of corporate strategy, as well as the absence of a mainframe product strategy, all of which could be cured with tough management and true leadership.

Gerstner impressed me because he had done his homework, he could identify the nature of what was wrong, and he conveyed confidence that he knew how to fix it. I believed him. Gerstner proved to be tremendously successful.

Business Model and Execution

Gerstner first needed decentralization, to change the risk-averse culture and reduce the remoteness from the customer. He then had to execute, but executing any plan was impossible until he fixed the foundation of the house.

One critical thing that Lou Gerstner did right away was to change the pricing of the mainframe computers. Mainframe revenues were plunging, and customers were disenchanted. Some managers at IBM did not want to lose revenues from their ailing company and would not drop prices in line with competitors such as Hitachi. They felt that it was too tough for customers to change to another computer company and that eventually IBM would have a cheaper technology coming along that would allow lower prices but retain the profit margins.

Gerstner realized that to save the customer base, and to move many customers from alienation and anger back to loyalty, he had to risk the profit stream by immediately lowering prices, and then push hard to improve the technologies that would lower IBM's costs. The price drops worked extremely well, as mainframe sales immediately turned around and rose strongly year after year.

The Big Lesson

A manager has to show that he can immediately identify what the real problems are in a troubled company. Only then can he put together a plan to fix things. If he has done number one expertly, then number two, the execution of the plans, will not be overly difficult. If he does not properly identify the problems, there can be no fix. Once the problem was properly identified, Gerstner showed that he could execute and immediately moved to save the customers, and the company.

This is what Gerstner did. Sculley, in contrast, had created a mind-set of what he wanted to do from his successes with Pepsi, and not from understanding the personal computer industry and Apple's place in it.

One of my sell disciplines says that when a company has troubles and changes management, sell the stock. An outfit should not experiment with *our* money to see if it can get things right. That rule works most of the time, and certainly would have been the case with Hewlett-Packard at the beginning of the twenty-first century.

Nevertheless, I have been using exceptions in this chapter to show you different facets of this generally correct rule, as this is how the case method can apply the rule differently with a mind not to cookie-cutter solutions, but to identifying specific needs and solutions. So Chrysler and IBM are good examples of when to go with new management.

Now, what if the business is managed well, but you have a specific need? In baseball, for instance, you might need a new pitcher, not a whole new strategy. This is what happens when a company based on style does not know how to fit the next move in consumer tastes or needs—car companies, clothing companies, and others in the style business are always looking for a style genius. (This can apply to other businesses also, though, such as a new head of research and development for a software company—tech companies are always trying to rob each other of talent. The same goes for big pharmaceutical companies and others.)

THE GAP

As I noted in chapter 5, the story of the Gap is a classic story of retailing, management, and merchandising, and illustrates how stockholders need to understand what a company needs to succeed at different times in its life.

Donald Fisher was a real-estate developer who had an idea for selling jeans, which were benefiting from exploding popularity in the late 1960s. He opened one store, and then several more stores, as his assortment of Levi Strauss jeans, popular styles, and very low prices made the operation successful. His target market was fourteen- to twenty-five-year-olds. He and his wife managed the operation for aggressive growth, trying to put themselves at an advantage in every possible way.

The operation continued to be successful for three major reasons:

(1) It replaced inventory with maximum speed, holding on to items that were selling strongly instead of changing over to new styles just for the sake of change.

(2) It concentrated on only a few items—jeans, a few shirts and light jackets—but maintained the inventory for each in a wide range of sizes and colors in order to avoid disappointing the customers.

(3) It maintained rock-bottom prices.

Within five years, sales had skyrocketed to $97 million, and there were 186 Gap stores spread over twenty-one states. The company wisely began selling some of its own private-label jeans to partly diversify away from its total dependence on Levi Strauss, while promoting its own name. Very smart. Then, the Gap offered stock to the public in 1976. The stock immediately went down. Lots of IPOs do that, and this industry was in a soft patch.

But, for me, I just was not close enough to the Gap when its stock went from an $18 initial price down to $7.25, a relative bargain. I just had no real feel for the company's management. The stock began to recover as sales climbed and new stores were opened, but I did not know what merchandising advantage the Gap might have, since customers were changing to some extent.

The kids of the 1960s were older by the late 1970s, and they wanted different things. Holding on to a customer base is not easy. Also, as 1980 approached, J. C. Penney, Sears, and a variety of other discounters sold Levis. I wondered how the Gap would deal with these things and at the same time be able to differentiate itself from the pack—a key criterion. The stock was moving up without me.

Solving a "Gap"

There was a clear gap between the time that the huge discount-store competition came into the jeans market and the time that Gap Stores did something about it. Nevertheless, the Gap was growing fast and did not wait for real trouble to brew before making a big move. Fisher understood the classic problem for a founder/entrepreneur—knowing (or not knowing) when to let go and bring in new management talent. He also knew that the Gap could not thrive in a competitive environment where selling at the lowest possible price was the dominant strategy. So he brought in Millard "Mickey" Drexler, a Macy's executive who had become the president of Ann Taylor three years earlier. Under Drexler, Ann Taylor revamped its line and style, enabling the company to quadruple its sales almost immediately.

He successfully pursued a similar strategy at the Gap. Drexler caught my eye, and that of other investors. Hearing him speak, we knew he had a clear vision and the talent to do what he knew was needed. I bought a little stock. Changing management, as I said, can be a warning sign in my disciplines, but fortifying management and filling a clear need are just the opposite. When his strategy dramatically increased the Gap's appeal in the marketplace, we bought more stock, even though it was at higher prices than our first purchase. This happens a lot, and if you have more knowledge and more confidence in the longer term, avoiding a short-term mentality and paying more can be very enriching.

So I was paying $8 per share, and $11 per share, and higher, and the stock kept going up, on into the $40s.

Mickey Drexler had created what would become a nationally famous and appealing look: the Gap look. Some years later Tommy Hilfiger also created his own unique "look," one with broad appeal. I bought all the Tommy Hilfiger stock I could and did roughly 7X my money in the mutual funds I managed, in less than four years.

The concept that you learn certain lessons in the marketplace and get better at applying them every year was alive and well. I had learned a lot from the Gap and used that education in most other retailing situations from then on. Sometimes you learn about semiconductors from airline cycles, or medical-device product cycles from electronics technologies. It all adds up, and the more case experience you accumulate, the more money you are bound to make.

Lesson

The combination of Fisher's savvy in making the moves he needed to make and Mickey Drexler's genius for consumer tastes and merchandising created a home run.

This is a special kind of company—but there are a bunch of them—and it offers a certain kind of stock lesson for investors:

What about the many, many companies that offer huge returns but are volatile and hard to predict?

If you cannot identify them as great companies, your nerves will be tested, each time they make a sharp move, and you will not know what to do. Volatile companies that do not have a great business model, a great customer base, name recognition, market share, and share growth—some or many of these attributes—are going to be too tricky.

Let's not forget about one of your most valuable investing resources: time. I think many investors would just as soon walk away from companies that are too tough for them, that test their nerves with volatility, and that require constant checking. First of all, the great companies do not require constant checking. Second, there are a lot of companies out there, and you must devote your time to the ones that you think you can understand the best. Spend your valuable time on those. Nevertheless, if you do understand the company, then do not shy away from volatility. You have more opportunities when you are confident enough to buy stocks at lower prices.

The secret to having patience with volatility is the confidence that you may be wrong on short-term timing, but you have enough knowledge to be sure that you are right about the company. Institutional investors do have trouble holding large positions of a stock during tough times, since we have committees and trustees to review buy and sell decisions, and we can strike a balance in investment strategy by having some funds that offset the short-term risks of our others. I did lose money in the 1987 crash—fortunately, crashes are rare—and it did take a few years to make it back, but ultimately I made a tremendous gain. This was a great recovery stock. The recovery was all based on knowing the company.

Individuals who know a company can be long-term holders and make some amazing gains. Somebody who bought the Gap when Mickey Drexler arrived and held the stock for eight years made 40X his or her money. The volatility might make it unrealistic that the average investor could hold all the stock. The average investor does not fully use BASM and the Seven Steps. As a result, he gets frightened by stock swings and loses opportunity after opportunity.

What is realistic, though, is for an investor to define great management and strategy and a great company that is the product of the ability of management to create, and to cope, and to stay close to the customer most of the time. There were many opportunities for the knowledgeable investor to make a lot of money in various time periods along the way. This is why you must remember the Seven Steps: knowledge, patience, disciplines, emotions, time horizon, market timing, and benchmarks.

So an investor could have taken part in many of the moves the Gap's stock made. Even without grabbing the entire move, he could have had a part of a greater than 4X move from 1980 to 1982; then, after the stock corrected, another move from that bottom to more than 17X from 1982 to 1983. Holding through the correction would have meant one move of 12X to 13X, which is terrific.

By the way, this stock multiplied in value by 100X in the first fourteen years after Mickey came on board. The Gap went from being a very good company with choices to make to a great company, by virtue of its choices—choices made by management.

CHAPTER SEVEN

BEAR MARKETS, BUBBLES, AND MARKET TIMING

How to Invest in Different Environments

Those who have knowledge don't predict. Those who predict
don't have knowledge.
> —LAO-TZU, SIXTH-CENTURY B.C. CHINESE POET

I always avoid prophesying beforehand, because it is much
better to prophesy after the event has taken place.
> —WINSTON CHURCHILL

THE MARKET IS INFLUENCED BY AS MANY VARIABLES AS THE WEATHER

The beautiful *Caligo atreus* butterfly rested on one of the reeds protruding from the calm blue waters of the Okavango Delta. It was very quiet as the hot midday sun baked the southern African landscape of Botswana with a golden hue. Suddenly a nearby hippo made a low bellowing sound. Startled, the *Caligo* flapped its wings and rapidly flew off in a swish of gorgeous blue and yellow and black colors, darting over the water.

The movement of those delicate wings was the only thing that intruded on the hot, still air. Waves of energy, generated by the fluttering butterfly wings, now moved through the air, and were amplified as they traveled higher and higher into the African atmosphere. Unseen energy transferred in a continuously amplified manner across the land and, eventually, above the Atlantic Ocean.

It was weeks later, when those atmospheric disturbances had traveled many thousands of miles north and east, in the early summer of the southwestern United States. The forecast that day for Colby, a small town of 5,900 persons in northwest Kansas, was for hot, clear, sunny weather. The tornado warning came from nowhere, and people scurried indoors at the sound of the sirens. Then they heard the sound of that tornado, like the rumble of an approaching freight train. As luck would have it, there was little damage.

"Well, I guess we might as well be back in the Stone Age, for all the good our so-called modern weather station does us," mused Jed Stevens that night, sitting with his pals on the long bench in front of the general store.

In the early 1960s, a meteorologist theorized that the flapping of a seagull's wings could initiate disturbances that would amplify and affect weather a continent away. Later, the seagull in this theoretical model was replaced by a butterfly, and as scientists incorporated this butterfly effect into their thinking about why weather is too complex to be predicted, mathematicians formulated all of this into what we know as chaos theory. Financial people now use chaos theory to explain why the tremendous number of variables and the unpredictable nature of many of them preclude predicting the movements of financial markets. Good stock pickers discover this very early from experience.

Any attempts to try to predict the direction of the stock market are called market timing. I will explain in this chapter why academicians and professionals as a group agree that it *cannot* be done; in fact, it will cost you money or opportunities.

Fear, greed, and a basic human desire to think we can know or control our future all drive us to try to predict short-term market movements. That is why the Seven Steps are essential if you want to be rich. If you flip a coin ten times and it comes up heads ten times, that is random luck, not a "system." We know that over time it will be fifty–fifty, heads and tails. Many who guess which way the market will move and guess correctly think they have a system and really can do it. Yet if you guess correctly and try to time the market a number of times in succession, it is most likely that you will guess wrong at some point and more than wipe out all your prior gains and be well behind (see the Long-Term Capital Management story later in this chapter). How do I know that? Both from reading academic studies on the subject and from observing what has happened in the markets over the decades. Stick with the Seven Steps and BASM, and be a stock picker.

One of the Seven Steps is to avoid timing the market, but just as running coordinates all the muscles of the arms and legs, the other steps coordinate to make it possible for you to easily resist the temptations posed by events or rapid market moves. First and most important is to have buy and sell disciplines, and right after that a proper time horizon. Emotions are an important step, for as soon as you feel the pull of fear in a down market or a down stock, or the magnetism of greed in sharp upward moves for the market or a stock, you know that you do not have enough knowledge to know what to do. Knowledge, disciplines, and the other Seven Steps can be called upon to resist emotion-driven timing.

Computers and sophisticated software programs for determining weather changes or changes in the direction of the stock market have been developed and refined over the last two decades. But computer software cannot properly account for all of the linked factors that influence weather changes or market changes.

EARNINGS AND FUNDAMENTALS DO AFFECT STOCK VALUES

I have observed two kinds of market timing over the decades. One is a system that is used analytically or methodically to determine when the overall stock market is going to change direction or make a significant move in one direction or the other. Thus it supposedly does not have to do with whims or emotions but rather has to do with some system that would be applied consistently for a portfolio or another pool of assets. Systems can involve mathematical models, technical charts, or other seemingly sophisticated methods, but they do not work any better than weekly weather forecasts made with supercomputers.

The other kind of market timing has to do with a judgment made after taking into account all the information about stocks and the market that you get from research and the media. Emotions may or may not be a driver, but either way, this kind leaves a lot to chance.

This book is not going to cite all the academic and professional studies, but just let me say that I do read what comes out of academia, I do read the best books about our business, and I do talk these things over with other money managers. Even if I disagree with colleagues about issues that affect wealth building through stocks, or concern any of the subjects I cover, I discuss those ideas that have merit in the eyes of my best stock-picking friends, since I am trying to help people become the best investors they can be. This is true throughout *The Big Money.* No one I respect and work with embraces any overt methods to time the market. Everyone is aware of the importance of the safeguard included in the Seven Steps to counterbalance the emotional pull in declining markets for many investors that has all too often shaken them out of stocks that could have made them wealthy.

Interest rate moves, acceleration or deceleration in the growth rate of corporate earnings, changes in dividend yields of stocks versus bonds, and some other key fundamentals do influence how stocks should be valued. That is not disputed among academicians or professionals in the mainstream.

Interest-rate increases decrease the value of stocks, whereas faster growth of corporate earnings increases the value of stocks based on higher expected earnings levels and growth rates. Usually, though, higher levels of demand for products and services cause the faster pace of earnings. That happens when the economy is growing faster, and that growth often causes higher interest rates. So we have two opposing factors involved in valuations.

There are many more factors, including how our currency is doing in relation to foreign currency, whether or not money is flowing out of or into our financial markets from abroad and how long that will last, and of course many other economic factors that suggest what earnings will be doing in the future. Forecasting interest rates and earnings with any decent accuracy is also not always possible.

Have I mentioned market psychology yet? Expert investors, including Warren Buffett, say that the markets can detach from fundaments for periods as long as a year or even longer. Therefore market timing is a form of gambling. It is easier to understand a stock you know well, and value that stock with reasonable accuracy, particularly if it is for a time horizon of a couple of years.

These days, minor market-moving news and events are more and more frequent and could have you trading (at a dizzying and counterproductive pace) into and out of some of the companies that you would want for long-term investing and wealth. The Seven Steps can save you from getting caught up in this self-defeating behavior.

There are countless small but violent moves in the markets, let alone the many corrections and periodic bear markets that occur. It seems as if almost every two years something of significance happens to the markets, such as the tech boom and bust in 1983; the 1987 crash; a big decline as the economy slowed in 1990, and actually went into recession later in the year as consumer confidence slipped (although it was a 1990–1991 recession—not long after we attacked Iraq in January of 1991, the market became strong, moving up sharply); a correction in the NASDAQ in 1992; fears of inflation and the tightening in 1994; the Asian crisis in 1997; more global problems in 1998; the huge bubble bursting in 2000; the terrorist attacks of September 11, 2001; and the big rallies that followed the 2003 invasion of Iraq and the 2004 presidential election results. In between, there have been many, many short, sharp moves that gave those interested in timing something to consider.

Just the moves above amounted to nine significant events in nineteen years—that is, *frequent* events. In every case, as with the market crash of 1987, using knowledge and disciplines instead of being driven by raw emotion and using a "timing" approach were the keys to investment success.

Over the years, volatility in market averages and individual stock prices has increased, not decreased, so that there have been many more sharp moves and many more reversals. Many factors are responsible. Some of the reasons are computerized stock trading, huge increases in the size of the largest institutional portfolios, the proliferation of aggressive hedge funds, and the complexity of the task of properly interpreting information that develops at a dizzying pace in our globalized markets.

Interestingly enough, there are typically more 3 percent and 5 percent daily upward moves in stock-market averages during bear markets than in bull markets. The basic nature of market moves, and the psychology that affects those moves, coupled with the complex financial variables, makes the process of trying to determine the short-term direction of markets a very tricky game of chance, and one that can be immensely costly.

HERE IS THE BEST WAY
TO AVOID TIMING THE MARKET

Once you have started to practice using buy and sell disciplines, and as you find how much simpler they make your investing life by giving you a focus, a compass, and a framework, you will find many practical applications for them. Remember that they are not without exceptions, since formulas and rigid rules are not the best way to invest. Instead they are what everybody does need: a discipline.

Buying stocks that are well above their own valuation history without a compelling reason (such as your knowledge telling you that big, positive changes are coming) is a bad idea. When markets are becoming overvalued, you will naturally have trouble finding good stocks to buy at reasonable prices, and you may not find replacements for stocks that you sell. That is OK; just wait and keep looking. So two of the Seven Steps—buy and sell disciplines, and patience—come into play at such a time to help you stay focused.

The converse is true for selling. Selling out of fear or a feeling that the market will keep going down could lead you to dump stocks that could make you wealthy. This has been the experience of countless investors. Again, look at valuations.

I remind you that lots of companies do become undervalued and are good buys: you can make some money even without great BASM. I am not against buying them, and often did buy them for my mutual funds. We, like many funds with an eye to risk, had a mandate to be very diversified. I often owned over one hundred stocks, even when I could not find one hundred of the greatest companies to buy all at once. Good BASM is necessary for companies that you hope will stay great and make you independently wealthy. You do not have to be diversified at all with BASM stocks after you have placed your essential money in some less risky mutual funds and go on to concentrate remaining funds in wealth stocks.

Selling a lot before the 1973–1974 great bear market would have been a good idea, not because somebody should have tried to predict the market, but because the great blue chips, then called the "Nifty Fifty," had been driven up by a kind of mania. Not only were they substantially overvalued, but they also had affected the broad market and caused most stocks to be very overvalued. Using the Seven Steps would have kept you from being trapped in those stocks. Earlier, you read about the crash of 1987 and saw how some people floundered and sold what they should have bought, and vice versa, yet it was clear that buy and sell disciplines coupled with knowledge worked well during that period. Finally, I used the disciplines to go against natural tendencies and made huge returns during the first Gulf War and the Asian crisis, when market timing by investors was rampant and costly to them.

When stocks like Disney or McDonald's—in their greatest periods of stock performance—went down temporarily, individuals were selling en masse, yet some of my colleagues who had done their homework bought more. Making decisions based on short-term market moves or listening to professionals (called "technicians" or "market technicians" or "chartists") who claim they are able to "read" stock charts and predict from them can result in your selling when you should hold the stock. Time horizon, patience, disciplines, and, above all, emotions are the steps you need to stick with. For example, those who reacted to a roughly 23 percent price correction for Disney over a few months during my first full year in the business (1971) by selling missed out when the stock came out of its correction, doubled in nine months, and rose by about 150 percent in fifteen months.

Disney was the first of many really important learning experiences I was to have. They all helped me to get better and better at avoiding those urges we all have to trade on the basis of market momentum. During the rapid and sharp price drops at the beginning of the first Gulf War, in 1991, I could see emotional selling at play, which tempted me to be just as emotional. But I avoided following the herd, sticking to my disciplines to temper my emotions.

The principles and disciplines of the Seven Steps helped me to take advantage of terrific opportunities. I bought lots of great growth stocks at very attractive prices. This resulted in huge stock profits for my public mutual fund, which won the Lipper Fund of the Year Award for 1991 (the best performance in the country in my category). So did the annuity fund I managed for the MetLife insurance company.

BULL OR BEAR MARKET

While various people can legitimately pick factors that trigger bear markets, or those stock-market environments that result in declines that are long, very significant, or both, there are five factors which I have seen great investors center on, and which I, in turn, have centered on. These elements of a bear market can be present individually to create falling prices, or they can appear in combination.

Markets have a habit of discounting good and bad events in advance. This explains why a company's stock may make a big move before its earnings are made public, or why the market may hit the doldrums for three weeks prior to a rise in interest rates. The reason is anticipation. Savvy investors must take into account that reaction to a future event may already be reflected in current prices. I discuss this in more detail when I deal with valuations and earnings in chapter 4, but the key point is this: Investors have to start noticing the patterns of price movements in stocks before and after news releases and events. This is neither particularly difficult nor time-consuming. You can learn how these patterns manifest themselves by watching, but you will not learn them from reading a book or a chapter or two trying to give you lots of rules. Practice doing it, and you will catch on pretty quickly, I assure you.

The five possible factors that cause bear markets are:

1. Persistent overvaluation.
2. High or rising interest rates or rising inflation that leads to them.
3. Weakness in company earnings. (By the time people know they are in a recession, normally weak earnings have already been evident, and if high interest rates cause economic weakness, then those rates have been present for a time.)
4. Oil shocks.
5. Wars (but not always).

The first three are, to me, "the big three"; and those who ignored them suffered much greater losses than those who did not, in tough times like the terrible 1973–1974 market, the 1983 tech boom and bust, and the 1987 stock-market crash, as well as numerous other instances over time.

Note: In each of these instances, as well as the 2000 Internet and technology bubble burst, there was a general disregard for valuations of individual stocks leading up to the collapses. Each collapse was related to this factor. They did not descend upon the markets out of nowhere, like locusts or hurricanes.

Things can appear a bit more complex, with news reports citing a falling dollar or a rising trade deficit, or diminished consumer confidence, or debt loads of the federal government. But these factors would probably be reflected in the five elements listed above.

When I studied economics in school, I, like most, used the great textbooks written by economist Paul Samuelson, who won the Nobel Prize in economics in 1970. Many years ago, he joked, "Wall Street indices predicted nine out of the last five recessions." This quip has become a favorite of many professionals on Wall Street. Although to those who concentrate more on the overall movements of the market indices than on individual companies and their earnings, it always looks as though a big market move "is telling them something," in reality that is not the case.

Samuelson shows that the market itself is not the forecasting tool that many people think it is. Some investors think that each drop means an impending recession, or impending doom of some kind. Most frequently that is quite wrong. Certainly this was a key factor that could make or break somebody's investment year (or maybe many years), as you will see for yourself as I review events in 1997 and 1998, in this chapter. Having said this, I must mention that, aside from the many violent and perhaps meaningless short-term market moves, a longer-term, sustained market move can influence people's feelings and spending behavior, and then become a bit of a self-fulfilling prophecy, influencing changes in the economy. The so-called wealth effect means that when your house price or stock portfolio appreciates a lot in your eyes, you will spend more money (and conversely, that you will spend less in the reverse situation).

It is useful, at this point, to take a few instances of sharp and emotional drops in the stock market and trace what happened. Look for yourself and judge whether market moves predicted real events or reflected emotions. Decide what was related to tangible fundamental events and read how the episode turned out for investors. (As for sharp or sustained moves the other way, the second half of this chapter, which is devoted to the tech bubble of the late 1990s, discusses manias and emotional upward moves.)

Investors who act emotionally and join the herd do not know where they are going. Investors who use BASM and the Seven Steps actually do know where they are going.

BUT THE BAHT SHOULDN'T COUNT: 1997

One can wonder if the long-term worth of Dell, Yahoo, Intel, and Wal-Mart, to name a few broadly owned stocks, should have any sensitivity to events other than management decisions, the competitive environment, interest rates, and, ultimately, earnings and growth rates. The key to that question is *long term*. Anything can happen in the short term.

In January 1997, Hanbo Steel, a large Korean *chaebol* (conglomerate), collapsed under $6 billion of debt. On February 7, Somprasong Land Public Co. was the first Thai company to miss payments on foreign debt. The huge growth of the region had been funded with huge debt, both by governments and by companies, and the chickens were coming home to roost.

There were rumblings of trouble from Malaysia, Korea, and Japan, and then, on May 23, 1997, moves to save Finance One, Thailand's largest finance company, failed. It was like the proverbial domino effect, but the U.S. markets ignored it.

Through the summer and into the early fall, debt troubles spread to many more companies and geographic areas, and Asian currencies began suffering severe declines. U.S. stocks continued to rise. But when late October arrived, the Taiwanese dollar had been devalued, and the Hong Kong stock market was beaten up badly, so U.S. stockholders finally reacted, suddenly and emotionally. On Monday, October 24, 1997, the Dow Jones industrial average posted its single biggest point loss ever, falling 554.26 points, or 7.18 percent, to 7,161.15. The NASDAQ plunged over 118 points to about 1,532, a percentage drop about the same as that for the Dow. Panic selling of many stocks continued for some days.

Dell Computer, which had been trading at over $100 per share in mid-October, fell to about $73. Worried investors had suddenly taken 27 percent off the value of this company, even though there had been no change in the fundamentals.

About five months later, in March, Dell was at $135, a rise of 85 percent from $73, in a very short time. Eleven months later, Dell had split twice and was now selling at $66.87, which would have been $266 on the presplit shares. Wise investors who bought or held made 3.6X their money, in eleven months.

Yahoo had dropped from about $53 to $38 in three trading days, but by March, Yahoo had risen 130 percent from that price of $38, so those who bought had made 2.3X their money in five months, and actually made an astounding 11X their money in only thirteen months following those panicky few days of late October 1997. The pattern was the same for many stocks, including some blue chips, although blue chips in general did the best and technology did the worst before the snapback in prices.

The difference between emotional selling (timing the market) and disciplines with knowledge was huge. This is how the Seven Steps work to help investors avoid typical herd behavior.

BUTTERFLY OR HIPPO?

Was the Thai currency, the *baht,* a "butterfly," so to speak, when it was devalued? Were any of the bankruptcies or other financial events in Asia at that time butterfly events?

Maybe Hanbo Steel was the first butterfly, or maybe Somprasong was. On the other hand, the butterfly could have really been some of the excessive lending and borrowing going on in the heated Asian economies during the years leading up to the region's financial troubles.

The real point is that many things go on in a global economy that are unknown, and even when they do become known, there is no way to understand the totality of their effects. This is no better than trying to understand what can happen when a hippo bellows and a *Caligo atreus* butterfly takes off in Botswana.

The examples of Dell and Yahoo! represent countless instances in almost every market environment that show how people fall into the trap of timing, and are shaken out of great companies that can make them the big money. Each year, and each of the many times the market drops, there are choices to be made on individual stocks.

As for me, I had already learned to avoid being emotional or acting without knowledge from a number of experiences with news events and market reactions. For instance, during the 1990 recession, I bought stocks that were great opportunities.

The year 1997 was not "typical" for me. I was raising money for new funds and told prospective investors exactly how we saw the environment. I had been calling lots of companies and, importantly, looking at their news and earnings releases, and comparing them with what the companies had said earlier in the year or even more recently about what kind of sales and results they expected. Things were looking much healthier than you would have expected if you were just listening to the news about Asia. It may sound trite, but don't run your life savings on the basis of a newspaper.

I pointed out that uncertainties from Asia's troubles had created great opportunities in great stocks. Many companies were doing well and had attractive PEG ratios, the price-earnings ratios divided by the growth rates.

That is a quick way to compare companies with their own history and with one another. I was buying in late in 1997, since my buy and sell disciplines said that many stocks I had a keen interest in looked like buys, not sells.

None of the great fears of recession or poor consumer spending that worried investors came true. Once again, the world did not come to an end. Once again, market timers did very poorly, as I observed things, and stock pickers did exceptionally well, taking advantage of other people's panic selling.

Early in 1998, with stocks doing well, I was fully invested. During the summer, as stocks corrected sharply, I was also fully invested in stocks that met my disciplines. Little did I know that a big event and an even bigger scare were just around the corner: a situation was about to present itself that would put everything on the table.

THE 1998 SCARE:
GLOBAL FINANCIAL CRISIS, AND SWEATY PALMS

Less than a year later, in August and September 1998, the American markets encountered another scare, triggered by global factors, and by something that started many thousands of miles from Wall Street. As far as most investors were concerned, it might as well have been light-years away. It was Moscow, and the problems were the debts and currency (the ruble) of Russia.

There is an old story in our business about the hippie, the priest, and the world's smartest investor, who were passengers in a small, two-engine propeller plane. It was an excursion over a remote part of Alaska. The pilot announced that mechanical problems had developed in one engine, and he would have to shut it down, but they would be just fine on the other engine. Shortly afterward, the pilot announced that fuel line problems had developed, and the other engine was not going to last either and the passengers must use the parachutes in the back, before the plane crashed.

Unfortunately, somebody had made an error, and there were only two chutes for the three passengers. As they looked at one another in horror, with ashen faces and trembling voices, the priest said, "I am the only one who can take care of my parish in a remote part of the West, where many families totally rely on me for help and guidance." The investor said, "I am the world's smartest investor. I cannot just die like this." Finally, the hippie said, "I want to live; I don't want to go down with this plane."

The world's smartest investor did not wait for more. He grabbed one of the parachutes and jerked the door open with one swift motion, yelling "Geronimo!" as he leaped from the plane. As the priest looked at the hippie with fear on his face, the hippie smiled and said, "Do not be afraid, Father. We still have two chutes. The world's smartest investor just jumped out of the plane with my knapsack."

Many of us in the investment world enjoy this little joke because we know how easy it is for so-called smart people to outsmart themselves. We further understand that investment success is not an IQ contest, and that paying attention to many things, while being somewhat humble in deference to how tough it is to predict the future, is healthy, to say the least.

In late 1993 a few of the other "smartest investors in the world" got together and formed an investment firm called Long-Term Capital Management, otherwise known as LTCM. Much has been written about what happened to this firm, which became famous, if not notorious, in the financial world, so I will be brief.

The brilliant people who put together the firm believed that those who thought market actions were random and unpredictable were missing a lot, and that they must be wrong. LTCM wanted to manage bonds, issued in different countries, and take advantage of the *spreads,* or price and yield differentials, that market moves would create. They saw short-term opportunities to give themselves an advantage when markets acted irrationally, feeling confident that a market would always come back to where it was "supposed to be," according to models they would build.

STRIKE ONE, STRIKE TWO, STRIKE THREE, YER OUT!

Remember that I said earlier that timing the market successfully once, twice, or more could be totally undone if you miss one market call. The case of LTCM proves this point, since its systems made a fortune for people, generating very high returns four years in a row and predicting the markets well. Then the firm lost virtually all of it and essentially failed.

LTCM had two Nobel Prize winners, and a former vice chairman of the Federal Reserve Board (he resigned from the Fed when LTCM opened), and some other brilliant professionals. These were some of the best minds in the world of finance, and they built a system that they claimed was infallible. But a funny thing happened on the way to the bank.

On August 17, 1998, a startling and unpredictable event resounded through the world's financial markets. Russia devalued its currency, the ruble, and declared a "debt moratorium." This meant that the country might default, or fail to pay, on its bonds. In fact, $13.5 billion in local ruble debt was instantly in default. These effects just "couldn't happen in a thousand years," according to what some at LTCM had supposed. But they did happen.

LTCM had always assumed that when liquidity (ability to buy and sell securities in a market, provided by plenty of willing buyers and sellers) dried up in one particular market, most other markets would have substantial liquidity, and various strategies could be executed. Wrong.

Long-Term Capital's portfolio was immediately in trouble. The size of its debt, or *portfolio leverage,* was so monstrous that U.S. financial markets were endangered. The LTCM way of trading and operating was paralyzed.

The rumor around Wall Street was that LTCM might not make it, and that major disruptions and losses were threatened. Going to other firms for help, such as George Soros's huge hedge-fund operation, did not work. Soros had a belief from his own experiences in the market that was contrary to the models and beliefs of LTCM. His beliefs had helped him build a personal fortune in the billions.

Soros felt strongly that you cannot predict the markets—rather, you take advantage of their moves, because markets are naturally chaotic.

The evidence over time supports the "chaotic" view, I concluded long ago. The events of 1998 bring forth various important lessons, and support for this view of chaos is the most important.

THE TRIPLE WHAMMY
THAT TRULY TESTED INVESTORS

Early in 1998, earnings looked strong, and the markets were strong. But when normal market correction appeared, headlines about the market being high as well as problems in Asia accentuated fears, and whammy number one was that many investors were scared out of their stocks.

By August, questions on the overall health of the market and the possibilities of a bear market (a substantial drop) were frequently in the news. More people sold. Then a prominent chartist (technical analyst) said on TV that we were definitely going into a bear market. Immediately, the market plunged by one hundred points in a day, and mutual fund redemptions (sales) by the public were reportedly becoming large. The action of the market itself created a poor psychology, and that created more weakness. That was whammy number two.

I am human, so I was nervous, yet my disciplines and research said everything was okay. I did no selling.

THE THIRD WHAMMY IS THE BIGGEST

Then came whammy number three. One of the main definitions of *whammy* from the dictionary is the following: "A potent force or attack: *specifically:* a paralyzing or lethal blow."

That is what the situation felt like when Russia devalued and defaulted on August 17. It was not just one event; it was a trigger. By now, most of the strong gains earlier in the year were gone, as markets declined. As Russia's actions rippled through all the markets of the world, and a flight to quality began with a rush, not only did we have the financial and emotional impact of rapid losses in stocks, but it became more of a mystery as to where all this would end. The pressure was building every day.

I did not want to give in to emotion, although some days I would start to feel warm in my air-conditioned office and wipe a bead of sweat from my brow, or feel my palms dampen as I penciled numbers into my notebook depicting what sales and earnings of companies were going to be.

On August 27 the Dow Jones industrials suffered their third-largest point drop ever, falling 357 points (these days that would rank twelfth after the 2000–2002 markets).

With everything else going on, in the late summer *Money* magazine wanted to write an article about my funds and why I had done so well over time, and also what I owned in the funds. I could have refused the interview or put it off for another time, but I felt that the public might be doing itself a disservice by responding to bearish news stories instead of looking at stocks and knowing what it owned. Whenever I am interviewed by the press—be it print, TV, or radio—I say only what is true and will help the public. I never use this venue as a forum for promoting my funds. I feel this is the only way. I had confidence in what I held.

I did the *Money* interview. My biggest exposure was in consumer stocks, and within that, the largest area was specialty retailing, where I owned a number of different companies, including Timberland, Men's Wearhouse, Proffitt's department store chain, and Family Dollar Stores, which were all featured in the next issue of the magazine.

A comment in that article stated, "Fund manager Fred Kobrick believes that low inflation and unemployment are prompting consumers to open their wallets." My work told me the consumer-spending environment was still healthy, despite Asia and despite the worries depicted on the evening news.

SEPTEMBER

Crisis conditions seemed to be spreading through European markets, Latin America, and Asia. Even Merrill Lynch's stock price went down by 50 percent. This was because of the trading situation and the terrible losses it was taking, particularly in the bond-market rout. The efforts of LTCM to find rescue capital had the normal effect on the community. Information about LTCM and the dangers in the markets began to leak around Wall Street.

The year 1998 brought tough tests for investors, as markets were some-what of a roller coaster. A 600-point drop of the Dow in June had started a fear syndrome, as more and more investors felt confused. The NASDAQ had lost 25 percent of its value in six weeks beginning in late July, and now the September rumors were tough on us.

HOW IT ALL ENDED

With no new events or reason at all, the market started to do better. To the bears it was just a typical bear-market rally; things were still bad. Market timers were out of the market, citing things like the dark and mysterious rumors about LTCM, Russia's troubles, those ripple effects that were still worsening, and more.

Stocks I owned or was buying a bit of started to come to life. Genzyme, a biotechnology company, had dropped from $31 to $25. Then it moved up steadily and closed the year at $49, for a nice 58 percent run. The discount retailer Costco, enjoying strong earnings growth, had dropped from the mid-$60s to about $45, which had made my heart sink, but I had confidence. It was wonderful to see that when Costco reversed, it had a powerful advance of 60 percent, closing the year at $72.

The stocks I mentioned to the public in *Money* magazine were great stocks.

What about some of my technology favorites? Dell experienced a sharp drop, followed by recovery and a big advance. Yahoo, almost $200 per share in early July, had dropped as low as $104. But then it ran to $475 ($236.50 after a two-for-one split) on December 31. Blue chips and other stocks rewarded their owners substantially. It seemed that greed had replaced fear once again, and in a short time.

My funds? The sweat and research were well worth it. *USA Today* had named my fund one of its twenty-five all-star funds. We all compete for the top spot every year. We far outdistanced both the market and the competition, and had an almost 50 percent year at the February fiscal close of the *USA Today* rankings. The definition of the group, by *USA Today*, says: *"All-stars are designed to be long-term, core holdings, but they're supposed to be consistent performers."*

I had already established one of the five best records in the country for mutual funds over a fifteen-year period when I was chosen to be in the all-star group of twenty-five for 1998. The calendar year and all-star fiscal-year results were pretty much the same. The final report and ranking from *USA Today* stated that the average all-star fund was up 11 percent for the twelve months ending February 18, versus 5.9 percent for the average stock mutual fund. Kobrick Capital was up 46.4 percent. We easily took first place, as *USA Today's* 1998 All-Star Fund of the Year.

BUTTERFLIES VERSUS THE SEVEN STEPS

There will always be butterfly events, and we may or may not know about them or about the bellowing or coughing hippos, for that matter. When we do know, the complexity of the global economy suggests that we are not going to understand the ramifications and ripple effects of these things well enough to time the market and sell everything or buy everything as events unfold rapidly, and we get the news.

Many people decide they can time the markets, and do so for emotional reasons or what they feel are fundamental reasons that they have read about. But history shows that timing simply does not work and will cost them a lot of money in most cases. In fact, none of the greatest portfolio managers I know and respect have ever created their long-term records by attempting to time the market.

People like Jack Bogle, the highly sophisticated guru who founded the Vanguard Group mutual funds (and who was part of my training when I began), tells investors over and over again not to try to time the markets, as do some highly regarded books and many top investment professionals. As Bogle points out, even professionally managed mutual funds seem to have more cash near the bottom of a market drop, and no cash at tops.

Know what you own.

So, if you thought you had stocks that could multiply your money by 5X or 10X or perhaps even some really great opportunities that could develop into a Cisco, a Wal-Mart, or others that mean over 100X your money, would you be timing the market? Here are the key things that lead to emotional timing by individuals:

1. Lack of confidence in the stocks you own. Troubling markets test you on this.
2. Investing money you might soon need for other important things.
3. Getting a bit greedy and taking more risk than is appropriate for your financial profile or your personality.
4. Lack of patience—taking a short time horizon instead of several years.
5. A desire to gamble or a belief that you actually can time the market.

Meanwhile, countless individuals and firms sell services to investors that are supposed to really work in timing the market. Some of those are the technicians' tools, or reading the price charts of stocks and the market averages.

TECHNICIANS: THE CHARTS AND TEA LEAVES— WHO IS ON THE CORNER WITH A TIN CUP, ANYWAY?

Wise investors know that using charts is no substitute for the Seven Steps and doing some work. Some professionals know how to work with the tiny number of technicians who actually do good work, and use charts to reinforce good or bad findings on stocks through research. It is an assist, but it is not a method in itself to the really good investors I have known, and woe unto those who fall into the trap of thinking that all of the good work the professionals do is not necessary because the "charts know all." I have heard this a thousand times and do not believe a word of it. During the summer of the Russian devaluation and LTCM that I just described, recall that one of the more expert and famous chartists went on TV and called it a bear market. Those who went with that advice missed out on some huge returns on investment.

One report, after talking about this chartist's call (on Wall Street we call this particular chartist "Mr. Bigchart"), said: "His analysis relies heavily on arcane comparisons of changing trend lines in market averages. Many professional portfolio managers say such so-called technical analysis is fickle and delivers no more insight than a reader of tea leaves."

Finally, I recall what a strategist on Wall Street told me in my early days in the business, after hearing me quote a technician (when I did not know better). His remark to me is what I would repeat to you right now if you told me you were going to use these chart methods for more than supplemental information. He said, "If I hear you using these technicians any more, the next place I am going to find you is on the corner with a tin cup."

I use charts to look at how stocks trend with earnings, since some of the better charts—like those from Securities Research Corp. (SRC)—chart the stock price and also have a chart of earnings reported by quarter. I find this a good fundamental tool, since the comparisons help you to visualize when valuations are getting more or less expensive. But I am not timing the market or using charts to tell me what to invest in. No "tea leaves," and no tin cups. Just buy great stocks and use disciplines, and you will do very, very well.

BUBBLE TROUBLE: THE REAL STORY

Bubbles and bear markets are two separate and distinct things. Investors truly need to understand the differences when using the Seven Steps and BASM. As is the case with any other tool kit, you need to understand which tool to apply when, and not use a hammer when you need a screwdriver. Once you see the straightforward differences, though, you will know what to do, and you will find it simple if you are using the disciplines outlined in this book. One buys in a bear market and sells in a bubble. You have read that I bought in bad markets and made a lot of money. This approach avoids the pitfalls of market timing and uses knowledge of what you own or want to own to maximum advantage. A bubble results from a mania, meaning that either valuations or fundamentals are highly suspect or totally wrong, since emotions and perceptions have overwhelmed what is "real." It is better to run— meaning sell—if you recognize a bubble.

Some people wonder why the NASDAQ remained 3,000 points below its old 2000 high for more than five years. They wonder why they had trouble making back their money that was lost in the 2000 bubble. That is because they think of bubbles like bear markets and do not realize the incredible excesses of bubbles that have to be worked off. But the most important difference is the cause.

Bear markets are caused mainly by fundamental problems. The five main causes of a bear market are listed earlier in the chapter. It runs its course, and so does the poor market. Then things normalize. You buy into a bear market, since you get great prices on stocks; then stocks come back and you make more money. Bubbles are not caused by fundamental events. It is investors themselves who create them. Investors come to believe some things that are not true or not rational and thus create a mania in a stock, in an industry, or in the overall market. If the mania goes on for a time, a bubble is created, and that builds until its inherent instability leads it to break.

One of the interesting differences between bubbles and bear markets is that in a bear market, there are plenty of bulls *and* bears. In a bubble, the few bears are drowned out by the loud and almost universal bullishness. This happened with the Internet, because a mania is normally caused by a belief in something that is supposed to be new and amazing, even though this cannot be proved.

It is natural to like momentum and money, but if investors have no disciplines and no sense of bubbles, then they are headed not for the big money, but for quite the opposite.

With bear markets, one wants to use buy and sell disciplines and buy when prices and fundamentals would dictate that. This is the Seven Steps.

There are market bubbles once in a great while, perhaps once in a lifetime, but individual stock bubbles are far more common. All bubbles have some similarities that concern how perceptions, emotions, and a lack of accurate information combine to set an investor trap.

On March 6, 2000, Alan Greeenspan's seventy-fourth birthday, I was privileged to be in a group that met with Greenspan, Summers, Arthur Levitt—the chairman of the U.S. Securities and Exchange Commission

(SEC)—Lou Gerstner, and a number of other executives who ran Internet and communications companies that were integral to the new economy. Bernie Ebbers, chairman of WorldCom, was one of them. It was sort of a gathering of eagles to talk about what the new economy really meant and where we were going. I was excited that I had an invitation and looked forward to what many of them had to say.

Levitt spoke about the regulatory climate and the needs of individual investors. While he was disturbed that investors were so excited about the new economy that they were totally disregarding risk, he never said anything to derail our concept that the new economy was here to stay. Larry Summers and Alan Greenspan and many of the senior executives actually waxed poetic about the productivity gains, the technologies, the confluence of our capital markets and great new technological advances, and the fact that it meant great things for our future.

Four days after that March 6, 2000, gathering, on March 10, the bubble burst and the game was over. All had changed.

On the other hand, I did not then, nor do I now, blame Greenspan, or Summers, or Gerstner, or even the CEOs of many of the Internet companies.

It all seemed very real at the time, and the senior people in our government were getting their information from the sources that had proved the most valuable and trustworthy in the past for all of us: real economic data generated by consumers and corporations, as well as the very best information that the executives running those corporations could give them. *We all had seen the same things, and we all had believed.*

> Trying to understand is like straining through muddy water.
> Be still and allow the mud to settle.
>
> Lao-tzu

The lessons from this recent bubble are important for three reasons. First, there is the unlikely possibility that we may encounter another stock market bubble in our investing lifetime. One per lifetime seems the "rule," but we cannot rule out anything completely. Second, we do have small bubbles in the market (smaller than in 1929 and 2000 is how I define this myself) periodically. These include the one caused by a mania in blue chips (called the "Nifty Fifty") from the late 1960s into early 1973, a moderate technology stock bubble in 1983, and the overvaluation in the market before the 1987 stock market "crash." Third and most important, bubbles occur in *individual stocks* fairly frequently.

We have all heard the term *bubble* and also the term *mania* used over the past few years very, very frequently—when people have talked about possible bubbles in real estate or housing, in financial instruments in foreign countries, and at times even in the Chinese economy, which has had some startling growth numbers that are far above anything seen before.

Bubbles, like those from bubble gum or soap, come in all different sizes, but they all have one thing in common with each other, including the gum and the soap bubbles: they are going to burst. *They are unsustainable because they are not built on enough real substance to support themselves. Thus, many bubbles develop from a mania. A mania is simply something that is more emotional than tangible or rational, so it can be thought of as irrationality.*

The irrationality that leads to the inflating in price beyond what complete knowledge and good analysis would suggest can be the result of one thing or of two or more things in combination. The irrationality itself is not very easy to see at the beginning, since there would be no bubble if it were apparent. The causes start with beliefs that are exciting, but the crowd does not know what it does not know. *Knowledge is incomplete or just wrong.*

When something appears that is new, and seems to have unlimited potential and some mystery about it, that, to me, is "the big one." This has happened many times in history, as when electricity first came to the household; or with the advent of canals, railroads, and radio in the 1920s; and so forth. It can even be Krispy Kreme Doughnuts—not all that mysterious or technological, but driven by perceptions, desires, and emotions. Perceptions, not analysis, drove this stock to ridiculous levels and then that bubble popped.

Bubble lessons never go out of style, and not only are going to help you with big bubbles, or individual stock bubbles, but will focus you on which information is real and what is perception in almost all of your investing. Learn the lessons well.

With bubbles, there is an element of mystery. To cope with that, start with the first of the Seven Steps, knowledge, and combine that with BASM, since in a bubble it is likely that the beliefs of the crowd cannot be supported by real knowledge. With a well-defined BASM, this can be clearly understood.

A considerable number of people (but not all) in the investment community regarded a wide range of technology, communications, and Internet stocks as having almost unlimited demand for their products and unlimited potential—all of which assumptions proved to be incorrect. Yet the entire crowd thought in this way about many Internet companies because of incorrect and incomplete information. Emotions temporarily filled that void. Behind it was what one of the Seven Steps helps you control: emotion.

The other big factor in irrational behavior comes when the crowd is deliberately fooled, so some bubbles are either accompanied by or built upon fraud or swindles. This is not how I see the 2000 Internet bubble, even though the atmosphere of greed it created did bring out the worst in a number of executives who engaged in what proved to be criminal behavior, either outright stealing from their companies (as executives of Tyco International and Adelphia Communications did), or engaging in accounting and financial fraud (which is what Bernie Ebbers, WorldCom's chairman was convicted of in March 2005.)

Personally, I think there were three bubbles that burst in 2000, and they were all related to one another. The first was the most obvious: the stock market bubble, which had component bubbles in Internet, telecommunications, and various technology stocks. The excitement over those took almost all other stocks into overvaluation.

The second was the bubble in capital spending by corporations in the great telecommunications build-out that was going to accommodate all the new traffic, create broadband access for most businesses and consumers, and handle all the new uses of the Internet. The same beliefs that caused stocks to soar were also driving this corporate capital spending, since the new information about the potential of all sorts of technologies appeared to offer great opportunities. Ultimately, the Internet has proved to be a transforming force (just as, say, the railroads were in the nineteenth century here and in Europe) and is changing business and life for many people.

Thus not everything that created the mania was false, and this fact just compounded the confusion.

The third bubble was the overall U.S. economy, which reached peak growth rates that were more than twice the long-term average real growth. The other two bubbles caused that to happen, so when stocks came down, lower stock values and fear caused consumers and corporations to spend less. The biggest effect on the economy was the loss of the part of corporate spending that had been directed into telecommunications, since that was an incredibly large part of the overall picture.

DOES HISTORY GUIDE US?

Bubbles have appeared for millennia, actually. A lot of speculation occurred in the Roman economy, which included money lending and some other aspects of capitalism. One of the most famous manias and bubbles of all time was the tulip mania in Holland in the early 1630s. People believed that ordinary tulip bulbs, which collectors prized, had greater and greater value. A virus randomly made bulbs of one strain change and become more valuable, introducing an unknown into the game with a gambling or speculative element. Bulbs went up in price as people simply bid them up, and one bulb could be a lot more valuable than an expensive town house. Naturally, there came a point when the market got a bit soft, and rumors went around that there were no more buyers, and so the market crashed.

Call this crazy, if you will, but it is a great lesson in how the combination of human emotions and misinformation can mislead and fool even sophisticated people, and create powerful forces.

There were manias surrounding the building of the railroads and canals in both England and the United States, since amazing leaps in productivity and economic advantages flowed from these developments.

The reality was there and lasted for a long time—twenty years in England, actually—but people just got too emotional, and their emotions led them to believe that this economic expansion would last forever. Crashes were always the way these mania-driven phenomena ended. In the United Kingdom, the famous railway mania led to the British financial crisis of 1847. October 17, 1897, was known in London as the week of terror.

Interestingly, the canals and railroads in England created a genuine and huge economic expansion, which in turn created a great deal of wealth before the situation slipped into mania territory. Thus when stocks started to come down in price, the crowd, many of whom were very sophisticated, truly believed it was only a temporary pullback in an expansion that would go on indefinitely. Most of those who got rich on the *reality* of the expansion were so caught up in the mania that they could not distinguish reality from wishful thinking, so they eventually lost all or most of their wealth.

A historical perspective is an excellent place for everyone to start. It is not the only tool, but it is a beginning. History is some help if one stands back and looks at things from the standpoint of fundamentals. But if we have misinformation, or are misled by fraud or lies, then history can be outweighed and we need to add other tools to the historical perspective.

Looking at our own economy in the 1990s, we were seeing a terrific decade of expansion, and that in itself built a great deal of confidence. The general feeling was that the elimination of federal budget deficits, coupled with higher productivity and less personal and corporate debt, could generate many more years of growth. Economists, including those in the U.S. government, were very optimistic.

COMPUTERS, BIOTECHNOLOGY, INTERNET

Cisco was actually selling its routers and switches over the Internet to corporate customers well before it went public in 1990. The Internet was alive and well, but hardly the force it is today—there were no real uses developed for the public yet. Along came Netscape with its browser in 1995, and its public offering ushered in a new mentality. Investors, investment bankers, and venture capitalists all recognized the reality of what a real browser for everyone could mean. By giving people a tool that enabled them to use the Internet in an easy, practical way, the Internet became accessible and used in a seemingly endless number of ways by endless millions of people.

Various revolutions had already occurred in our economy, society, and stock markets in the recent past, so public and professional investors alike were very receptive to tremendous and new moneymaking ideas. One idea that really had stood out, of course, was the personal computer, which had spawned hardware and software revolutions far beyond even what optimists had envisioned at the beginning. The same thing had happened with biotechnology, particularly in the stock market, where many biotech issues far surpassed expectations. Such developments provided the conditions for "the perfect storm."

Given the enthusiasm stirred up by developments in biotechnology and computers, the amazing performance of companies like Microsoft and Dell, and countless more technology success stories, the time was ripe for a company to come up with something that looked like magic. But it was real. The product enabled anyone to go anywhere on the Internet to find information. It was a compass, a navigator, and more.

When Netscape went public, it had only a couple of quarters of operating experience and no profits, yet the stock not only soared; it paved the way for many others to follow. Some people remembered that Cisco had grown at 60 percent per quarter in its early days, with no sales force, by selling over the Internet. Now masses of people were about to become Internet users.

I met with all the Internet companies that went public—industry leaders like Netscape, then Yahoo!, theglobe.com, Amazon, eBay, CMGI, and Lycos, as well as smaller companies like drkoop.com, Webvan, and, of course, Martha Stewart's newly expanded operation. There were a lot of copycat companies, but there seemed to be room for all of these offerings to reach astronomical heights. I met with most of the interesting companies and not only did I get to know them, but by meeting with so many, I came to understand what the Internet might become. I absorbed and pondered a huge amount of information on technologies, business ideas, and new market opportunities that came from all of the top management.

I recall that Joy Covey, the first chief financial officer of Amazon.com, who had known me from an earlier tech company she was with, kindly told Amazon's founder, Jeff Bezos, as they came up in the elevator to meet with me in my office, that he was about to have his best meeting in Boston. Whether or not that was the case, I was pleased that people felt I had good techniques in meetings with management, and as a result, Jeff, Joy, and I had a really great meeting in which I learned a tremendous amount. I was also very impressed. Each time I met with Jeff over the years, I was impressed. Some years later, as I sat under a tree with him in Sun Valley, Idaho, we discussed whether or not his business plan, as it was then structured, was going to work. He had an open mind as well as conviction—a good combination.

Each company envisioned new markets opening up, with huge growth and almost unlimited potential. The business models had not been tested by time, so we could not know if any of these companies was going to move from a good investment to a potentially great company. Today we know that some of the companies became *great* companies, such as eBay, Yahoo!, and Amazon.

HOW WE ALWAYS INVESTED

I knew from the preceding decades the best way to invest in new companies. My experience curve included the early days of biotechnology, a sector in which I had done exceptionally well. The methods were the same, actually, regardless of whether I was considering a technology company such as Compaq, Sun, Microsoft, Dell, and others—we started with these on their public offerings, and invested successfully over time—or a retailer, restaurant, or media company. The more I learned, the more I used BASM for my analysis. You can, as I did, apply BASM to avoid investing in just a glamorous new concept or product. Instead you learn to fit concepts, ideas and products into your overall understanding of the business, and how it will succeed.

Most of the expert and experienced portfolio managers I knew, the ones with good records, understood that the best way to invest was to buy a little of each company of interest, and participate in the market performance to be competitive and fulfill our fund shareholders' or clients' mandates, as long as these new companies satisfied our criteria in areas like management, business model, vision, and strategy. Then we carefully watched how these companies performed over time, and how they developed and met new challenges either from competition or from changes in customers' needs.

Things moved, it seemed, at the speed of light. Stocks soared, and we all know today that many of these small companies came to be worth billions of dollars in the marketplace (market cap) before it was clear how everything would work out in the end markets for Internet companies. Many stocks reached prices of $100, $200, or even $300 (Amazon went to $400 on the famous or infamous recommendation of analyst Henry Blodgett). However, most of them ultimately crashed down to earth and either the company went bankrupt or the stock was traded at very low prices—in some instances for only cents per share, not dollars. Pretty amazing in magnitude, but also in how all of this cycled faster than at any time in financial history.

Some of the more value-oriented investors who normally did not do well on high-growth and technology stocks had serious reservations about the fast pace of everything, the seemingly high valuations, and the high expectations for the so-called new-economy stocks.

I say "seemingly" high valuations, since those of us who had successfully invested in companies with no earnings at their beginning had known for decades that valuations of new companies depend on what they become in future years, not in the early years when they are not making money.

One makes estimates and then makes adjustments for the uncertainty or risk, and that is what we all did in my firm. So, when Amgen, Genzyme, and others went public, we made enormous gains on those stocks, and for solid reasons. Today most of the good biotechnology companies (seen by many when they went public as long shots) are established, successful companies that some see as blue chips. Amgen became not only the most successful biotechnology outfit, but an excellent performer in comparison with companies in any industry. Amgen finished 2004 with revenues of $10.4 billion and earnings of $3.148 billion.

Among the Internet companies, eBay finished 2004 with revenues of $3.27 billion and earnings of $778.2 million. Yahoo! finished 2004 with revenues of $3.57 billion and earnings of $839.5 million.

Two points of note: First, the successful Internet companies generated big revenues and profits faster than biotechnology and probably just about anything else that came before, while the losers went bankrupt—but that is what happened in every other new industry in the past. Yahoo!, eBay, and some others are still growing revenues at 50 to 60 percent annual rates, and have been growing a bit faster recently in profits.

Second, these two companies are great examples of organizations that spell out information in clear detail in their financial releases, so you can see exactly how it is all going. Their mailings and Web sites are excellent.

So, if the Internet works so well, what happened?

There was a lot of misinformation going around, and things moved so fast in the stock market, as well as in the competitive scramble between telecom and Internet companies, that by the time the real truth started to come out, it was already over. The stocks, the economy, and the telecom boom had run out of steam.

Company managers made many solid presentations that Wall Street and institutional investors accepted as truth, and the investment community began to see this Internet-driven tech boom as something akin to the situation that prevailed in biotechnology, or even electricity or railroads. The company managers were almost all honest and believed what they were telling Wall Street. They also were to become victims of their misinformation and then their own, as well as some strange, economics.

Many well-respected technology gurus said wonderful things about the future. Even Bill Gates had stated in his 1996 book, *The Road Ahead,* that the impact of the Internet and other new technologies on society could equal that of the printing press.

Now, on the one hand, Bill Gates was not forecasting anything that had to do with the stock market; he was simply thinking about the overall future, and what he wrote may become true. He did not say how long it would take, and I am sure he did not expect the rise of a mania. I had learned in my very first meeting with Gates, when he brought Microsoft public, that he was an extraordinarily prescient and creative thinker, and what he said was something to seriously think about. At this time, the public saw Gates largely as a world-class tech guru, and many people interpreted his remarks in the most optimistic way.

Then in 2000 along came Super Bowl XXXIV, which later became known as the "Bubble Bowl" because a lot of the advertisers were dotcoms, many of which later went into bankruptcy. Pets.com spent *$2.6 million* on its commercial, and there were some other names that existed for only a short time, such as Computer.com, LifeMinder.com, Epidemic.com, and OurBeginning.com. (I never owned a share of any of these or any other companies that I could not figure out or whose managers I had not met with.) This lavish expenditure of ad money by these companies, when they were (briefly) at their peak, took place just two months before the beginning of the end. But it just fueled the mania.

THE EMPEROR'S NEW CLOTHES: MISINFORMATION AND THE "BIG LIE"

In addition to hype and ads and media cheerleading, three factors worked separately, as well as in concert, to create the bubble.

First, the Big Lie

WorldCom told customers, prospects, and the world that Internet traffic was doubling every one hundred days. Nothing of this magnitude had ever been seen before in any business or tech sector. WorldCom was a great growth company in both investors' and customers' minds, and had credibility. If a company were to double every one hundred days, it would be 8X its present size in a little more than two years—a nearly astronomical growth rate. This kind of traffic meant that even the most optimistic expectations were being exceeded. Given this, all an Internet company had to do to succeed was grab a small share of a market this big and grow this fast.

The public was told about this fantastic rise in traffic not only by WorldCom, but by the United States Department of Commerce, so it *had* to be true. The Commerce Department wrote a report which was very much relied on and which stated that Internet traffic was doubling every one hundred days. It gave the U.S. government's "seal of validity" to the forecast for growth and the measure of fundamental business strength.

But the Commerce Department had interviewed WorldCom, used its figure, and went no farther! It wasn't until after the bubble burst that this became known—these numbers had been made up out of thin air.

But in the manic atmosphere of those days, the "one hundred days" report spurred tremendous activity by investment bankers who saw great opportunities for virtually every new company. Countless start-ups emerged, were brought to market, and sold stock to the public without having created solid business plans. They found out later, as did we, that although it is fine to move fast and get that first-mover advantage, it means nothing if your business plan is not solid.

Why did WorldCom do it? The company felt that this would impress prospects and show them who was king. Then WorldCom would take the biggest market share. This was part of a scheme to become number one, no matter what it took. It not only made Internet companies misjudge the size of the future markets, expand too rapidly, and disseminate forecasts and plans that were based on incorrect information; it also influenced the telecom companies. They weren't prepared to let WorldCom take the lead, so the majors decided to expand, telling investors they were going to build out a huge network of broadband-capacity fiber optics and offer the best service to customers.

Internet companies also overspent and expanded as fast as they could, presented their plans to analysts—plans based on this "knowledge"—and made the situation even more frantic.

They all believed it. We all believed it.

Maybe this would have been enough, but there were two other factors that inflated the bubble.

Normally reliable information from traditionally reliable sources (like the Commerce Department), combined with what the corporations were telling both the government and the public, turned out to be horrendously misleading. The Wall Street analysts provided the rest of the misleading information. All of these sources were honest, but they were victims of misinformation, victims who in turn passed on misinformation. Neither

Treasury Secretary Larry Summers nor Federal Reserve Board Chairman Alan Greenspan was immune to this information infection. Summers and Greenspan were, like the vast majority of executives in the private sector, doing their jobs well and acting in good faith. Virtually everyone believed these marvelous stories. It is what the nineteenth-century philosopher William James called the "will to believe." People simply want to believe good news.

Second, a "Feeding Frenzy of Telecom Spending"

After it was all over, and the truth was known, Larry Summers explained to me at lunch what I call factor number two. It was, he said, an incredible "feeding frenzy of telecom spending."

Give Larry Summers truth and information, and he can figure things out better than just about anybody else. Whenever I talk to him about economics or business, I am reminded of what a great a mind he has, and how good a teacher he is. After the bubble burst, Larry was telling three of us at a lunch in New York how and why it had happened. He wanted to explain how the spending of telecom companies grew to be far in excess of what was needed (in large measure to create network capacity that was far greater than needed). He looked around the table and said, "Let's imagine that we all want this dollar and are going to start the bidding at five cents." We bid, and the bidding rose slowly to about seventy cents.

Larry continued, "The bidding represents the spending of the telecom companies to do their build-out and have available capacity for the future, as well as provide enough to impress customers. Each telecom company wants customers to have enough confidence in its capital spending and overall capacity now and in the future to 'lock-in' with it."

"Now, at some point as the bidding goes higher and higher, it dawns on the telecoms that whatever they sink into this bidding war is money they will never get back if they lose. So they conclude that they just cannot lose and will have to spend whatever it takes." Larry added. Thus the spending continues to escalate.

Ultimately, the overspending is so huge that they all lose. One more incident in which so-called sophisticated businesspeople get into exactly the same economic circumstances as a chicken farmer, who almost always overproduces at the end of a cycle when high prices induce him to do so.

Third, the Baseball Cap and the Backhoe

In a group meeting with Andy Grove, chairman of Intel, we learned about the third factor. Andy said that the telecom companies bought a lot of the components we all knew about to build their networks. These included endless miles of fiber-optic cable from Corning, lots of switches and routers from Cisco, and pump lasers from JDS Uniphase. The lasers split light into various wavelengths and sent it across the fiber optics. There were other technology products involved, and each of these companies had its own suppliers, of course. Cisco, for example, bought lots of specialized semiconductors from PMC-Sierra, Applied Microcircuits, and others.

But when the telecom companies figured out the economics of the whole build-out process, they saw that all of these technology purchases were only—we have to approximate here—maybe 25 percent of the entire build-out. The other 75 percent was the hugely expensive process of digging the trenches for the cables. With labor scarce at this time, it was actually guys wearing baseball caps and operating backhoes that cost so much.

Thus when a company dug a trench, it decided it never wanted to dig another one, so it laid in maybe ten or twelve times (I am approximating) more cable than was necessary. What was needed now was referred to as "lit up," and what was there for "someday" was called "dark fiber." That is how we got so much fiber-optic cable put in the ground that it could be stretched from the earth to the moon and back sixteen times or so—far, far more than the market needed.

Andy, in my opinion, was implying that for all the analysts to miss this economic reality and not understand how much bigger the telecom build-out was relative to what it should have been was a pretty dismal testimony to the quality of their work. All of the stock recommendations coming from Wall Street were based on figures that were very much inflated.

. . .

Those three factors all reinforced one another and created such an enormous market opportunity in investors' minds that stocks soared. If the numbers had been real, perhaps we would not have seen a mania.

Well, they were *not* real, and it *was* a mania.

When stocks started to come down in March 2000, at first this was universally considered a normal correction in a very strong market. Major publications were telling people that it looked like a great opportunity to buy Cisco and other glamour stocks as prices fell. Me? I stuck with my Seven Steps and I didn't try to time the market. As we saw earlier in this chapter, timing simply doesn't work.

When this technology and Internet market was climbing high before the 2000 crash, I had felt that Cisco and other big companies were just too expensive and could not keep up their blistering growth rates, so good little companies would be better to own for the future. Thus I sold Cisco before the top, and sold others and put the money into smaller companies to capitalize on their opportunities for the future. But, despite my sticking with my buy and sell disciplines, I took a beating along with everyone else. When the market collapsed, it took everything, and along with all the other individuals and professionals, I lost money in almost every stock.

In more than three decades, this was the only time that I lost money in a bad market that was not soon made up again, or more than made up in recovering markets. Even though virtually all high-growth investors lost, I focused on how to do things better. There are some lessons.

LESSONS FROM THE BUBBLE OF 2000
Lesson Number One

Understanding some things about past bubbles helps us to get a feel for the mentality of a mania, which is what leads to a bubble. Yet each bubble is different. There is no perfect insurance, then. One has to temper greed with disciplines and knowledge, part of the Seven Steps, and we need to know as much as possible about what we own. I think this is best done through the holistic approach, or business models, assumptions, strategy, and management: BASM.

I can ask myself over and over again whether I lost money in the first part of the bursting of this bubble *in spite of* all I knew about my companies, or *because* of it. Management had convinced me that things would work out. But none of us knew about the incredible misinformation we were being fed.

There is no single answer or easy answer. I did not own "bad" companies. I would not buy the little start-ups that seemed to have low scores for BASM.

Well, here is one lesson for me and for all of us.

As I rushed around from one meeting with management to another, and then another, trying to determine if things were as management had originally told me, I was not looking at other investors. A huge proportion of the investors in the general public did not practice investment disciplines and did not understand what they owned. They had just bought hot stocks because of all the press cheerleading from the very beginning, right through the Super Bowl ads. Then they read more articles that assured them that this was a buying opportunity, even as Cisco and other stocks declined. They believed what they read and bought the hot stocks. Unfortunately, a lot of professional investors did the same thing—not all pros, but enough to matter. Even if they had no deep knowledge of technologies, they wanted the extra performance. Had I been as aware of this as I should have been, I would have had more knowledge about what was pushing up stock prices. It might well have convinced me that mania was at work, and that I should sell a lot of stocks. I do know how manias end.

I will always find out the state of investors' knowledge in future bull markets, and I urge you to do the same. If we get another long, great bull market with very high valuations built on great expectations, we need to know that it is built on knowledge. We should know if there are elements of mania.

Investors who have little or no knowledge of what their money is going into warn us of possible manias when those investors become a majority.

Lesson Number Two

Do not let this recent experience (or advice from journalists and "technicians") motivate you to try to invest by timing the market, forecasting the short-term direction and then buying or selling with a great deal of your money. When even experts tell you that you will lose the greatest opportunities, and you follow their advice, you will also lose a lot of money sooner or later.

The other side of the coin is that by avoiding market timing, one can exercise knowledge and disciplines, and buy things that go down, as I did in many, many markets to make tremendous gains.

> **He burned his tongue on the soup, and now he is afraid of the yogurt.**
>
> —OLD TURKISH PROVERB

Lesson Number Three

I do know that one can still buy in downturns, and the fact that the pace of the developing Internet did not allow us to fully understand and differentiate between business models is no reason to be afraid and give up all future opportunities.

The key is that buying should be done stock by stock. I truly believe that the chances that the misinformation and other elements which combined to form the perfect storm could happen again are so unlikely that one should not avoid doing research and buying in areas of maximum opportunity.

Since knowledge is the antidote to fear, if you are buying new public offerings or other stocks with limited track records, it will be knowledge, not market timing and emotions, that generates the big money for you. This is what I had done successfully with Home Depot, Cisco, Microsoft, and so many other stocks.

Most often, people invest in new public offerings for some quick money, and run for the hills when things get a bit shaky. That happened with many of the early investors in Dell, Microsoft, Home Depot, Cisco, and countless others. That is often how people who invest with far more emotion than knowledge lose out on the stocks that would have made them 100X or 200X their money, and even more. Remember to let yourself be guided by the Seven Steps, particularly patience.

Dell came public at $8.50 in 1988. I was an investor then, and added shares on some of the pullbacks along the way. When it dropped to about $5 roughly 18 months later, emotions and selling ran pretty high. Well, those who bought and held from that price level, seven stock splits and sixteen years later closed 2004 with 768X their money.

Amgen came public in 1983, and I bought it. It was the dawn of biotechnology investing for many of us. Amgen showed the way. Nothing was any more certain in those days than the Internet, and most things were less so, actually. Amgen stock had dipped to less than a dollar (split-adjusted) in 1984, with doubters selling, and then went up 100X in seven years. Later on, it went up another sixfold. This was the kind of mentality (both bulls and bears) and performance that characterized the early Internet a dozen years later, but biotechnology was not a mania, and many of the companies, even those at an "early stage," had developed their businesses and business models much more than the crowd of Internet companies did in the late 1990s. So with biotech, there were some huge payoffs and no crashes. Biomet, a medical device company, was 35¢ adjusted in late 1984 and went up 95X in seven years; and Genzyme, another biotech company, went up by 9X in only three years, and then another 10X in the 1990s.

There are plenty more examples, but you get the point—aggressive investors saw good companies with something new and valuable create astronomic gains in short periods of time at various points in modern history. The emergence of the personal computer and semiconductors and software provides a long list of more examples. I was also there for the emergence of Informix, the database management software company that went from $2.75 adjusted to $36 in only a year and a half.

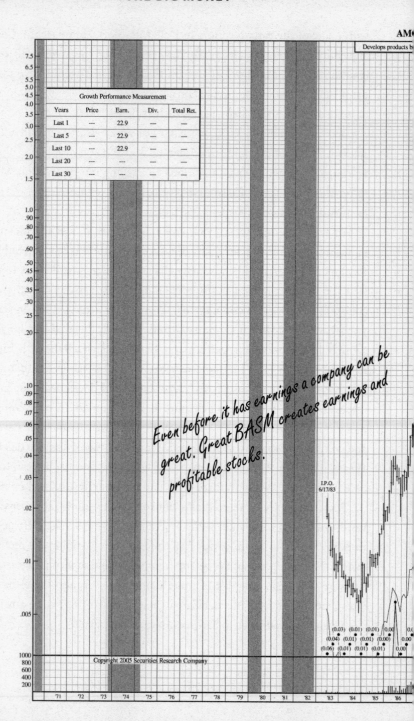

AM

Develops products b

	Growth Performance Measurement			
Years	Price	Earn.	Div.	Total Ret.
Last 1	---	22.9	---	---
Last 5	---	22.9	---	---
Last 10	---	22.9	---	---
Last 20	---	---	---	---
Last 30	---	---	---	---

Even before it has earnings a company can be great. Great BASM creates earnings and profitable stocks.

I.P.O.
6/17/83

(0.03) (0.01) (0.01) 0.00   0.0
(0.04) (0.01) (0.01) 0.00   0.00
(0.06) (0.01) (0.01) (0.01)   0.00

the doughnut maker took the glow off the shortage story, as it expanded from a few locations to many locations across the country in a few months.

Common sense was as good as (or better than) being a restaurant analyst on this one. You could see that it was a mania, since most people had no idea how the actual business model looked, or what the strategy was, or how the market would unfold. Another commonsense point is that when companies really mess up, as this one did, you always have some danger of fraud, because management may try to make the earnings look good through fancy accounting and other deceptive measures. In April 2005, the company kicked out the existing management, hired a "turnaround" CEO to run the company, and was responding to an SEC investigation of possible accounting fraud.

Be aware of stock manias; they can cost you just like a market mania. This brings me, one more time, back to Cisco, a kind of poster child for the big Internet expansion and subsequent decline. Cisco was selling all the routers and switches for the Internet build-out. I sold Cisco when valuations for the big companies were too high, feeling that I should move money into smaller companies because the ultimate market would give them many more years of open-ended expansion. This concept proved to make some sense on the sale—but obviously the little companies ran into trouble anyway.

Later on I took pencil and paper and figured out how big Cisco would get if it kept growing at its very peak growth rate, achieved in spring 2000. My arithmetic told me that continuing at the same growth rate, Cisco would become as large as the entire United States economy circa 2000 in only nine years! Something would have stopped the growth sooner or later.

An investor should watch not only for unreasonable conditions that spell mania, but also for things that make no common sense. Always look at how big a company is relative to its customers, never mind the whole country. When a company needs more customers than are actually available to make it grow more, it is time to sell. These are all back-of-the-envelope calculations coupled with common sense.

CHAPTER EIGHT

TECH INVESTING

From Microsoft and Dell to eBay and Google

There is nothing more difficult to take in hand, more perilous
to conduct, or more uncertain in its success than to take the
lead in the introduction of a new order of things.
—MACHIAVELLI, 1469–1527

He knew everything there was to know and had all the answers. He could
see around corners. He could see into the future, and even into the black-
ness of the vast unknown. Things that were to dramatically shape and affect our lives were in his power to create and to mold as he wanted them.

He was a wizard—and maybe even had the powers of the legendary
Merlin. We did not know. All that we did know was that the brokers and
others who talked about him spoke in grandiose and amazing terms. In
hushed voices, they would say, "He is coming. It is really him, and he is going to amaze you."

That may be an exaggeration, but this was the impression that many
people originally had when Wall Street firms brought Bill Gates and Microsoft to us at the time of the company's initial public offering. As that day
approached, in the waning days of winter 1986, the excitement was building. By this point, both personal computers and Microsoft were central to
the tech world. The personal-computer industry was on every investor's
mind—and in his or her portfolio. I had already profited nicely in this area,

241

but I still thought that the best days were yet to come. That, of course, turned out to be very true, and things would be much better than my own optimistic projections or those of many others.

> There is never a reliable map for unexplored territory, but we can learn important lessons from the creation and evolution of the $120 billion personal-computer industry.
> —BILL GATES IN 1995

That quotation from Bill Gates is very true. It is the reason why investors should understand how Microsoft and Dell came along, well behind those that originally dominated their respective industries, and won the game.

Microsoft and Dell not only came from behind to dominate their industries, but became two of the greatest companies and greatest stocks in history. Yet even today, many who want to make a lot of money in tech stocks are unclear about how this all happened, and how they should look for the next Bill Gates or Michael Dell.

Management did it for Microsoft and Dell, and did it for all the greatest technology companies that I know.

The winning technologies, and more important, the winning strategy and business models, are created and executed by great management. Then they are also modified or evolved to meet changing technology or competitive challenges by those same great leaders. Now, for the most part, the elements of the business model are created to make the strategy work, and the strategy in many cases is designed the way Gates designed his: around goals based on the management's critical assumptions about how to win.

How do technologies fit into this winning recipe, and what kinds of assumptions drive the whole process? Microsoft, Dell, and eBay are among the greatest examples. By contrast, some of the failed Internet companies, although often having good technology, are models for the opposite of Bill Gates's model for success—I call some of those the "un-Microsoft." We will start with Bill Gates and his assumptions.

When Bill Gates quit college at Harvard University, it was because he had a burning desire to get into the brand-new computer industry before it was too late. He foresaw that being first or at least early was critical. Perhaps the most important reason in Gates's mind was that the customers for computers would want software to carry out powerful functions for them, but they would want software built around standards. That meant with uniformity and continuity, so a businessperson or consumer would not learn something only to have a better technology come along—perhaps from a different company—and require an entirely new learning process. Gates realized this would be a giant handicap that could deter the blossoming and growth of the industry, and it had to be avoided by the early birds, who would establish dominance and standards. He desperately wanted to be the early bird.

The big assumption that drove it all was the assumption that customers would have a critical need for standards, and they would stay with one company's products cycle after cycle if those products met their needs and were competitive in new technologies. Assumption number two was that the standards would be set by those early companies—perhaps only one company. Therefore those standards had to dominate early.

Assumption number three was that the technology had to be either the best, at the very beginning, or close to the best, and customers had to believe this. Assumption number four was built on the knowledge that it is very tough for any one company to always have the best technology, product after product, year after year. So management assumed that once a company came to dominate the industry by becoming the standard, each new product only had to be *competitive*. It did not have to be the absolute best, for customers were not going to walk away from the standards they wanted. Yes, the organization would strive to be the best at all times, but a great strategy was critical to maintaining leadership.

Setting standards and achieving early domination flowed from those assumptions as the core company strategy was formulated at the beginning, in the mid- to late 1970s, long before Microsoft had products in the market and was ready to go public.

We understood in that very first meeting with Gates in 1986 that he had not simply been pursuing the computer market with good technology. Had he done that, he would have been prominent in the high-tech race and maybe even had the best products for a while. But he would not have had a strategy that locked in customers, created repeatability in product cycles and results, and made Microsoft the long-distance runner it became. This is in stark contrast to the vast majority of high-tech companies that are hot for a few years, then give way to others. The best of those companies may multiply their investors' money 3X, 5X, or more, but they are not the big-money stocks, since they do not have repeatability for the long run.

It was clear from what I read and what I heard that day that the operating systems of computers like DOS (and later Windows—embedded in the computer so that the computer can understand and run applications programs) were the first standard. Then came the individual applications programs (like spreadsheets and word processing). They would all coordinate with that standard operating system, so that customers would never have to fear being forced to hop around among vendors to get what they wanted.

The strategy, then, was to capture as much market share as early as possible, no matter what. Profits were not the highest priority in this original strategy, which was different from that of most other companies. Market share and market dominance were the goals and strategy, and the business model was built to accomplish this.

Thus, management—Bill Gates and other key people, such as his friend and company cofounder, Paul Allen—developed tools for computer programmers at the beginning, so that they would be accepted by those who wrote software for the industry. This was a way of pursuing a goal of controlling as much intellectual property as possible. Next Microsoft knew that to have a standard operating system from which it could write and sell standard applications to do word processing and more, it would have to be accepted by the big computer manufacturers. The biggest was IBM, which totally dominated the industry in the early phase of PCs' going mainstream.

At the very beginning, there were some exciting early success stories of small PC companies, and they had excellent technology. Yet none of them actually had good enough business models and strategies to fend off the giant IBM when "Big Blue" decided to enter the PC market in a big way. Once again, not technology but management—and more completely, BASM—was to determine who won and who lost. Technology had to be developed and managed in a way that supported a winning strategy. Technology is critical, but not as critical as BASM, which defines who will become the real winners.

Once you understand how BASM within a company "aims" and develops technologies, and then use the Seven Steps to apply investment disciplines to manage greed, fear, and so on, you become a successful tech investor.

Bill Gates knew that he must capture IBM. That fit with the entire strategy built on those first two assumptions. He made a secret, exclusive deal with IBM to develop an operating system for its PC. Then, when he was not ready early enough with a finished operating system, he took his knowledge of the technologies developed so far by Microsoft and others he had studied, and went across the bay in Seattle to a little garage shop—one of countless tiny groups developing software for the new, exciting PC industry. Gates bought what this shop had called QDOS, for Quick and Dirty Operating System—for a mere $50,000 for the software.

Next, Gates licensed, rather than sold, this operating system to IBM, dropping the Q and calling it DOS, for Disc Operating System. IBM had its own operating system, but it sold for a hefty price, so Gates decided to price his at only $40, a fraction of the price of the IBM system. This was another great move, based on his original assumption that early dominance was more important than early profits. He accomplished dominance with the combination of the IBM deal and the low price, and the profits came later. His strategy and business plan never strayed from the ultimate goal of great profits and growth, but he knew that if he went into a technology-only race, it was very uncertain how many competitors would eventually look alike to the corporate and consumer markets, and that would not have been the ultimate winning strategy.

Some people debate what might have happened if the garage shop had sold DOS to IBM instead of Microsoft. Would history have been different? I believe that it is all about management (and BASM), and that Bill Gates and his vision and assumptions would have simply found another route to winning.

Could Bill Gates really see around corners and see the future? Once you have some key assumptions about how things can be in the future, and what customers will truly want and need—since it is easier and even more important to understand customers' behavior than to know or guess future technologies—the idea is to create products that make this future happen. Then it looks as if you foresaw it! Bill Gates's assumptions were powerful, and he built everything on them. Great software development came from Microsoft, but it was not substituted for great BASM; it was *driven by* BASM. It is management that creates great technologies, repeatability, and a winning strategy virtually every time.

Once again, reading is important. Much was written about computers and software in general, and Bill Gates in particular. Even if I had never met with Bill Gates, reading about him as a focused, competitive person; reading about Microsoft; and looking at the original prospectus and later the company's annual reports would have made it plain that the elements of success were there. Just as BASM helps management create the future and succeed, BASM helps investors predict the future. It is a much more powerful tool than basing predictions on great quarterly-earnings reports, which hot technology companies have for a time. But some of these companies stay around, while most do not.

The business model of Microsoft was to set standards and combine them with aggressive pricing for an early market-share lead, knowing that the volume would come. This would create huge incremental profitability, since all the costs were in software development rather than at the manufacturing end.

Think about the brilliance of the razor-and-blades business model pioneered by Gillette in its early days: sell razors cheap, or even give them away, so that people will buy your blades, where the real profits are. That's repeatability. This was also what Eastman Kodak did in its early days. Kodak was a great technology company developing films that were a leading technology of their day. The company wanted to put cameras in the hands of consumers, so that photography would be a mass market. By selling cameras really cheaply, it could develop a market for its film.

THE INTERNET AND THE UN-MICROSOFT

With Microsoft realizing that everybody can copy and develop good technologies, and one had to avoid being part of a crowd, it is kind of amazing that so many other technology companies—from Wang, a quarter of a century ago, to the Internet days—ignore this and fail to develop good BASM with their technologies. Maybe it is not so amazing when you consider that there seem to be a lot more innovative and brilliant engineers and technologists than brilliant management and strategists. Good BASM is hard to come by.

The Internet has become an even greater force in our lives than was foreseen in the late 1990s. Companies like eBay, Yahoo!, and others with great business models have become successful and truly great. However, early in the torrent of new Internet companies, it was very tough to know for sure which companies had the right stuff and which did not. It turned out that most of them did not have great management and business models, and for that reason, even though they might have had excellent technology, most failed.

The idea of selling toys over the Internet, as with many other products, was a good idea, but there seemed no barriers to entry and the field quickly became too crowded. Still, big companies stepped in to buy Internet toy companies to give them money and make them stronger, since even after some of them began to struggle, the idea seemed to have promise. Disney bought Toysmart, but the big parent and extra money did not save it. Another entertainment giant, Viacom, bought Red Rocket. Viacom had two brilliant managers, among the greatest in America: Sumner Redstone and Mel Karmazin. If Mel had run Red Rocket, he surely would have developed a stronger business model for it, but he was running the parent along with Sumner. Red Rocket was the opposite of Microsoft—it had as good a technology as anyone, but nothing that was proprietary and no unique strategy to set it apart and help it take market share from other electronic retailers, or "e-tailers." Anyone with technology could do what Red Rocket did, and the field was becoming more crowded.

Red Rocket was the un-Microsoft because it lacked great BASM and tried to succeed on technology and an idea alone. Therefore it was destined to fail, and did, along with countless other un-Microsoft companies.

Mel Karmazin is today the chairman and CEO of Sirius Satellite Radio, one of two leaders of a new, fast-growing industry. There is lots of great technology, but it is easy to see that Mel, a superb manager, is deploying a great business model and strategy, since he knows what it takes to win.

EBAY AND INTERNET SUCCESS

The ancient Greek historian Herodotus wrote about Greek real-estate auctions in the year 500 BC. Imperial Rome also was known for auctions. Ancient times saw slave auctions in many parts of the world, and while it is difficult to know how far back in human history the first auctions go, the auction is clearly something that has economic usefulness in bringing together buyers and sellers, and in setting prices. It is also clear that auctions are interesting and fun for many and have a psychological attraction that goes beyond economics and convenience.

Today, many people say that the biggest auction markets in the world are the trading markets for stocks, bonds, and commodities, in which buyers and sellers have a bid price and an ask price, and meet in an exchange or electronic network, which facilitates the auction. The format is basically the same as it was in ancient Greek and Roman times.

Think, then, about the brilliance of the Internet auction idea that arose not many years ago, which eBay grasped and perfected.

Since most people like auctions, the potential market is really big. At the time that eBay was founded in September 1995, the Internet had come of age, and computers were being used in almost all businesses as well as tens of millions of homes. All one had to do, then, was apply technology to facilitate bringing together buyers and sellers over the Internet. Others tried it, but eBay succeeded best.

The company had, in my mind, just the right cocktail of excellence in combining first-rate technology with BASM: business model, assumptions, strategy, and management.

People spend more time on eBay than at any other site, making it the most popular shopping destination on the Internet, according to company information. The company makes no secret of its business model. eBay provides very good information, and is the type of company that makes it easy for investors to understand what it intends to do, how well it does this, and what to expect.

As with most companies, you can look at annual reports, quarterly reports, and other corporate statements that are available to you on its Web site, through the mail, or by way of the Securities and Exchange Commission. The eBay prospectus, when it went public, was full of terrific information, and so are its other filings with the SEC and all of its quarterly and annual reports. Like most great companies, eBay makes things very simple and clear, and lists the specific metrics for you, such as how many people use the site and for how much commerce.

One of eBay's statements about the business model tells you how it conducts business and the factors that make it unique. The one below is from the original prospectus, the offering statement filed by eBay when it was in the process of going public:

> The company's business model is significantly different from many existing online-auction and other electronic-commerce businesses. Because individual sellers and not the company sell the items listed, the company has no product cost of goods sold, no procurement, carrying, or shipping costs, and no inventory risk. The company's rate of expense growth is primarily driven by increases in head count and expenditures on advertising and promotion.

I met with the company's managers, and I really liked what I saw about their plans, strategy, and business model. I also liked eBay's high level of profitability and the management, starting with CEO Meg Whitman. It seemed very solid and very promising, so even though eBay was a hot IPO—and priced like one—I bought stock as it went public on September 24, 1998, when it was already making money and growing fast.

Along the way, eBay became overvalued by some of the ordinary valuation formulas. In order to keep it and make the big money, we had to un-

derstand that the business model would continue to succeed in (1) generating great growth, (2) generating high profitability, and (3) making eBay
relatively immunized to other companies that wanted to get in on this
action and take away some of its customers. The power of the BASM
seemed to us to offer these elements. As I look at it today, it still does, as the
company racks up terrific numbers.

Use valuation disciplines to have frameworks (already given to you in
chapter 5) and benchmarks. Yet keep in mind that many investors try to
boil things down to simple formulas and often allow those formulas to
overshadow BASM. This is why they sell stocks that could have made them
the big money. The holistic approach can incorporate the valuation disciplines as well, as long as you keep in mind that you cannot allow the tail
to wag the dog. You look to the future when you see a winning business
model that does what eBay's showed us it could do (and the same is true of
Microsoft, Cisco, Dell, and others).

THE "NEW WORLD" OF GOOGLE

Each time there is a new technology with one or more new, exciting leaders, that tends to make people drop the kind of disciplines we use in the
Seven Steps, or forget BASM for a time, as investors simply enjoy the excitement and the initial success of a great new stock that is making them
money. Obviously, I think that behavior is trouble in the making most of
the time. Google has great technology and is the leader, but investors forget
about AltaVista, HotBot, and other prior leaders in search, and do not
study what happened to them. As Google reached its first anniversary of
being a public company, its stock had performed extremely well, trading at
prices that made it nearly a quadruple for investors who bought it when it
went public.

I hear from investors all the time about Google, and invariably they ask
if it is a buy or a sell or a hold, or what I think about the high price (valuation). They do not ask about what they should look at to see if it can be a
great company or have a great future, yet that is what BASM is all about,
and that is what will determine what will happen to the stock.

Whether you invested in biotechnology in the early days, or in other companies we have talked about along the way, or will invest in new things that come along, such as the exciting, unfolding world of nanotechnology (the science of the small, which could be revolutionary for many applications), it should all be the same: look at how technology companies are managed, look at their managements and business models, and understand what can make them great.

With Google, just as we did with Microsoft when it met challenges from competitors such as Borland and Lotus, we need to watch how Google will meet the strong competitive challenges that will come along from Microsoft and Yahoo!, two great, well-established companies that are developing technology products and strategies to try to snatch the leadership in the search market. The first thing you can easily spot is the fact that Google is doing a lot of new things, from expanding search into universities to launching an instant-messaging product. It is trying to lock in customers to a brand name, as part of a strategy to protect itself against competitors.

I took sharp note (and so should you) of the fact that in Google's 2004 public-offering documents, it conceded that Microsoft will be a competitor to contend with. Yet the business plan did not detail the company's own competitive strategies. Watching Google's strategy unfold after Microsoft and Yahoo! unveil their strategies and offerings in 2006 is the first thing investors should do if they want to understand whether or not Google will make them several times their stock or make them really rich.

The last thing to know is that as companies get bigger and bigger, and have an increasingly dominant share of a market, they have to act more like the whole market or even the economy, because they are so big and have so many customers whose spending may be sensitive to changes in industry spending or the economy. As long as a company can avoid being too tied to cycles outside of its own control, such as economic cycles, it can be a true growth stock. And growth stocks are more likely to make you wealthy than those more cyclical stocks that have lost some control over their own destinies by virtue of their size or dominance, or both. The leading semiconductor stocks are large and sell to many economically sensitive customers, so it is new and smaller companies that are more likely to make you all the money, rather than established blue chips that may take a position in your portfolio, but not the position they did when they were baby companies just starting out.

Control over destiny is an important element, as I have said before, of a company's being able to remain great. It is a key with Google, it will be a key in the future, and it was a key to Dell's emerging from a thousand other PC companies, as we are about to see.

DELL: ONE FROM MANY—PICKING A WINNER FROM ONE THOUSAND CLONES

Be the change you wish to see in the world.
—MAHATMA GANDHI

One day in 1982, two experienced managers from one of the leading semi-conductor companies, Texas Instruments, along with a tech-savvy venture capitalist, sat down to lunch together in the House of Pies restaurant in Houston. There they planned and brainstormed about starting a PC company to go after a piece of IBM's dominant share of what was already a large and burgeoning market. They outlined their ideas on a place mat, which they took with them.

The three men started this company—Compaq Computer Corporation—almost immediately after that meeting. They incorporated it and began operations, selling their first computers by January 1983. In their first year they achieved sales of $111 million, the highest first-year sales in the history of American business.

Compaq quickly went public in late 1983 (impressed, I bought stock on the offering), and rapidly became the youngest public company ever to be included in the Fortune 500 (the five hundred largest corporations) and the youngest to reach $1 billion in sales. Roughly ten years later, its stock had performed so well that Compaq became, at that time, the best-performing stock of any venture-backed IPO in history.

The year 1983 was one in which tech had become too expensive. Some fundamental disappointments triggered the bursting of what was a decent-size bubble for those times, the market was lackluster, and

Compaq's stock plummeted shortly after it began trading, dropping by roughly 70 percent or so before turning around and skyrocketing.

A number of investors who were just looking for a hot IPO were shaken out by Compaq's initial plunge, and they missed later opportunities. Many others did some homework and found that they liked the company's business model. The excellent products and performance also excited those investors, and they saw that the pricing was lower than that of the leader, IBM. They were buying Compaq stock, and they made tons of money.

The earnings were growing rapidly but were not substantial for such a new entity, so—as is true of many baby companies with great promise for the future—the stock was very expensive, with lots of market risk and volatility. I had bought some in my funds because I liked the management, the business plan, and the fact that Compaq computers boasted higher performance and lower prices than IBM's—in other words, better *price performance* for customers, and a good chance to grow faster than the market. I did not see a reason for the big price drop other than the stock market itself, and still very much liked all of the qualities that had originally attracted me to the company—as well as the really bright outlook for the PC market at large.

Since I had some uncertainty about this new company, though, I did temper the risk and bought only small positions. I lost some money on the IPO stock, then bought a little more later on, so that I ended up breaking even. Then I bought still more on the way up as I learned more about both the company and the personal-computer market and saw the rave reviews of Compaq's products. My buy disciplines were met, and I looked at valuations the way I did with any new company, projecting sales and earnings out about three years.

FAST-FORWARD TO 1988: DELL GOES PUBLIC

Five years went by. The growth for the PC industry, and specifically for Compaq and IBM's personal-computer division, had been tremendous. Industry sales of Intel-based PCs had leaped over tenfold, from 698,000 units in 1983 to over 7 million in 1988.

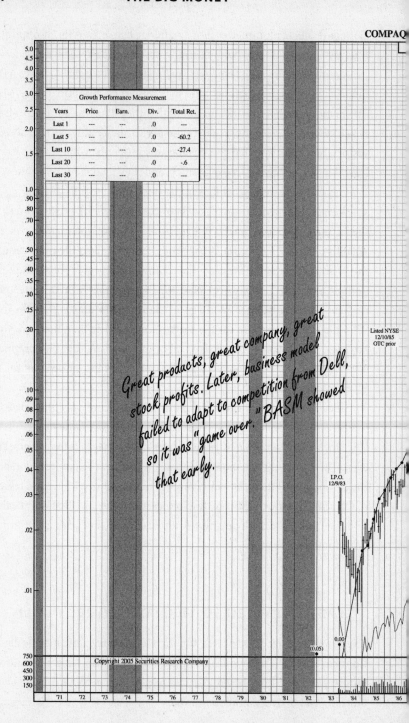

COMPAQ

Growth Performance Measurement				
Years	Price	Earn.	Div.	Total Ret.
Last 1	---	---	.0	---
Last 5	---	---	.0	-60.2
Last 10	---	---	.0	-27.4
Last 20	---	---	.0	-.6
Last 30	---	---	.0	---

Great products, great company, great stock profits. Later, business model failed to adapt to competition from Dell, so it was "game over." BASM showed that early.

Listed NYSE
12/10/85
OTC prior

I.P.O.
12/9/83

0.00

(0.05)

'71 '72 '73 '74 '75 '76 '77 '78 '79 '80 '81 '82 '83 '84 '85 '86

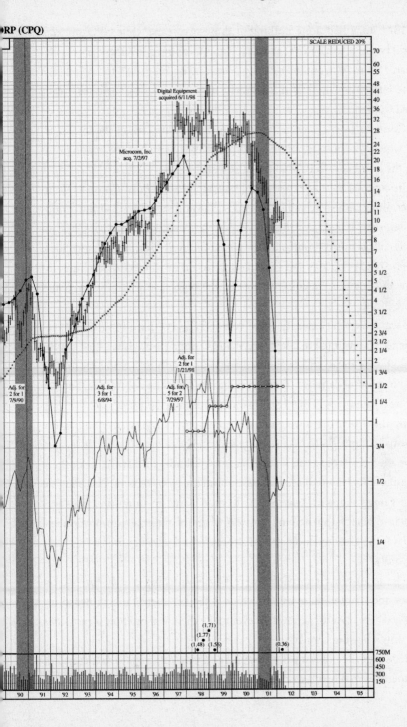

RP (CPQ)

SCALE REDUCED 20%

Digital Equipment
acquired 6/11/98

Microcom, Inc.
acq. 7/2/97

Adj. for
2 for 1
1/21/98

Adj. for
2 for 1
7/9/90

Adj. for
3 for 1
6/8/94

Adj. for
5 for 2
7/29/97

(1.71)
(1.77)
(1.48) (1.55)

(0.36)

750M
600
450
300
150

'90 '91 '92 '93 '94 '95 '96 '97 '98 '99 '00 '01 '02 '03 '04 '05

IBM stock had done nothing in those five years, while CPQ stock, as might be expected, had been spectacular, multiplying investors' money between 4X and 5X from the offering price, and by about 11X to 12X when it came back from the low it hit shortly after the offering. Investors really loved Compaq.

Compaq, by the way, had reached just over 5 percent of the total market, which was only about one-quarter of IBM's size but still made Compaq the number-two PC maker in the world.

In contrast to that experienced management team of Compaq Computer, along came Michael Dell in mid-1988 and took Dell Computer public. Before he started Dell, his only experience was that he had sold PCs out of his college dorm room and then gotten the bug to start a company. So he dropped out of college and started one. He said he wanted to be a big company and felt that he could be one of the biggest in the industry, if not number one.

I was looking at a twenty-three-year-old CEO with a tiny amount of experience who wanted to take on IBM and Compaq, as well as a host of others that were ahead and established and doing really well, and beat them. I liked him immediately. I liked his ambition, his quiet confidence, and the way he thought, and I liked his vision and his business plan.

By this time, there were countless companies trying to manufacture personal computers to take advantage of the huge opportunity. It seemed to be the great gold rush all over again. We know that at the peak there were about *one thousand companies* around the globe making PCs, ranging from garage shops in Asia to IBM to other large corporations. This was similar to what happened in the 1920s when the internal-combustion engine was the great technology of that period, and sales of autos were growing wildly.

The top twenty companies were worth watching closely for market shares and market-share trends, which is the key metric in a crowded industry where investors know that eventually there will be endless casualties and only a few big winners.

IBM had the highest prices around and was losing share to a bunch of competitors that had lower prices, including CPQ and Dell. Although Dell was much smaller than Compaq and was reaching only about 1 percent of the market, that put it into the dozen or so top companies.

Since I could see from the prospectus that sales were growing by leaps and bounds, it was obvious that Compaq was taking market share by the minute. It had even passed Digital Equipment Corp. in market share, and Digital was the leading manufacturer of minicomputers (mid-range in power).

Clearly, Dell was doing a lot of things right, and I wanted to know exactly what the company was doing to create rapid sales growth, expanding profit margins, and solid market-share gains, all great barometers of a business that should generate great stock-market gains.

A DIRECT ROUTE TO BETTER PROFITS: SELL DIRECT

Dell did not use middlemen or dealers to sell computers. The heart of the business plan was different from the rest of the industry—selling directly to customers, primarily through telemarketing. Michael Dell said that he had learned early in his college days that this approach meant better profit margins for the manufacturer as well as the economic ability to cut prices more than competitors did.

A third advantage, according to Dell, might have been at least as significant as the others: to really be close to the customers, get a great feel for what they wanted and needed, and collect information and data from customers instead of just completing a sale. Dell maintained that this was very important and a huge advantage.

Dell had described the process of marketing computers directly to customers and stated the reasons for doing so in very succinct fashion in the original prospectus:

The company markets a broad line of personal-computer products directly to end users through a telemarketing sales force and a national advertising campaign [its "direct response" approach]. Direct-response distribution permits the company to price its products aggressively by eliminating dealer markups and provides the company with access to end users without having to compete for limited retail shelf space. All of the company's personal computers are backed by a comprehensive service and support program.

Well, over the years to come, Dell said exactly what it was going to do and *did* what it said it would do—and did it consistently.

Even when Michael Dell sold computers from his dorm room, he knew enough to collect information on buyers, feeling that he was in business to understand customers. Anyone who later on read about this or heard about it would realize that this kind of prescience is rare, and that it was not only the beginning of an astute business model, but a good read on a potentially great manager. Later, Michael did expand on this information gathering, and did it for 100,000 customers and more, and ultimately millions. Along the way, it was a key element in a business model designed to capture the customer. I was reminded of Molex and others, of course. Dell made assumptions about understanding customers and how to win in this business, followed up, and made those assumptions work well for him all along the way. Somehow, with him, BASM developed early because of this.

Lesson Number One

Here is why I really liked seeing this brilliant business plan. First, in any crowded field, whether it be specialty retail, search engines, software, hardware—just about anything at all—there will be a lot of price competition, and some companies will *not* be able to maintain decent profit margins and returns on capital. Second, most companies will eventually disappear.

Third, it is very speculative and risky both for companies and for investors to bank on having the best price/performance indefinitely. This is particularly true for companies that rely partially on the technology of a supplier. In this case, it was Intel, the developer and manufacturer of the central processing units (CPU), or the semiconductor chips that determine the speed of the computer.

So, whether it is a star designer for clothing, such as Mickey Drexler at

Gap Stores, brilliant systems for McDonald's, or something else, you do need that something else to create enough differentiation so that your company—your investment—can simultaneously maintain a lead and make good profits, and perhaps become a great company.

Not only did I love the concept of the direct-selling model, which was unique, and the heart of the business model for Dell; I also thought the assumptions were great, and it all gave me great insight into Michael as well. So, very early there was a lot of differentiation and, in my mind, a potential big winner.

What I and other investors were facing with Dell, we all will face with many industries and companies as we move into the future of our investing: a need to find and invest in a business that can build and maintain a lead by combining excellence and differentiation, while remaining highly profitable. Along with that, we need to avoid the also-rans that will fail as companies and investments.

I had invested in technology and nontechnology areas such as restaurants and retail, where I had searched for winners out of a pack. I knew that hot products or low prices alone were not enough to create a tremendous winner in the personal-computer area.

Not long after Dell went public, market conditions were already showing signs of changing, and the great engineering expertise of IBM and Compaq was not the only factor that would determine future success. For those of us who carefully watched industry trends—something investors should do on top of just watching the companies they own—we saw emerging changes. Not only pricing was added to what a company did to compete, but also new elements: distribution, service, technical support, and understanding customers' needs. Dell was aggressively pushing ahead on all of them.

This is precisely why Dell's business model excited me. After watching Compaq succeed for over five years in a free-for-all against an almost endless list of competitors, I was increasingly concerned that neither Compaq nor anyone else had yet come up with something that would enable the company to secure a long-term winning position.

I was looking for two things. First was repeatability, that core concept we have talked about before. In technology, repeatability typically does not come from a horse race to have faster and better products; it comes from something deep within the business model.

Second was another core concept from the business model: "moats," or how a company would protect itself from competition. Technologies get copied and are not normally all you need to have a good moat.

What Compaq was doing to IBM could be done back to Compaq later: lower prices and better performance. Actually, Dell already had both of those advantages, and more.

More comments from the offering prospectus of Dell:

> The company's direct contact with its customers provides its telemarketing and technical-support personnel with an opportunity to influence customer purchase decisions and to receive valuable input from customers regarding product design, delivery, and service. . . . Direct-response marketing reduces obsolescence risks and time delays associated with new-product introductions because the company does not have to support a pipeline of dealer inventory.

One other thing that I thought reinforced the case, as detailed in that prospectus:

> The company's forty-one telemarketing-sales representatives respond to telephone inquiries, assist customers in defining their computer-system needs, provide information on the company's products, including comparisons to competing products, and provide pricing and delivery information. When appropriate, these sales representatives are assisted by technical-support personnel.

Now, my experience with companies such as Molex had taught me very early about the value of being close to the customers. There were other investment experiences, certainly including the experience with Sun Microsystems, and how it used knowledge of customers' needs to drive its technical development to astounding success over its competitors.

There is no question that Molex helped me with Sun, and that Sun helped me with Cisco when it came public, and on to eBAY and Google, and so it goes. That is the reason for this book's case approach urging you to do the same—use the Seven Steps (knowledge, patience, disciplines, emotions, time horizon, market timing, and benchmarks) and build from experience.

Lesson Number Two

First, because I believed that all investment experiences should build on one another and the aforementioned experiences were doing just that, I had an easier time than most seeing the huge value in Dell's approach and model in those early days when most investors were totally focused on pricing and product performance.

Second, I had notes in my spiral notebooks that helped me to key in on these experiences to reinforce my memory and remind me to look for benchmarks again and again. Third, this really turned out to give me a huge advantage over other investors, who simply did not use this type of approach or did not have the kind of close experiences with management that I'd had with Molex, Sun, and others. Even my experience with companies such as American Airlines and McDonald's lent something to the calculations. Investing is investing, no matter what the company sells.

But airlines cannot be growth companies because of their lack of control over destiny, and technology companies will disappear unless they have great repeatability and more. Thus, while we focus on management that gives birth to a great business model, we still need to see key differences in industry dynamics, also, so we can properly assess what it is that management can and must do to be great.

ONE-TWO PUNCH

The key to understanding Dell was to start with the one-two punch of management and business model.

If you have confidence in the management and business model, this can get you through some rough spots with a company on its way to big successes, and it can get you through some temporary screwups.

And screw up it did: After great-sounding meetings and lots of promises following the initial road show and stock offering, it was not long before Dell mismanaged inventory in memory chips. Apple had done things like that and suffered, as had a bunch of other computer companies. It was a very tough, tricky management job. Compaq's management was very seasoned and shone the best in those days, and IBM's was also very impressive.

Even though Dell's stock sold off, dropping a lot, and that cost me a lot of money, I was unwilling to just walk away.

LOVE AND HATE FOR STOCKS

By now, I knew enough about investing to have the Seven Steps in my head, and I knew that really, really loving a stock that was going up a lot could be a dangerous and costly emotion; or, if kept in check and balanced by the rest of the Seven Steps, it could be a positive factor.

Investors started to really hate Dell. Brokers, money managers, and analysts were being rather emotional. They hated the operating problems that cost them money, and they hated what seemed like broken promises. They felt that Michael was an inexperienced kid with little chance of making this thing work. They sold the stock down to much lower than its offering price. At one point it was trading at around $5.75, about two-thirds the initial offering price of $8.50.

If you read about Michael, there were people who thought he was just a twenty-three-year-old upstart who would be a flash in the pan, and others who kind of liked him but felt it was hard to tell. I felt he was very ambitious, but very honest and unable and unwilling to deceive or exaggerate to get shareholders. He was committed, he held 100 percent of the stock, and he had a plan that pretty much worked.

From all of my business and personal experiences, I believed in him as a person and as a CEO. I do think that if you read a lot—and there was plenty to read about Dell the company and Dell the person—you get a good feel for a person. Just as with the lesson with Howard Schultz of Starbucks, sometimes even a great business plan is great only if the right person is creating it, evolving it, and managing it. Therefore you should read about the person, not just the building blocks of a business.

I felt that when you saw someone with a history of what Michael had done, and wanted to do, it was likely that all those who had never met him would still come away from their reading and research realizing that he had a winner's qualities, and that his perseverance and long-term goals were not going out the window. He was a real competitor—we all could see that—and he had all this stock. Thus I felt that those who were selling his stock were emotional more than reasonable.

So I bought more, with my heart in my mouth, for there was an element of fear. But the Seven Steps helped. Patience—knowing that this opportunity would be huge and be there for a long time, and that capturing it would also take some time. Emotions—those who hated the stock were driving the value down too far and giving me an opportunity.

Buy and sell disciplines said sell on short-term failure to execute, but buy on the value opportunity and the fact that I decided that this management would learn to execute fast. Why? Because Michael Dell showed that every mistake was an opportunity to learn, as he did in the case of managing chip inventories, and get better. In contrast to many aggressive executives who tried to cover up problems or just find reasons to be optimistic, Michael freely admitted his mistakes. And he learned fast.

Time horizon and benchmarks—I decided that I would give Dell a year, and would be reasonable in expectations and hope that as the company fixed problems, initially I would recoup some stock losses and start to make money. I also avoided market timing and concentrated only on the fundamental progress of this company.

The most important thing of all was knowledge. I knew that this differentiated business model had the potential to create a big winner; I knew from my experiences with many other stocks that Dell's ability to know its customers was a huge asset that the competition lacked; and I knew that in a marketplace putting more stress on service and support, Dell was gaining.

I felt really great when I saw in the annual report that the company had won awards for customer satisfaction and service. This, to me, meant that the direct model was working just as Dell had said it was supposed to work. This was a big deal.

Then, there was a more personal thing.

I tend to go into stores and check out products and talk to airline pilots and truck drivers. This approach really helps me build knowledge and confidence. It is something that individual investors can do at least as well as pros, and they are missing the boat when they do not.

I bought a Dell computer early on because I needed a computer, and I felt that this was a good one. The company's information on its product performance and prices was very impressive, and counted for a lot.

Well, one day I needed more capacity in my hard-drive memory. By today's standards, it was nothing, but these were the early days. I had a 100-megabyte hard disk and needed to double that. People hated taking their machines to the stores, and corporations hated to deal with service issues.

I talked on the phone to a Dell customer-service rep, calling in without saying anything about being a shareholder, but just a person with a need for memory. In truth, computers intimidated me, and I did not know what to do, and I did not want to have to do anything.

The guy at Dell said, "I can overnight to you another one hundred megabytes of hard disk. Then you can call back, and we can tell you how to take a screwdriver and install it in less than ten minutes." I was amazed and somewhat skeptical, but excited at the possibility that this actually could be done.

I agreed, and the next day got the memory board, made the call, and ten minutes later was in business. I had seen with my own eyes that the service and technical support of Dell Computer were everything the company claimed and perhaps even more. To me, it was not merely a personal experience; it was confirmation of something important, and actually one kind of analysis. This is something all investors can and should do. When you cannot directly experience for yourself what a company does, talk to friends, neighbors, or perfect strangers in stores. Just look with your own eyes and listen with your own ears. That is often better than twenty pounds of paper covered with complex analysis.

More knowledge meant more confidence, and I could see that Dell's business model could really differentiate the company from the crowded field. Also, I now knew firsthand that Dell made great computers. Differentiation—that was the key criterion in a dog-eat-dog industry, but an industry with huge growth and profits and worth investing in.

Dell was doing better than Compaq, as well as IBM, on pricing and performance. Back when Dell went public, Compaq PCs were priced at a 20 percent premium over Dell, so Dell's direct model already allowed it to sell equal or better computers at lower cost in a market that was quite sensitive to relative pricing. Compaq had to pay dealer margins, and Dell advertised in magazines that were read by computer shoppers.

List prices were discounted by PC retailers to what was termed the "street price," just as you see in many products today. Dell ran ads that compared its list price with Compaq's list price, ignoring street prices, and thereby created a strong impression in buyers' minds that Compaq was actually about *50 percent* more expensive than Dell. This worked well. Aggressive marketing coupled with the Dell business model and its lower costs propelled Dell. When I saw the original numbers as Dell went public, it was clear that sales had been soaring in the two years leading up to the IPO. Now, as I owned the public company and watched the marketing, the sales, despite the operational problems in manufacturing and memory inventories, grew by leaps and bounds, and Dell was taking market share away from bigger companies. Market-share gains and keeping customers are the heart of many of the greatest success stories, as we have discussed.

DELL STARTS TO ACCELERATE MARKET-SHARE GAINS

Two and a half years after going public, Dell had more than twice the market share of the leading minicomputer company, Digital Equipment, and was accelerating the gains in market share taken from many other vendors.

Dell was still a lot smaller than Compaq but was gaining, Because of Dell's higher market-share numbers, Compaq's share of industry sales had actually slipped since Dell had gone public.

On a calendar-year basis, Dell's strategy had grown sales by amazing amounts, from less than $250 million in 1988 to well over $825 million in 1991.

While I kicked myself for being chicken and not buying massive amounts of the stock when it was being "hated," I did own a normal or average position, which for my funds then was about 1 percent or so. By 1992 the stock had moved up to over $32, which meant it was almost 4X the offering price in three and a half years, and more than 6X the lows at which it traded. Fortunately, I added to that original position even at higher prices as I saw things unfolding.

It was already a great investment. I did not know at the time that it was only just beginning, and I did not know that Dell and I as an investor would have one tougher hurdle, the next year.

NO RESPECT

Even so, Dell was still very much below most people's radar and somewhat mistrusted by those who had walked away and not noticed enough—they hadn't acquired enough knowledge—to see the abundant reasons to own it. Like the comedian Rodney Dangerfield, this company and stock were getting "no respect." That was very interesting, since gigantic investment opportunities lay ahead.

One could have bought Dell any time around then and had one of the best investments of all time. All it took was knowing what was really happening in the industry.

In 1992 one of the great books on Silicon Valley dismissed Dell in only two sentences. Most brokers did not like the company, because of its operational problems from time to time as Dell figured out how to handle huge growth with rapid product introductions.

I found only one analyst on Wall Street who really thought the way I did and had centered on the business model and the opportunity. Michael Kwatinetz and I had liked working together from his first day at Sanford Bernstein, the great Wall Street research firm. I have come to know him as a professional and good personal friend. Over the years, we have gone out to hunt stocks together and share thoughts, and we have discussed or even argued about stocks. After becoming a top analyst in both the computer arena and software—for his work on Microsoft and others—he left First Boston a few years ago to found Azure Capital Management, an excellent technology venture-capital firm in Silicon Valley, and we continue to have the same discussions.

Mike was the only one I found who felt that the number one thing to look at with Dell was the business model, even more so than the bumps in its road, its computer sales, and so forth. He and I agreed.

It turned out that this focus and the belief in the success of the business model to take market share was what made us and other investors more money on Dell than on almost any other stock. I made a much higher return than the other portfolio managers that I competed with. For similar reasons, Mike Kwatinetz was voted (*Institutional Investor* poll) the number one computer analyst on Wall Street for six years in a row, ending in 1999 when he formed Azure Capital. Paul Weinstein, before he helped Mike form Azure, thought the way we did about his own stocks, and he was a great Cisco analyst. He was number one in the *Institutional Investor* poll five years in a row, ending in 1999.

This is *exactly* why I feel that if you think in terms of BASM, *you will also win in your own quest for wealth.*

THE INDUSTRY PLAYS HARDBALL

The intensity of industry competition and the growing price discounting, the market-share changes, the confusing and mushrooming number of new vendors, and more and more new product introductions were making it more difficult for corporate and individual customers, and these factors were taking their toll on the whole industry by the early 1990s.

There were more and more companies selling PCs. Some of their names consumers did know, but there were many more whose names they did not know, and the unknowns were getting sales by tremendous price discounting. Profitability was not good except for the best-managed companies.

Compaq saw that an increasing number of the chains that sold its computers were having trouble with thin profit margins, and the eight biggest chains merged into four. Compaq was roughly a $4 billion company and had had an incredible run in its stock for almost eight years. Yet distribution problems and a minor recession combined to put pressure on earnings and sales, which dropped in 1991 for the first time ever. This drop not only killed the stock for over a year, but shocked investors and industry watchers, many of whom began to think that perhaps this PC phenomenon was not going to be so great going forward.

Compaq was resilient and smart, and changed some of its distribution. The company authorized some computer consultants and discount chains to sell its products, and experimented with—yes—direct selling by establishing a toll-free hotline. How interesting that Dell still did not have great credibility in general, and yet Compaq had noticed its success and was interested in experimenting with direct selling. Lots of those who sold Compaq during this period decided that the big stock moves for all the PC companies were all over.

Apple stock was doing only marginally better after floundering for some years. Commodore, an early entrant, was having a tougher time, and its stock showed that, while IBM stock remained flat for some time.

But after Compaq regrouped, it had a huge move from the oversold depths that the pessimists had sold it down to, multiplying investors' money by more than 30X over the next seven years, and participating very profitably in the next huge expansion of the personal-computer industry. I captured part of the move, watching to see if strategy and execution made sense, and then moving in. I was not first, but I did not walk away. The most profitable course is to buy on disciplines and knowledge, and I did.

Meanwhile, Dell had been on a tear from 1990 to 1993, and the stock had been great.

1993 AND DELL'S BIG TEST

A company growing 127 percent in one year is either on its way to huge success or spinning out of control. In 1993 Dell went from supergrowth to a quarter when it actually lost money because of messy operations. The company had far too much on its plate, ranging from day-to-day operations to very big decisions on whether or not to change the batteries in its laptops

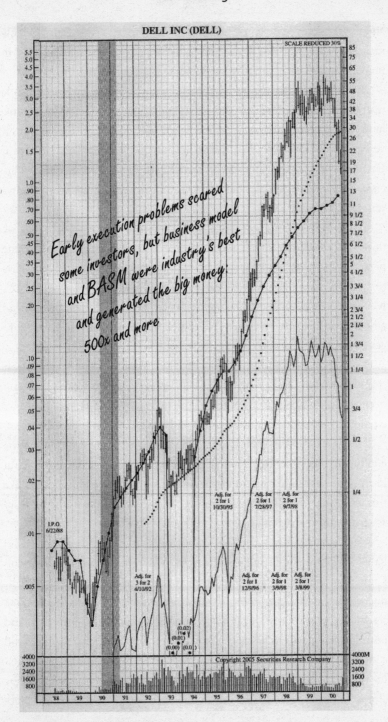

DELL INC (DELL)

SCALE REDUCED 30%

Early execution problems scared some investors, but business model and BASM were industry's best and generated the big money. 500x and more

I.P.O.
6/22/88

Adj. for
3 for 2
4/10/92

Adj. for
2 for 1
10/30/95

Adj. for
2 for 1
7/28/97

Adj. for
2 for 1
9/7/98

Adj. for
2 for 1
12/9/96

Adj. for
2 for 1
3/9/98

Adj. for
2 for 1
3/8/99

(0.02)
(0.01)
(0.00)   (0.01)

Copyright 2005 Securities Research Company

'88 '89 '90 '91 '92 '93 '94 '95 '96 '97 '98 '99 '00

and use those based on a new technology: lithium ion. Then Dell suddenly realized that its huge growth rate had outstripped the information it had to manage the business. There was some serious revamping to do.

The stock market is generally unkind and impatient, and most people really do not center on great companies and business models. Most people have little patience and are emotional. So, once again, Dell stock sold off very sharply. I sold a good part of mine, but kept some, trying to decide if Dell's inability to cope with success would outweigh the power of its differentiated business model, or if Michael Dell would get his arms around things before long.

Both Mike Kwatinetz and I were very worried and irritated by these problems. Mike had written a 143-page initial report on the personal-computer industry in July 1992 and recommended purchase of Dell. By early 1993, only months later, Dell and its stock—and Mike's recommendation—were being victimized by the huge growth that we had all expected, and the fact that Dell did not have the internal controls to cope with it all.

I still liked it for the longer term, so both Mike and I took a little heat from other Wall Street analysts and our colleagues. Yet when we talked it over, we saw that we had confidence both in Michael and in the company's strengths. It was a tough time, though, and sweaty palms were the least of it.

I must say that I thought a lot about the emotions involved, both mine and the market's, and the Seven Steps were not in the back of my mind but in the forefront—every minute for a while. My decisions on matters like this were not snap decisions. I wrestled with the elements of the buy and sell disciplines all the time.

Naturally, I talked with Dell executives and also with analysts who hated Dell, and got all sides of the story. Mike Kwatinetz and I were too knowledgeable to just try to make each other feel more confident. Self-questioning and talking to those who disagree are great assets to investors, since they help increase both knowledge and confidence. I recommend both as ways to save you money and make you more money. Mike and I did a lot of both. Also, these days, reading releases from companies and industry reports to beef up knowledge, and analysts' comments as well, will be almost as useful to you as sitting down with management, since management does not play favorites and everybody has access to what is important these days. You will get what you need.

I had various discussions with Michael Dell over time, and certainly at this juncture (reading continuously is also a route to take). More than once I was polite but very challenging. I remember once when he commented to me face to face that his quarter would have been fine if he'd had enough parts. I told him bluntly that parts were his business, and thus that could not be offered as an excuse. I was used to hearing a lot of tech executives continuing the excuses and giving more complicated reasons. Michael pleasantly surprised me. His exact words were, "You're right, Fred, and I am going to fix that right away."

Not long ago, talking about those tough days, Michael told me a story he thought I had known. Just before going public, Dell was growing so fast that it could not get enough Intel microprocessors to meet the growing demand. At that time, Dell was just an unknown blip to Intel—one of many, many companies springing up to take advantage of the PC-market opportunity and the new Intel processors.

Michael told me how he flew to San Jose, California; walked into Intel headquarters; and said that he was Michael Dell of Dell Computer, and he wanted to meet with Mr. Grove (Andy Grove, chairman of Intel). Grove was busy, the staff told him. He waited, and when the day passed and the same thing happened the next day, Dell said he would camp in the lobby until he got ten minutes.

They eventually relented, and Michael's ten minutes became an hour's meeting with Andy. The plea for parts was honored, and the two have had an excellent personal and business relationship ever since, built on a great deal of mutual respect. While I did not know this story in 1993, I saw that Michael Dell showed, in his meeting with Grove, the same character and drive to be number one, and the same perseverance—something just as true today.

TURNAROUND, VICTORY, HUGE GAINS

My experiences told me to stick with it, but I did not enlarge my small position until I saw tangible evidence that the turnaround was for real. Then I bought the stock back at somewhat higher prices than I had sold it at. Doing that with conviction is always the right thing, rather than speculating on the top or bottom price without understanding what you are doing, or what the company is doing.

Michael Dell had fixed it, and for those who had stayed close to the situation (including Mike Kwatinetz and some other very good money managers), the stock worked out very well. *Upside* magazine named Dell the Turnaround CEO of the Year, and this stock went on to be the number one stock of the 1990s.

We won, but I like to think that what always wins is knowledge, and other elements of good investing. I knew from the start that Dell had all of the elements of BASM in place. Good disciplines won, and elements of the Seven Steps that I and others practiced, even though not everybody thinks of the method as seven steps. It doesn't matter what you call it, but when you replace emotions with knowledge and disciplines—as well as patience, time horizon, market timing, and benchmarks—you will win.

Sure, there were more challenges and tests, but by now we knew this was a great company, so for us the tough part was over.

In less than five years from that bottom price of 1993, Dell had multiplied its share price by over 100X, and it kept on going.

During the decade when Dell skyrocketed, there were more questions, developments, and doubts, but some of us, including Kwatinetz and I, never wavered.

In fact, once during the 1990s when Dell stock was not going anywhere for a while, because people were worried about the economy or the PC market in general, Mike Kwatinetz got frustrated by the number of people who looked too much at the galactic stuff that one can never predict and not enough at Dell's progress and business model, which give you a basis from which you really can predict.

He put out a research report that was only a little tongue-in-cheek when he suggested a bet. Since stock in Kellogg, the cereal company, was going up sharply and was hugely expensive and loved by the market, and Dell stock was hated (yes, again) and really cheap and Dell was doing very well as a company, you should buy Dell and sell Kellogg. Not only *sell* Kellogg, but *short* it. Then you could profit from the coming downfall of Kellogg stock by borrowing it and selling the borrowed stock to buy it back later at lower prices. His recommendation was right on.

What is the lesson? All too often those without disciplines and knowledge rely much more on crowd psychology and emotions than they want to, or than they even realize they are doing.

It is always relevant to look at these things: the emotional avoidance of a controversial stock, and, conversely, crowding into a "safe" stock. The momentum buying of blue chips (the Nifty Fifty) from 1969 to 1973 was a mania that cost people gigantic money after that market collapsed. This has happened many times, and it will happen many times again. You can be prepared, though. Always bear in mind: fortune favors the prepared.

FINAL LESSONS OF DELL

Keep in mind that, very important, the Dell personal-computer technology was great and continued to be great even during times when operations got messy.

Biggest Lesson

Great management has people who create great technologies, but this does not happen the other way around.

Second

Compaq had a five-year lead on Dell in going public, many others preceded Dell, and ultimately Dell was in an industry that had as many as one thousand worldwide PC vendors at the peak. While there were volatile times, and rocky times, the key element in winning in a crowded field with look-alikes was differentiation. Dell had it, and others did not. Compaq ultimately struggled; bought Digital Equipment (bad idea); and when that did little for the company, sold out to Hewlett-Packard.

Even though Hewlett and CPQ are combined, Dell is the number one manufacturer of personal computers in the world. Differentiation of the business model and Michael Dell's vision and drive to be number one were what created the technologies and the overall success.

Third

When Dell would mess up periodically, a few quarters after coming public, and then again in 1993, I used my buy and sell disciplines and patience: cutting position size; buying back, even at a bit higher price; and avoiding the outright anger of some analysts and shareholders when the stock was going down, for anger muddies the whole process of investing. *Emotions have to be countered with disciplines, and this was one of my earliest and best and most profitable examples.*

Finally

Even if somebody did not catch highs or lows, and waited to accumulate knowledge, paying attention and doing research on this company instead of just looking at it as a possible fast-buck IPO, he or she could have become wealthy in this one stock.

Dell stock closed 2004 at over $42.14, after reporting a spectacular earnings quarter. Along the way, Dell has had seven splits. That means an original investor would have ninety-six shares for each original share. *Thus the stock has multiplied by roughly 476X the offering price, or 47,500 percent.*

By the way, from the price it dropped to while straightening itself out that first public year, around $5.13 unadjusted (the intraday low was $5), *the gain has been almost 789X on investors' money, or 78,800 percent.*

All it takes is one, as my friend Dave, who invested in small companies, found out. He was looking for that one great company, and found it in Xerox when it was a fledgling, untested company. He lived though the ups and downs by acquiring ever more knowledge along the way, so the stock made him very wealthy. I never forgot that. Nor did I ever forget all my other experiences that led up to Dell, and I have continued to build from these experiences and knowledge.

All it takes is one. The Seven Steps helped me along the way, and they can help you find and keep that one.

CHAPTER NINE

SNAKE OIL:
HOW TO PROTECT
YOUR MONEY FROM
LIARS AND DUMMIES

Fraud, Liars, and Fools

WHAT KIND OF VISION WAS THAT?

In the early 1990s, in a more or less normal period of a good market, and a good market for technology stocks as well, I sat down in my office with the managers of a company called MediaVision. They were on their "road show," going around with investment bankers to see possible investors for their initial public offering. Their technology seemed new, and they talked in wondrous terms about how the future could be very bright. Word had gotten around that this would be a stock in high demand, so it would be one of those hot IPOs where investors could expect to get a lot less stock than they wanted, but the shares might go up a lot right away. This was a typical market environment, before Internet stocks became frothy or there were any elements of the late 1990s bubble.

They wanted to concentrate on how great their technology was, and you know by now that I feel we all see lots of great technologies arise, but we cannot be blinded by those headlights, and we must decide if the management and business model make success probable. The assumptions part of BASM means that I want to know what management assumes for the most important factors: market size, protections against competitors, growth, resources it will need to compete (mainly people and money), and so forth. This gives you some yardsticks to see if you think a plan makes sense.

Commonsense assumptions are very important and should be presented by any management of any company so that they are very easy to understand by anyone, regardless of background.

MediaVision's business was digital interactive entertainment, in which the audience can be participatory, as opposed to passive books and movies. Products included interactive movies, games, and three-dimensional Web-based movies. All this obviously required a lot of complex software, and nobody would understand the whole technology or business model unless the company made an effort to ensure that it was made plain and simple. MediaVision did not make *anything* plain or simple.

Instead, the managers waxed poetic about how great this was all going to be, and how I should see their demo on the big TV they had lugged into the office with their software demonstrations. I asked straightforward questions, the kind that you would probably want answered if you were sitting there, particularly after you have absorbed a bunch of the cases and lessons in this book, and have an idea of what makes a good company or good management. Nothing I asked was complicated; I just wanted them to lay out a business plan in simple terms.

Well, they just hyped their product and frustrated my efforts to know the business. So I got tougher and bored into the business model. Finally the CEO said, "Fred, Fred, if you are not a lot nicer to me, I won't show you the demo." Well, I chuckled to myself, since it was not the demo I wanted but some facts. I told him I just wanted to understand and needed his help getting there, and bored in some more.

I never got a decent explanation of the whole plan. I wasn't all that much easier on the CEO, but he did show me the demo anyway. I must say, it was awesome, and I could see that it would sell the stock to many buyers. But by my rules, there was nothing substantive about the business model.

There was no management person of Michael Dell's caliber, nothing to make me feel strongly about the company.

So I bought stock on the IPO, made some quick money for my shareholders, sold it, and never went back. I looked once in a while to see how the business fared, but saw nothing of interest. Eventually, the company floundered. Its officers were accused of lies and fraudulent accounting, and the whole thing turned into a mess and went bankrupt. (Today, by the way, the technology lives on with a new management and a new company with a new name.) Whatever kind of vision MediaVision had, it was not a business vision, for sure.

YOU CAN DO THE SAME THING

This is the kind of situation in which, yes, it is an advantage to be sitting there with the management, but anyone who invests—let alone reads this book—can evaluate an IPO by looking at the prospectus and looking for the BASM. I harp on looking for consistency, so I stress the importance of acquiring knowledge, sticking to disciplines, and the rest of the Seven Steps. The key is that many investors do not do their homework; they just read or listen to stuff in the media.

> If we all did the things we are capable of, we would astound ourselves.
>
> —THOMAS EDISON

Just as a kid is intimidated before getting on a bike for the first time or trying to catch or hit a ball, investors on the sidelines think there is more mystery to investing than there is. I have avoided getting burned not because of what I learned in business school, but because I read annual reports and listen to management or read the earnings releases on the Internet, and act on this information in the same commonsense way that I urge you to: look at consistency, look at what the company said it would do, and look at what it did do.

After a while you see patterns. To understand is to perceive patterns. Sir

Isaiah Berlin, a legendary British philosopher known for his history of ideas, said that there are two forms of knowledge: that of the proverbial fox, who knows and pays attention to many things; and that of the hedgehog, who knows one big, important thing. In this book, I stress a few important things that you have to know and caution you not to let yourself be drowned in data that you don't need. So I urge you to watch for certain important things and then act. This book is about doing.

A KEY GUIDELINE

When more knowledge does not mean more understanding, you have a bunch of facts that mean nothing, and they may get you into real trouble. This is not the same as sniffing out trouble, data you must pay attention to. Remember that a crucial step in the Seven Steps is building knowledge, so you can have confidence and conviction and take larger positions or hold great companies through shaky markets. One important function of knowledge is that it enables you to sense trouble, and then run from it and save lots of money. The other function is to reinforce conviction and stick with what can make you a fortune. Both functions require the same disciplines. That is exactly why trying to be alert for trouble is a key way to use the Seven Steps, and not just to avoid troubles and untrustworthy management, but also to build wealth.

I certainly had to deal with my share of lying management long before the great bull market of the 1990s, which became a breeding ground, it seems, for unfettered greed and lying on the part of many businesspeople. The biggest bankruptcies in history erupted with the closing of that decade and the century, as Enron and WorldCom became financial scandals, and a long string of crooked accounting, financial, and business policies were uncovered.

You too will have to cope with deception. It is a fact of life, and should not be a deterrent to good investing, any more than rain should stop you from going to work. That's what raincoats and umbrellas are for, and that is what the simple, commonsense techniques in this chapter are for.

After New York State Attorney General Eliot Spitzer spoke at a financial

gathering I attended, I talked with him about a few things. I asked him if being really tough on those who were convicted would keep us stock people safe for some time to come.

Eliot smiled and said, "Fred, when people go speeding down a super-highway and then see that a cop has pulled someone over to the side for speeding, they all slow down, of course. But do they slow down for one mile, or two? The crowd certainly doesn't slow down for the rest of the trip, does it?"

I got Eliot Spitzer's point, and I think I really knew it all along, but my question was born of wishful thinking. We all want human nature to be such that we are fully protected from people who don't always have our best interests at heart. From the first day I entered the investment business, wise people told me how we had the greatest markets in the world, and that part of the reason was our economic system of promoting entrepreneurial activity, and another part was that other countries as well as Americans had learned to trust our accounting and financial disclosures and our over-all system of reporting more than any others on earth. This led to better market participation by domestic and foreign investors, capital flows into our country, and better valuations and prosperity along the way. All true.

Japan learned the hard way that if people lose faith, they leave and it is hard to get them back. So a couple of years ago, Japan's stock market, once a signpost for financial prosperity in our times, hit a nineteen-year low. This happened partially because of poor economic policies rooted more in culture than in logic, but also very much because the markets were exposed as having untrustworthy elements in them, and the public wanted nothing to do with a rigged game.

Despite the recent exposure of financial and accounting scandals in-volving some prominent American companies, you should know that this has happened every time there has been a huge boom period. It has never affected the health of our underlying system, and it has not done so this time either. In fact, it is this health of the American system that exposes and deals with these scandals.

STRONG, SOUND, SECURE

In our country, we all should be glad that the system is not only intact but so very strong, and that the surfacing of all these false or otherwise unreliable financial reports is a good thing—not the lies or other problems themselves, of course, but the fact that we have a system that surfaces these things, and takes care of them and makes the system strong again. As I have said, each time there is a giant financial boom, greedy people get out of hand and try to take advantage or cut corners; so do not feel that, because of the boom of the 1990s and the resultant problems, this is a new turn in human nature and the entire system is suspect.

We are strong, sound, and secure, and the overwhelming majority of management is honest, and we have good accountants and regulators. We also have very skilled financial analysts and portfolio managers who are doing their best to keep the investment business transparent and honest. We are cleaning up after a party that got out of hand, as it has done on several occasions before in history.

But for thousands of years and for all the years of our modern stock markets, there have been lies, and it cannot be entirely left up to regulators to protect our money before it is too late. We must and can do some things ourselves. There are amazingly simple ways to do this, and one does not have to leave the game and hide and miss the huge opportunities of the next five, ten, or twenty years, and more. We do want to know about financial lies and other investment pitfalls before we get stung.

Good news: you do not have to be an accounting genius or a financial sleuth. What you must do is quite simple and straightforward—learn to recognize inconsistencies and problems that common sense can warn you against, and acquire information as you learn and have experiences of your own. Learn from common sense and from observing lots of companies for consistency, and comparison gets much easier as you go along. Protecting yourself means heeding a few tips and acquiring a few techniques and learning how to recognize and avoid certain types of situations. Having knowledge and disciplines is a great place to start, so the Seven Steps really do help to keep your money protected to a certain extent, but there will be some situations where knowing what to look for is invaluable. You are inevitably going to encounter these situations and can handle the flow of information—or lack thereof—from the company itself most of the time.

SAMBO'S WAS MY FIRST ENRON
One of the Biggest of All Investment Lessons

There is a great difference between knowing and understanding: You can know a lot about something and not really understand it.
—CHARLES F. KETTERING

Sambo's Restaurants was a hot stock in the 1970s, and more people knew things about how well Sambo's was doing than truly understood why it was doing so well.

But the stock went up, and that often makes people think that there are great and good reasons for the rise, even if they are not sure of how great and how good.

Does this sound familiar? It should, particularly after the early 2000s, when each discovered fraud or set of muddy financials was matched by tales of the losses and woes of those stockholders who stuck with companies they really did not understand all that well, because they loved the profits the stocks were racking up. One of the most important investment lessons is that when even the best financial experts cannot properly interpret or figure out a company's financial reports, it is best to run away, rather than wait around in a stock to see if there is fraud. Generally problems in understanding financials are more common than not in a very strong market. After all, why should you do research when you are making money and all seems well? Naturally, there might be a lot fewer Enrons, Tycos, Adelphias, and other frauds if people used one simple rule: Understand, truly understand what you own, and why the stock is going up so strongly—or walk away.

I was an analyst for Wellington Management Company (today a giant firm managing most of the Vanguard Mutual Funds and a great deal of retirement-plan money). One of my primary responsibilities was restaurants, including McDonald's, Steak and Ale (Norman Brinker, who founded many great restaurant companies including Chili's), and others, including Sambo's.

Sambo's at one point had some trouble because the name reminded people of a children's book that had racist overtones, *The Story of Little Black Sambo;* but the management defended it, saying it was not that name, but a contraction of the founders' names: Sam Battistone and Newell "Bo" Bohnett.

Sambo's competed with casual dining spots like Denny's, appealing to a mass market that liked Sambo's convenient locations and the good-quality food, and the terrific value of the low prices. My favorite part of the annual reports in the 1970s, actually, was the menus showing how wide a selection of food was offered and at low prices. Sambo's attracted great business, and the company grew very fast, doing more than $250 million in restaurant revenues in 1975.

I felt there was a direct link between the great menu and great prices and the fact that people loved the restaurant, went there in ever larger numbers, and during one two-year period drove such a high growth rate that total revenues actually doubled.

The stock had a great run over a few years, multiplying investors' money by almost 7X. I had recommended it strongly; many of our portfolio managers owned it and captured much of the good gains.

The company had partnerships for each and every restaurant unit, retaining 50 to 60 percent ownership, but selling off the rest to each partner, and booking the revenues when the restaurant was opened. This format complicated the analysis of the operations quite a bit; and instead of just food sales and royalties from franchisees selling food, as was the case with other casual restaurants, we were dealing with various real-estate matters and lots of noncash earnings derived from depreciation and amortization, as well as deferred income taxes. On top of that, there were very significant financing transactions such as sales and leaseback of land and buildings, which amounted to a very large part of the whole earnings picture.

Yes, it was more than enough to make your head spin, even if you were hard pressed to come up with an earnings estimate for future quarters. It was enough to confuse me, and I was a recent graduate of Harvard Business School and had taken a financial accounting course in which I had done very well. Others in the investment community also had a bit of a problem with this kind of earnings formula, and wished that, since Sambo's was so good at selling pancakes, chicken, and hamburgers, it would just stick to those things without the fancy real estate and partnerships, collect its money, and that would be that. Oh, lest I forget, the company also had what it called a "fraction of the action" program, which gave incentives to each level of employees such as restaurant managers, district managers, and so forth by cutting them into a percentage of the profits their operations generated.

As time passed, this operation of hundreds of restaurants got to the point where it added well over one hundred new restaurant units per year, which meant that everything was "pyramided," the nonfood revenues increased, and the complexity of the whole thing was increasing by the day.

From the 1976 Sambo's annual report:

> The sales of the remaining interests (40 percent to 50 percent—Note A) of each restaurant joint venture is made in the following manner. The manager of a particular restaurant is sold 20 percent ("manager's interest") and the remaining 20 percent to 30 percent is sold to either a joint venture investment group ("Investment Group") or a real estate joint venture group ("Real Estate Group").
>
> These Investment and Real Estate groups provide incentive compensation to employees through cash investment opportunities.

This is as complicated as I will allow this section to get. The point is that we all tried to convince ourselves that we understood how the whole thing worked because we were all supposedly good enough analysts to figure anything out. Yet it was a pretty good version of "The Emperor's New Clothes," because we finally figured it all out when the chief financial officer (CFO), Owen G. Johnston, came around to the big cities and gave general presentations or personal ones in our offices and those of other big stockholders, and whizzed through numbers and arrows on an easel. As we watched him, it all seemed so simple—just like the traveling salesman's pitches in the late 1800s.

After he was gone, and we had our basis for the earnings going forward, we would rub our eyes and scratch our heads and try to remember exactly how he had put together all the numbers. We did think it was great that he came all the way to Boston (and New York and elsewhere) so frequently from Santa Barbara, California.

A CORE PART OF THE SEVEN STEPS

One day I was arranging a business trip to Los Angeles to visit companies, and I realized that I was going all the way across the country and would be only about ninety miles from Santa Barbara, the corporate headquarters of Sambo's.

My worries about the real core of Sambo's earnings, and my trouble getting all the figures to add up, made me feel strongly that despite all the visits we regularly got from Sambo's top management people, it would be worthwhile to spend half a day with Sambo's management people and get everything straight in my mind.

Now, almost all of the time more and more knowledge means more and more understanding. This is why knowledge is a core part of the Seven Steps. The more you know, the more you understand something, gain conviction and confidence, and thus make more money—or learn when to get out.

When more knowledge does not necessarily lead to more understanding, this often gives you some kind of warning alarm. Yes, an alarm can mean other things, like a need to find a new way of looking at something; but in understanding a company, as you learn more about the products, customers, management, model, and so forth, you really understand a lot more of its operations, its future, and its potential.

I did my work on Sambo's and knew more and more, but my knowledge did not lead to a real understanding of how this financial sleight of hand worked with the partnerships, revenues, and so forth. This was becoming increasingly worrisome to me, despite the fact that most others in the investment community seemed to continue to feel that everything was great, and the stock was making us all a lot of money in our client portfolios. None of the Wall Street research reports got any deeper than we did, but this should not have been an accounting job—most things are easily explained in annual reports and in the information that management puts out.

Keep in mind the following.

First: Management does not want to make it hard for people to know where earnings come from. It can be tough to forecast earnings, but just understanding the report should not take a degree in finance or qualifying as an analyst. The really good companies make sure of that. Some companies even give a little education along with their reports, to help people. If you go to the IBM Web site today, you will see that it is one of those really good companies that do this. Things were no different in those times from what they are today. It was rare to have an "understanding" problem.

Second: The better a stock is doing, the less digging people are inclined to do, and this generalization does include some professional analysts. Put it down to human nature and the fact that people are very busy and are attending to the next idea or looking into what does not seem to be working. What counters these tendencies is having discipline and something like the Seven Steps, so there are known things to do.

Accordingly, I spent more than half a day at Sambo's, and it all it accomplished was to make me feel stupid. The managers were very friendly, but they went quickly through things that were tough to follow. The remarks that I quoted above from an annual report were only the tip of the iceberg. The footnotes to Sambo's annuals were long and not very illuminating. The managers went over everything orally, and had no paper or handouts of any kind that I could take with me.

When I was ready to leave, the president, Sam Battistone Jr. (his father, the founder, was chairman, and was in my meetings, as was the chief financial officer), asked me how I was getting back to L.A. I said I had an Avis car, and he said I should let him give my car keys to his assistant to return it for me, since he could take me in his plane, because L.A. was where he was heading. Okay, so we went to the airstrip in his Ferrari, at great speed, and he flew me back in his plane.

It was fun, and I was suitably impressed, but I also felt more uncomfortable than when I had started out earlier that day. I scratched my head and worked over all my notes and the available figures on the long plane ride back east, but I continued to remain confused. I knew that this was it. I had to recommend selling this stock, for sure. My only question was, Do I blame myself for being unable to do the analysis, or do I say that there is something wrong, even though I could not figure out what was wrong? It was very stressful, and I was unsure about what course of action to take.

SAVED: THE BELL IS RUNG

I got back, and sat down at my desk to write my recommendation report shortly thereafter. Well, I wrote and rewrote it, and I was not having an easy time. All of a sudden, something happened. Fortuna, the Roman goddess of good fortune and luck, walked into my office, and said, "Fred, you have been a good boy this month, and you have worked very hard, and it is not your fault that you cannot figure out Sambo's. I am going to come and rescue you." With that she disappeared, and I thought I must have been dreaming.

Okay, she didn't walk into my office—at least, I did not see her. But all of a sudden news came over the Dow Jones newswires that W. R. Grace & Co., a very large conglomerate, which had been buying up small- and medium-size restaurant chains, had made a bid for all of Sambo's stock and wanted to acquire the company. Sambo's stock zoomed up by about 35 percent on top of the nice gains that the stock had recently been posting. We had a really big profit in that stock, and it was getting expensive as measured by the current earnings estimates.

So I quickly wrote a memo of less than a page, saying that the stock was very much overvalued, and we should sell all we had immediately. I actually hand-delivered it to the portfolio managers that I had put into those shares. We sold all the stock. It was a victory, or maybe I should say an escape and a big relief. That night I had a better night's sleep than I had been having recently.

Time went by, maybe a few weeks at most. We were all occupied with other things, and Sambo's stock had not budged, as holders waited for the actual transaction to be done. All of a sudden, an ill wind blew through the world of Sambo's. W. R. Grace was back on the Dow Jones newswires announcing that it could not figure out Sambo's accounting, and it could not figure out the "fraction of the action" program, and it could not get to the bottom of the company's books. The deal was off.

Naturally, the stock plummeted, not only because it no longer had merger support for the high price, but because holders were rattled by the fact that a very sophisticated buyer of restaurants, with great experience and a large financial staff that was used to working on deals, could not figure out where Sambo's numbers came from.

Sambo's got increasing scrutiny and had increasing troubles, and lower and lower stock prices continued for some time after that until eventually charges were filed against some management people, suits were filed, and Sambo's went into bankruptcy, selling a lot of units to a big company called Vicorp Restaurants.

The warning signals at Sambo's were very similar to those at Enron two decades later. The two companies had similar and complex partnerships, accounting, and financials that made it almost impossible for experts to determine how they made their money.

Along the way, of course, I benefited from the Sambo's example many times and in many ways. When Enron was running "hot," I avoided it because I could not figure it out, and this made me feel that something was very, very wrong. I could see shades of Sambo's Restaurants. Sambo's was my first Enron.

HUGE LESSONS FROM THIS ONE

Everything repeats. Learning to recognize patterns is a path to making or saving significant amounts of money.

My early experiences—and Sambo's was a very critical one—taught me to check whatever management said and read various other sources of information. I got better and better at checking and reading every year, and every decade, and all the way up through Enron and WorldCom and to today. I found that just looking at the right things is what counts. You do not have to be a supersleuth or financial crackerjack. Just look.

Here is your advantage: you can run. You do not have to write reports and then defend them; you can sell a stock and not be made to defend the sale before a committee; you can sell and not have to prove your decision to a senior investor; you can just plain sell when something makes you uncomfortable or worried, whether your concern comes from your common sense or intuition or research.

Now, as I said earlier, the better a stock is doing, the less people want to check things or dig, or read, or believe that the music has to stop. But you have the Seven Steps, including knowledge and buy and sell disciplines, and this should control the instincts that could make you get too greedy, by giving you a framework for decision making.

Biggest lesson: Always admit it to yourself when you do not understand what a company is reporting or telling its shareholders. Do not gloss it over because everybody loves the company and the stock is going up. Once you are at that point, you can at least deal with the situation. You can decide to ignore this, and be at risk, knowing you are speculating, or you can work on this by talking to others or looking into it, or you can sell and just walk away.

For decades I have met, spoken to, and known investors who are truly embarrassed that they do not know enough to defend their buys and sells, and cannot follow intuition or their gut, or use common sense. Well, I was afraid of looking stupid when I thought everybody should know the things that I could not figure out. This is a consequence of being human, but we learn to deal with our emotions on the road to investment success.

You can save a lot of money and grief if you never buy what you do not understand. If you do not understand a stock, then you are acquiring knowledge or using any of the Seven Steps or other disciplines and techniques that are straightforward and well within your ability. You might save even more money and grief if something changes with a company, and you find that it is not sticking to its business plan, or you no longer understand its reports or operations. Just sell.

Why would this happen? Well, lots of times when companies see that they are having trouble keeping up the growth trend they have enjoyed, they do things that are honest but nonsensical and that just make the situation worse, as Hewlett-Packard did when it bought Compaq, in my opinion; but a small number of companies do things that are fraudulent, like cooking the books.

MANY EXAMPLES; ALL SAY THE SAME THING: SELL!

You cannot imagine how simple and straightforward it is to avoid the bad apples, and how much you can build the confidence to stay with the world-class winners during poor markets if you can just learn this.

In the 1980s, I had experiences with a hospital information-systems company in Atlanta, HBO and Company. I spent a day there with the leading Wall Street analyst on that stock, who wrote great reports and recommended it, to the great profit of his clients. It was a great stock. But the company claimed to us that it had no problems integrating two concurrent acquisitions, and a strange thing happened. I saw that the chairman and each of his next seven executives had the same style of cuff monogram. Unusual—and maybe it was a coincidence that they all had the same answers to the same questions, and appeared to be yes-men and possibly hiding something.

Strange? Maybe, but I went with that feeling of discomfort. We all sold the stock; the analyst strongly recommended it again; the company ran into huge problems with operations and credibility; and the earnings and stock blew up. Even in a big bull market, the stock collapsed, losing 60 percent of its value fairly quickly. We were out. The analyst left the industry and went into the music business. This is true.

Barron's wrote a column on this story, entitled "The Case of the Matching Cuff." It's amazing how often your own intuition and common sense will warn you when you can't get answers you need. You do not have to be in a room with management these days, but I feel you do have to read.

Each time you dig into one like HBO & Company, it may seem strange, yet they all have similarities, and all of them deprive you of knowledge you really need along the way.

Tyco, for instance, did not sting me, because of my discomfort with CEO Dennis Kozlowski and his decreasing ability to show he was in touch with its operations. Did meeting with him give me an advantage? Yes, definitely, but reading a lot about what is going on in a story which improbably just gets better and better, and in which the CEO spends a lot of time boating and partying—well, sometimes it is all there. I did meet with him, more than once. It seemed that the higher the stock went, the greater was my discomfort with management. My talks with him were producing less and less. He was not sharp, and he was distracted. HBO and Company, and Sambo's before that, and all the others made me better at boring in. You will get better just by reading and seeing what good companies disclose and make plain to you, so a little work goes a long way. Don't expect to get rich if you do not want to look into things that are not clear at first.

One day, I was a guest along with Kozlowski and a few others in the box of the owner of the Miami Dolphins football team. Normally, on such occasions, I do not bore in and try to get information about a company. But you invariably come away with some information, often very valuable information, acquired in a casual fashion. But it was a first that I came away from an entire football game with a CEO and knew absolutely nothing more after the game than I had known before. Zero.

I told this to a portfolio manager back in Boston, and he thought I was nuts. He continued to maintain a huge position in Tyco, even though he knew that I had sold all of my Tyco stock and that I thought something was amiss. Remember, the better the stock is doing, the more you want to be sure that the company is doing really well to support that.

The stock blew up, as everyone now knows. This other portfolio manager runs some money at a giant mutual-fund company. Most analysts and money managers in brokerage houses and investment firms are intelligent, but that does not mean they are any good at interviewing executives or making inferences from what they learn. Some people who work with their hands have more common sense, and some analysts are fabulous. It depends. Do not take things for granted, though. Plenty of people who do other things in life are going to get rich with stocks, and plenty, like this analyst I tried to warn, are just going to be working along very mechanically the rest of their lives.

Interestingly, our host that day was Wayne Huizenga, the owner of the Dolphins. He founded Waste Management, and then Blockbuster Video (later sold to Viacom), Auto Nation, and other companies. Now, for some investors who tend to think that all business leaders at the top must cut corners or lie or cheat, Wayne is a great example of *the opposite*. He is a self-made billionaire who has been my friend for a quarter of a century, not because he is successful with his companies but because he is truthful and honorable and a great business leader and person.

Lessons

Try to know all you can about the guy running the company your money is in. What does he do with his time—is he more on the social pages or the business pages? If he is working, what is his skill set? What does he do best? And so on.

Trust your own judgment, instincts, and, yes, intuition as much as possible if you are doing sufficient homework and using some disciplines.

Do not own what you cannot understand. Period. Never, ever.

NUMBERS WILL NOT DO IT FOR YOU

Do not fall in love with your stocks just because they have been good to you. Be objective. Sounds easy—and it really is, if you have a framework of buy and sell disciplines and do not let emotions play a bigger role than knowledge. I have to remind myself of this all the time; I have the same emotions as everybody who is just starting his investing life, but I have these other tools to use to control emotions.

Caveat emptor. Do some work. Do more when you do not understand and when a stock is a highflier. Never expect the analysts to warn you— they almost never do. And never, ever, buy into media hype. Reporters usually know much less than they think they know.

Use disciplines, the Seven Steps, and common sense. Remember to admit it when you do not understand, and if knowledge is not leading to understanding, sell and move on.

EPILOGUE:

DOWN THE PATH TO THE BIG MONEY

In the movie *Speed*, the bad guy bomber, played by Dennis Hopper, is on the phone with Jack, the good guy police detective, played by Keanu Reeves. Hopper has been telling Keanu what to do to get him money so that Hopper won't detonate his bomb. Keanu (Jack) is complaining about how many things he has to do and how little time he has to do them, and his mind is disorganized under the pressure. "Focus, Jack, focus!" Hopper tells Keanu. His sharp tone and words do get Jack very focused.

We live in an information world, and investing is an information business. Over the last couple of decades, the information age has brought investors such a torrent of available information that the excess has created a major problem: lack of focus. It is easy to tell yourself to focus. It is hard to actually do so when your stocks are under pressure or if you are unsure of what to focus *on*. The Seven Steps are invaluable in helping you to focus on BASM, the golden goose that creates those golden eggs, the earnings.

Now that you have finished *The Big Money*, you can see the logic of why simple is better, and you know what to focus on. You know why BASM helps to explain why most of the technology companies that became famous, with some years of terrific stock appreciation, eventually disappeared, and how the winners that defeated them achieved their victories.

We are not born as stock pickers; we become stock pickers using some straightforward methods and learning from investment experiences, and from our peers. Most of us are born with more than enough curiosity and common sense to succeed.

Investing can be like riding a bicycle. At first it looks almost impossible to a child. But we are all born with a sense of balance and just have to learn to use it. Soon it becomes easy, until the rider can say, "Look, Ma, no hands." In similar fashion, we are all born with common sense and curiosity and just have to mobilize them when we invest.

Some investors may want to know more about finance. There are countless books on simple, straightforward ways to read income statements and balance sheets, and use P/E ratios if you want to do so. I have explained a bit of that. More important, though, I have shown investors how to see where the numbers come from. When Amgen and Microsoft were emerging, they had no earnings, but you could understand these companies by using BASM.

The more I worked at the early detection of who has *repeatability* and who does not, using a holistic approach to understanding a business, the earlier I could identify what to own.

Many investors act as if management that has a couple of good years must be excellent, when that is far from true. Extrapolating great results then can be a very "Neanderthal" approach if one does not know what else to focus on. Only a small percentage of managers will be stars and create BASM, great repeatability, and great wealth for shareholders. If you have invested for years, you probably know this. You may be frustrated because traditional techniques have not shown you how to differentiate companies.

To the uninitiated, it all may seem like finding a needle in a haystack of earnings and other statistics. Yet for those who understand the holistic approach and focus on the right things, great companies become easier and easier to recognize, and at earlier stages of development.

In professional sports, a good scout or manager can cut through a blizzard of statistics and identify star athletes early in their careers. To me, it is easier to recognize great managers, particularly if they have businesses and business models in which they have great control over their own destiny.

Be the scout. Use and refer to the cases (or examples) in this book again and again, remembering that everything repeats. Keep notes on your own experiences, as I did. This will help you to become better and better at recognizing the great stocks early. Use BASM and the Seven Steps to guide you on the path to the big money.

ACKNOWLEDGMENTS

The members of my family were my first teachers. Those early-in-life dinner conversations with my parents and my brother Jeff, covering a wide range of subjects, helped me in life and also enabled me to be a more confident investor, seeing the key issues. I am grateful to them.

I wanted to go to Harvard Business School so I could study with a great teacher of investments, Colyer Crum. He taught me to look beneath the surface, which is what I have always tried to do, and I am glad for the time I spent with him.

Upon graduation I was advised to take a job with someone who was both a great investor and a great teacher. So I went to work at Wellington for David Ogden, and I am very grateful to him for his wisdom and patience in my early years. Wellington had some worldclass fund managers during that time, and while John Neff, still a legend, was creating his top record with Windsor Fund, I had the privilege and benefit of his teaching as I learned about analyzing companies and picking stocks. I continue to be thankful to him today as I mull over things he told me—things that I never forgot.

Very few analysts actually pick stocks well, and in fact, the analyst who did the best job of understanding company financials over the years, in my opinion, could not pick a stock. Yet analysts can be worth their weight in gold for each piece of the investment puzzle that they are expert in. Some pick stocks well, but I look for an ability to take apart companies and determine what makes them grow or an understanding of the key things about an industry, or both. Although I have mentioned a few analysts in this work, there are literally a few hundred who I found very helpful. I do not "rank" them, I value each for what he or she is good at. I am grateful to the countless honest analysts and the excellent brokerage firms that work very hard to make this the best and most open investment environment in the world and for helping people such as myself.

When I was starting out as an airline analyst, two Wall Street airline analysts who were great thinkers and great people took me under their wings and taught me a great deal, and I thank them. They are Ted Shen of Donaldson, Lufkin & Jenrette and Bert Fingerhut of Oppenheimer.

Along the way such people as Ben Bloomstone and Vic Linell of Cross Shore Capital (formerly of First Boston and Bernstein respectively), Jack Schneider of Allen & Co., Frank Gorky of Merrill Lynch, Jamie Blond of Lehman, Dick Hurd of Harris, Nesbitt (and way back, Kidder, Peabody and Donaldson, Lufkin and Jenrette), and T. J. Fitzgerald of Smith Barney were among a larger group of star institutional salespeople who were there for me when I needed assistance.

I thank David Sherman for allowing me to discuss some of the content of his fine book *Profits You Can Trust* as he was working away on it, and for urging me to not wait any longer and to begin to write this book I have wanted to write for a long time. My great thanks to Securities Research Corporation (SRC) for permission to reproduce their stock charts herein. I have used their charts for over three decades, and I have always found them to be the best.

Certainly I am very grateful to have such a fine editor as Bob Bender at Simon & Schuster, who patiently taught me the difference between good writing and writing a good book. I am also thankful for the help of Johanna Li, Bob's assistant. I also want to thank Jim Wade for his help with this book. Finally, I am also grateful to Nancy Inglis, the supervising copyeditor, and Phil Bashe, the copyeditor in the trenches.

My attorney, Robert Barnett of Williams and Connolly in Washington, was invaluable to me as a great adviser. He taught me the ropes and helped me through all stages of this endeavor, and I am very grateful.

INDEX